Contents

TEACHING FOR
Intelligence
SECOND EDITION

NCWC
Pearsall Library

Given in Memory of
Kathryn Dentler Oyler
By
Charles and Mary Jo
Godwin
2008

John I. Goodlad • Herbert P. Ginsburg
John Brockman interviews Howard Gardner
Robert J. Sternberg • Robert R. Spillane
Dorothy S. Strickland • Arthur L. Costa

TEACHING FOR
Intelligence
SECOND EDITION

Joseph S. Renzulli • Linda Darling-Hammond
Theodore R. Sizer • John Barell
Elliot W. Eisner • Richard L. Allington
Robin Fogarty • Eric J. Cooper
Maxine Greene • Daniel U. Levine
Rayna F. Levine • Jonathan Kozol
James Bellanca • James P. Comer
Joyce VanTassel-Baska

EDITED BY

BARBARA Z. PRESSEISEN

CORWIN PRESS
A SAGE Company
Thousand Oaks, CA 91320

For information:

Corwin Press
A SAGE Company
2455 Teller Road
Thousand Oaks, California 91320
www.corwinpress.com

SAGE Ltd.
1 Oliver's Yard
55 City Road
London EC1Y 1SP
United Kingdom

SAGE India Pvt. Ltd.
B 1/I 1 Mohan Cooperative
    Industrial Area
Mathura Road, New Delhi 110 044
India

SAGE Asia-Pacific Pte. Ltd.
33 Pekin Street #02–01
Far East Square
Singapore 048763

Printed in the United States of America

Library of Congress Cataloging-in-Publication Data

Teaching for intelligence / [edited by] Barbara Z. Presseisen. — 2nd ed.
    p. cm.
Rev. ed. of: Teaching for intelligence I. 1999.
Includes bibliographical references and index.
ISBN 978-1-4129-5554-6 (cloth)
ISBN 978-1-4129-5555-3 (pbk.)
    1. Thought and thinking—Study and teaching (Elementary)—United States—Congresses.
2. Teaching—United States—Congresses. 3. Intelligence—Congresses. I. Presseisen, Barbara Z. II. Title.

LB1590.3.T42 2008
372.11—dc22   2007020992
This book is printed on acid-free paper.

07   08   09   10   10   9   8   7   6   5   4   3   2   1

Acquisitions Editor:	Hudson Perigo
Editorial Assistants:	Jordan Barbakow, Lesley Blake
Production Editor:	Libby Larson
Typesetter:	C&M Digitals (P) Ltd.
Proofreader:	Charlotte J. Waisner
Indexer:	Michael Ferreira
Cover Designer:	Lisa Miller

Acknowledgments

Corwin Press would like to thank and acknowledge the following reviewers for their contributions to this new edition:

Dr. Douglas Bailer
Teacher
Earnest Pruett Center of Technology
Hollywood, AL

Linda L. Eisinger
Third Grade Teacher, West Elementary
2005 Missouri Teacher of the Year
Jefferson City, MO

Ganna Maymind
First Grade Teacher
Asher Holmes Elementary School
Morganville, NJ

Burt Saxon
Connecticut Teacher of the Year, 2004–2005
Adjunct Professor
Yale University and Southern Connecticut State University

Jolene Dockstader
Seventh Grade Language Arts Teacher
Jerome Middle School
Jerome, ID

Ellen E. Coulson, MA
Seventh Grade U.S. History Teacher
Sig Rogich Middle School
Las Vegas, NV

Gayla LeMay
Social Studies Teacher
Louise Radloff Middle School
Duluth, GA

Norma Barber
Language Arts Teacher
Ukiah School District 80R
Ukiah, OR

About the Editor

 Barbara Z. Presseisen is Chief Education Officer and Vice President of Education of Nobel Learning Communities, Inc., a network of private schools across the United States. She has served as both a director and consultant for several educational organizations and has trained educators in critical thinking, Holocaust education, and reasoning in teaching history and social studies. Dr. Presseisen taught at Swathmore College and Temple University and is the author and editor of numerous publications and articles on educational theory and practice.

Introduction

The second edition of this volume is a testament to a good idea that is much more than a decade old. *Teaching for Intelligence,* the record of a conference held in New York City at the end of the twentieth century, remains a powerful focus for education in the twenty-first century. This is due not only to the reasons cited at the original conference, but because we are in a post–September 11, 2001, world. Also, in America, the experience of an educational policy dominated by No Child Left Behind legislation makes this position of teaching for intelligence even more significant.

The first section of this volume examines what teaching for intelligence actually means: emphasizing the *intent* that students and teachers need in order to value inquiry, critical thinking, problem posing, and problem solving. This position suggests that *how one thinks* is a prime concern for classroom interaction. This target is a long way from testing goals that lie on a pass or fail continuum or that define 100 percent achievement as an assessment priority. Rather, one might examine Sizer's praise of the skeptical mind or Greene's faith in rich conversation and dialogue as important bases for instruction. How could you capture such objectives on a timed test? Cognitive scientists like Sternberg and Gardner emphasize *process* as well as *content,* and open the door to questions about teaching methodology and the pursuit of *depth of meaning* in classroom exchange. They raise issues such as who is the learner, and under what conditions can teachers actually instruct for intelligence development? In the second and third sections of this volume, writers such as Darling-Hammond, Barell, and Fogarty provide responses to these queries and report empirical research findings that demonstrate the efficacy of teaching for intelligence.

The papers in this collection also challenge educators to review the reform period in education at the end of the last century. They

1

suggest a need for examining how teaching for intelligence makes a difference to issues raised in several key documents of that period: *A Nation at Risk* (1983) and *Academic Preparation for College: What Students Need to Know and Be Able to Do* (1983), as well as those in the more recent No Child Left Behind Act (2001).

In terms of the first two documents, writers in this volume suggest American schools have failed to serve their constituencies well because the goal to have all students learn to be intelligent has not really been pursued. Every student can learn and, given appropriate conditions for learning, can succeed academically in terms of his or her potential. But merely covering curriculum or subject matter is not sufficient when the question of sound academic preparation is faced. The curriculum must also be *accessible* to the learner. Whether it is in reading or mathematics or the wisdom of making moral choices, according to Strickland, Gardner, Ginsburg, and Sternberg, teaching for intelligence enables learners to master the developmental skills and cognitive operations that underlie the "frames of mind" necessary for every thinker's lifelong learning.

Teaching for intelligence also highlights *how* students learn to think within and between content areas. In this context, the subject-specific medical model that underlies the basic approach to No Child Left Behind legislation requires further review. The so-called rigorous scientific evidence sought in the recommended content programs supported by this national effort *are* classroom interventions, to be sure, but they have not been found to be foolproof medications. As Eisner suggests in this volume, student outcomes measured by standardized tests of core subjects rarely assess the critical dimensions taught by experience and exposure in studying fine arts, for example—a subject matter not advocated by No Child Left Behind legislation. Nor can purposeful instruction to transfer reasoning to other forms of decision making be included in narrowly conceived, content-specific programs. There are many goals of learning involved in teaching for intelligence; they need to be addressed and researched to help students face the new and varied issues that arise in a complex, fast-changing, and terror-threatened world.

An important educational development is notably addressed in this unique volume. At the end of the last century, a great deal was learned about actual classroom instruction for intelligence. From understanding the requisites of a thinking classroom, to appreciating the importance of teacher support and building university partnerships with schools, to learning from research about thinking in specific student populations, the reform period of the 1990s provides sound guidance for practical implementation. Writers such as Cooper, Levine, and Renzulli demonstrate many successes of particular instructional implementations that prepare students for thinking. These research studies need to be followed up today by new efforts to apply this past research and to reclaim an empirical base on which to build further applications. Although the documents in this volume speak for themselves, it is important to see that their message is shared throughout.

Last, but hardly least, contributors to this volume address the needs of special students in their studies. The fourth section demonstrates how crucial teaching for intelligence is for children from poor, depressed, and immigrant backgrounds. These are children who are school-dependent for learning higher order thinking skills. Whether it is Kozol or Comer describing the desperate conditions of children with such needs, it is very important to know that here, too, there are successes to report. The importance of developing a *community* of learning is a well-known goal in a post-Vygotsky world. Child-centered environments—places that nurture thoughtfulness and focus on appropriate development-based learning and experiences—can make all the difference in a child's ultimate ability and skill. The continuing challenge today is to provide such rich and caring environments for all youngsters in need.

What can we learn by looking back at the educational movement centered on teaching for intelligence? We can see that such a movement still holds great promise for *all* of America's learners. It advises us to study more carefully where we have been educationally and where we can hope to go in the future. In a world overwhelmed by too much dumbed-down information, this past reform period encourages us to realize there are alternate paths. Beyond current schooling's narrow focus on IQs, standardized test scores, pass or fail assessment dimensions, and minimal curricular requirements, there is a vast and exciting world of knowledge, thought, inquiry, wisdom and beauty eager to help educate all children. Open this volume and see what a treasure we already have—pedagogical knowledge on *teaching for intelligence.*

—Barbara Z. Presseisen

SECTION 1

The Value of Intelligence Theory

For centuries, there have been numerous philosophers and educational theorists who have called for "intelligence" in schooling. In America, such advocacy has sometimes clashed with demands for practical knowledge and empirical application. During periods of reform, however, researchers and educational leaders become more energized about intelligent teaching because they actually see policies and practices in place that run counter to this long-held approach. They also see the potential and promise of bringing intelligence development to the center of American schools.

This initial section reveals many of the essential arguments embedded in the need for intelligence in schooling. They have emerged over the last half century of educational research and represent the philosophical, psychological, and sociological underpinnings of theory about pedagogy and achievement. Whether it is Sizer's informed skepticism or Goodlad's intended learning, these writers call for the development of an inquiring mind and the cultivation of critical skill. Above all, these experienced educators argue that habits of thoughtfulness need to be accessible to all students so that, as learners, they become part of a stimulating sensory environment—the "surround" of Goodlad's study. Such belongingness in a learning community is critical to upholding the basic ideals of democracy and capitalism.

The content or subjects of schooling are also entwined with their intelligent pursuit. Teaching thinking has long been associated with learning the disciplines of knowledge, but classroom educators are cautioned not to strive for mere "coverage" of academic content. Gardner and Greene both emphasize the importance of depth of

5

meaning in the student's developing mastery. Intelligent education requires more than the mere transmission of knowledge from one generation to another; rather, the active use of information calls for instruction that creates uncommon experience, forges new relationships, and sometimes raises uncomfortable issues and innovative challenges. Greene, in particular, emphasizes the importance of rich dialogue in learning, of conversation amidst new experience, so as to weave intricate nuances of thought into a creative, human act. The school of intelligent thinking must be a cauldron of invention and, at heart, advocates of teaching for intelligence believe it is important to be avid humanists as well.

Among the supporters of intelligent education, the cognitive scientists question what the abilities that constitute intelligent behavior are. Gardner's multiple "frames of mind" are held in high repute and, to Goodlad, are only a starting point of a more fully defined education. Sternberg acknowledges that teaching for intelligence, based in constantly growing memory, involves building analytic, creative, and practical skill, as he has long advocated in his triarchic theory. Sternberg also calls for a new understanding of wisdom, which he defines as an educated person's power to judge rightly, and ultimately select a sound course of action. Sternberg's approach emphasizes tacit knowing; the learner needs to become sensitive to what is not openly expressed, to what may only be implied and silently understood. It is in this sensitivity that intuition comes to play an important role in more complex thinking. It is in this sensitivity that values of the larger community can come to mediate the thought and reasoning generated by "book knowledge." Teaching for intelligence, with a goal to develop wisdom, can thus influence the moral base of society and, at the same time, strive for the achievement of the common good. In teaching for intelligence, then, Sternberg seeks to develop a new model of a balanced, wise education. He pushes the blueprint on teaching for intelligence forward into the realm of social, emotional, and ethical behavior.

The larger landscape of teaching for intelligence is outlined in the writings of this initial section. While not an easily mastered body of readings, they are rich in ideas and represent many years of research and thought about productive teaching and lifelong learning. These selections also raise many of the issues that others will address in later entries: the role of questioning in the interplay between teacher and student, the rare understandings built by study of the various arts, the interdisciplinary relationships among several academic content areas, and the special needs of certain groups and particular kinds of learners. Yet, these thoughtful studies speak in one voice about the importance of teaching for intelligence. In a world where communication grows so rapidly that how teaching occurs must be altered daily, these major educational thinkers underscore that the central importance of teaching has not changed for centuries.

On the Habit of Informed Skepticism

Theodore R. Sizer

Theodore R. Sizer *is founder and Chair Emeritus of the Coalition of Essential Schools at Brown University. He has worked extensively with secondary education to reshape the American high school so that all students can achieve academic success. The author of numerous seminal studies in education and history, Dr. Sizer served as Dean of Harvard's Graduate School of Education.*

Language tells us much about an age, including our own. It serves us always to listen to ourselves, testing the words we use, sensing what lies behind them. Words matter.

I recently received an invitation to a conference in Washington. Its focus was on what the conference announcement described as the "alignment of standards" for children, their schools, and their teachers. The conference invitation stated how vital standards were to improving education, yet how difficult they were to use effectively in practice because of their sheer number and complexity. The invitation called the alignment of standards one of the most essential and crucial issues facing educators today. This conference was to help bring order to what was assumed to be a chaotic and thus incompetent educational system.

I know that the term *standards* is today's hottest educational catchword. Usually it is preceded by adjectives such as "rigorous," "tough," and "world class" (whatever that means). Apparently, the simple word *standards* is not enough. But this topic's presence in the conference announcement was expected. The discussion of "standards" draws participants.

However, for me, the most interesting word in the announcement was alignment. While the conference description issued no apparent challenge to the emerging lists of "standards"—that is, of their substance, their political and educational legitimacy, or exactly how they might function as a "vital way to improve education"—a need was expressed to gather all of the standards together and string them into a usable and persuasive parade. A uniform set of national standards, not only in the schools but also in the teacher education and related communities, would thereby emerge to drive reform,. Americans would then have a describable, predictable, and measurable American educational system. Presumably, all the pieces of the complex educational structure would be, to a substantial degree, substantively united into a sweeping "One Best System" of education—one engineered in the name of high American standards.

The ambition as well as the arrogance of this conference was stunning.

I turned from reading this announcement to the Sunday newspapers, especially the Commentary section. I caught up on the Inter-American conference in Chile. In this country, we revel in the fact that most Latin American and Caribbean countries today have capitalist economic systems and democratic forms of government. I read here again what I have read often in the newspapers over the last decade: *The American way is now and inexorably the world's way.*

The key words that generally describe this American way are *democracy* and *capitalism.* Behind these two words are two fundamental ideas: *The people decide. Free and competitive markets count.* A wise nation prepares its youth well for such a world. Wise educators must look carefully at the intellectual essence of democracy and capitalism. What makes these globally triumphant enterprises tick?

What makes them tick is best expressed in demanding questions. Democracy and capitalism are necessarily supple enterprises, ones that give substantial freedom to individuals and bestow prominence and riches to those individuals who use that freedom in effective ways. It is questions that count, with informed answers forthcoming. *What is that? Why is it so? What does it matter? What if . . . ?* The answers to such questions draw their legitimacy from the respectful but insistent probing of *what is* in order to discover *what might be*.

Consider a few examples: digital computing was crafted out of new questions asked of old realities in mathematics and physics. New ways of effective management arose from a challenge to the deeply entrenched factory system. An unexpected interweaving of the arts led to powerful new forms of expression, and this interweaving still unsettles the traditional arts community. All these new realities emerged from smart people asking new sorts of questions, questions that the established order might understandably have found to be cheeky, not part of the anointed system, or indeed downright disorderly. They led to inventions, and these inventions demonstrably worked, at least in the view of enough serious people to sustain their existence. Our competitive and free market allowed the people to decide.

Democracy and capitalism depend on hard knowledge, on the disciplines of the past. However, their essence derives from their experiment with and beyond existing knowledge and practice, experimentation that arises from powerful questions—and hardly from a carefully "aligned" massing of conventional wisdom.

I often puzzle about the extraordinary gap between the politics of establishment educational reform and the politics of reform in other fields. In education we are betting on a strategy of centralizing control over what is taught and upon what basis that learning is assessed: nationally aligned goals and objectives. The people charged with that centralization are largely unelected and represent the existing power groups in American education. These are surely devoted and decent people, but they are rarely considered entrepreneurs in the best capitalist sense.

In education policy, there is limited attention paid to research on the process of learning, especially if that research suggests substantial change in the ways that formal education is defined and "delivered" or if the needed change is likely to cost substantial amounts of money. There is but a tiny investment by both the government and the private sector in educational research and, especially, development. The existing ways of defining schooling remain—to any noticeable official extent—largely unchallenged.

We seem to be pushing the safe, conventional reform vessels, even as there is sweeping evidence both that they work poorly and that the tests and mandates being imposed correlate little with desired behaviors. There is no "market" out there to remedy these weak arguments; the control and now the "aligned" standards and assessment remain closely controlled and centralized.

There are many historical and political reasons for this astonishing lack of boldness. What is particularly interesting is how these sorts of policies run absolutely counter to the critical ideas that inform the much-applauded American way, the basic ideas behind democracy and capitalism. Compounding the irony is the oft-heard and patronizing argument that centralized control is necessary to protect the poor, as though there were not equally effective and more democratic mechanisms available to accomplish that end.

Further, many argue that our schools today are too diverse, that standards suffer. Yes, student intellectual performance by any definition is low, but that is not inevitably to say that the means to raise performance is the introduction of centralized standards and assessments. Indeed, there is a wealth of evidence that the miserable showing of many students arises not from details found in a curriculum guide or a testing booklet but from much deeper, more profound causes.

Finally, as today's conference illustrates, there is at hand a provocative body of research in cognitive science that raises deep questions about the accepted ways or means of teaching and assessment. My request today is for us who are concerned about the intelligence of the people—that is, the aggregated wit, knowledge, conviction, and grit of the American population—to recognize the lack of connection between most contemporary education policy and the widely applauded character of democracy and capitalism.

A wise society is peopled by more than the merely adroit, the useful but conforming spinners of the familiar. It depends on people who are in the habit of asking questions that break new ground. Further, in an age when communications technology provides society's "teachers"—the spinmeisters of the advertising world—with unprecedented and sustained access into the lives of communities and families, the habitual questioner—the informed skeptic—becomes ever more important. The young person must be taught to say: What is the evidence? How might that task be done better, more effectively, and at less cost? What is really behind this message? What is for sale? Do I like it or not, and why? Is this all a lie, or is what I am told a truth of some sort?

The constructive questioner is necessarily informed and, thus, difficult to gull. The effective questioner wraps his or her questions around disciplined knowledge that emerges from incessant questioning, both of past scholarship and that of the present. A wise society will invest in intellectually competent citizens who persist in asking why, who, what, and especially what if—in thoughtful, *informed* ways.

An interest in questions comes at birth. The why questions abound, as many an exasperated parent will testify. That curiosity must be cultivated and encouraged, with all the nuisance it causes. It must not be crushed, however disrupting it may be.

> The effective questioner wraps their questions around disciplined knowledge that emerges from incessant questioning, asking why, who, what, and especially what if—in thoughtful, informed ways.

Nurturing a questing mind can make schooling, especially secondary schooling, a complicated task for teachers. A good question is rarely disposed of quickly. It takes time to form. It must be challenged, massaged, played with. It can rarely be rushed.

The Holocaust is a topic that very often provokes deep questions. Usually it is recounted in but a few paragraphs in a textbook, situated chronologically at the end of World War II when U.S. troops "liberated" the camps. Kids will ask, How can people do that to other people? The Nazis were people like us who had been to school. Nazis went to church. What did they think when they engaged in this barbarism? How could they justify it as fair? What about all the Germans who were not Nazis? Did they know? If not, why not? How not? How can one know that these German citizens actually knew?

As the discussion typically deepens, and, as the details of the Holocaust emerge in young minds, some student will ask, Do we have a Holocaust today that we do not "see"? Cambodia's Killing Fields and the Rwanda genocide usually come up. Are they similar to what happened to European Jews? Someone raises the matter of American slavery. Is that our Holocaust? Does it continue today? Is there a Holocaust in our midst? The discussion will explode.

Most teachers must acknowledge the issue and then, however reluctantly, move on. There is too much in the conventional history curriculum to "cover." There are tests on all the material covered to prepare for. Deep questions take too much time to answer. There are not enough hours for extensive reading on a complex topic, especially one that diverges from the syllabus, even if the class is captured by it. There is no expectation for intense discussion. Such discussion can become undisciplined, and the teacher's other section of U.S. history may not raise the same sort of questions. The two sections must be kept on the same schedule. The teacher, shouldering responsibility for 150 students, cannot be expected to do two "preps" for the "same" eleventh grade social studies classes.

Further, there is no right answer to all those questions. I remark to the class, How can I tell if you kids know this stuff? And a cheeky kid will surely ask, What does it mean to know this "stuff" and just how and on what basis will you "test" us?

The habit of questioning is both the heart of democracy and capitalism and at the heart of demanding pedagogy. *Why, why, why, why? What if? How do you know? What is the evidence? How sound is the evidence?* People's energies flow from questions. Questions capture the attention of people of all ages. Vibrant collective government and the exercise of informed free choice depend on it. However, conventional schooling, systematized in exquisite detail, usually trivializes this type of questioning. If schools do not value this habit, what is the cost to the culture?

> The habit of informed skepticism is the necessary habit of a vital democracy and creative capitalism. We adults must practice this habit in all that we do in schooling.

The habit of informed skepticism is the necessary habit of a vital democracy and creative capitalism. Generations of young people schooled to parrot other people's answers to other people's questions will not be the seed bed for a good society.

Educators and political leaders themselves must ask deep and troubling questions about our own system of public schools, questioning even the meaning of that too-readily-accepted word system. They must inform themselves deeply about learning, about why people try to learn, about intelligence, and about the expression of informed ideas. Simply, they must open their eyes to the possibility that there are very different ways to educate America's young than merely making traditional notions about learning and schooling more systematic and "aligned." That is, we adults must practice the habit of informed skepticism about all that we do in schooling. It is a worthy habit. Let us exercise it, boldly.

Let me go back to the ideas of democracy and capitalism, and the words behind them: *The people decide. Free and competitive markets count.* If applied to education, what might this mean?

If one assumes, as I do, that beyond the rudiments of linguistic and mathematical literacy, reasonable people can and should disagree about the substance and standard of a serious education, then families must have a choice among schools for their children. "Choice" has a long history in America, but it is enjoyed almost entirely by those in upper-income levels. People choose a town with schools they trust or a private school. Realtors tell us that the "quality of the schools" is a major criterion governing a move. If choice among schools is undeniably good for rich folks, it should be for poor folks as well. Let the people decide which school among many they want their child to attend.

What, then, is the role of government?

- To insist on tested evidence of each student's mastery of basic literacy and numeracy skills and on continued effort in some acceptable setting for learning beyond that.
- To provide adequate financial support for settings in which students are admitted by lottery and which serve no special interest in violation of the Constitution, this most likely made possible by means of a system whereby the money follows the child.
- To make available funds in excess of the basic per-child support for children with special needs or from highly stressed or dysfunctional families.
- To promote the creation of schools in underserved areas.
- To make available evidence and examples of good practice and to support research and development to study and create such examples.
- To financially support the recruitment and preparation of each generation of new teachers and administrators.
- To insist upon "transparency." All schools should be required to report fully and publicly, on an annual and comprehensive basis, on their programs and the performance of their students.
- To have the power to shut down schools that either lie about their offerings and performance or that demonstrably hurt children.

These ideas will not be popular in many quarters. Many will say they spell the end of public education. The opposite will be the truth. American public education today is profoundly segregated by social class, is inequitably funded, has massive and repeatedly reported shortcomings, and is in the effective control of a very small number of people, many of them unelected. If anything, that control is being extended; witness the many calls for "alignment."

Many Americans will be terrified to try something so new. And yet, there are indications that a grassroots movement in such a direction is already underway. Home schooling is reportedly one of the fastest growing reform efforts in the country. The demand for charter schools and their equivalents is heard in every state. "Upstart" schools within many public systems are struggling into existence, usually in the teeth of top-down regulation. There is a constructive restlessness in communities across this country.

Most telling, however, is the unwillingness of governments to put financial muscle behind their calls for reform. As always, Americans should attend carefully to what their governments *do* and pay only skeptical attention to what their governments *say*. For a quarter century we have had national political posturing, much of it studded with self-righteous and apocalyptic rhetoric. However, there has been no serious and sustained outpouring of funds to make significant educational reform possible.

The launch of *Sputnik* was the catalyst for getting a man on the moon. Conversely, the 1983 *A Nation at Risk* report began the establishment of low-cost standards and assessment schemes, precipitated a sea of studies and reports and a plethora of name calling, and ultimately sustained little attention to the central problems facing the country's children. The signal here is clear—government itself has deep doubts about the existing system. If it did not, it would have acted decisively as it has in other areas of national life.

In 1974, David Tyack, one of America's most respected historians of education, published a history of American urban education. Tyack's final words, written a quarter century ago, still ring true:

> Old reforms need to be reformed anew, for today many lack confidence in the familiar patterns of power and authority that developed at the turn of the century. Substantial segments of this society no longer believe in centralism as an effective response to human needs, no longer trust an enlightened paternalism of elites and experts, and no longer accept the inevitability or justice of the distribution of power and wealth along existing class and racial lines. To create urban schools which really teach students, which reflect the pluralism of the society, which serve the quest for social justice—this is a task which will take persistent imagination, wisdom, and will.[1]

The intelligence of the American people requires an end to careful and highly controlled tinkering with the old system and a scary leap into something that promises to be better. We must turn to our persistent imagination, wisdom, and will. Democracy, much less capitalism, cannot survive without them.

America must prepare its students well to be informed skeptics. America must itself become an informed skeptic about its system of schooling—and act accordingly.

Note

1. Tyack, D. B. (2005). *The one best system: A history of American urban education* (p. 291). Cambridge, MA: Harvard University Press. Tyack and his Stanford colleague Larry Cuban also published with the Harvard University Press a further critique of school reform: *Tinkering Toward Utopia: A Century of Public School Reform* (1997).

Narratives of the Educative Surround

John I. Goodlad

__John I. Goodlad__ is Professor Emeritus, Codirector of the Center for Educational Renewal at the University of Washington and President of the Institute for Educational Inquiry in Seattle. He has been awarded numerous prizes for his contributions to the study of education, and holds honorary doctorates from twenty colleges and universities in the United States and Canada.

EDUCATION VIS-À-VIS TEACHING

Seeking to tidy my mind somewhat regarding the work I'm in, I find it helpful to distinguish sharply between education and teaching. Education is of the self: partaken by the self, driven by the self. Education is not a commodity that can be given or taken away by somebody else. Yet it is not context-free. What the self is at any given time is the consequence of personal, evolving interactions with the surround.[1] There is no such thing as an autonomous self.[2]

One's education is both deliberate and serendipitous—that is, it is both sought for and not sought for. When one appears to have developed a measure of expertise without benefit of tutoring or some form of schooling, we say that she or he is self-taught. This, for me, is not helpful. Education is self-teaching: a process of preparing for and making choices—some deliberately, some not—that determine one's view of selected elements of the surround and, indeed, the

17

whole of it. "Self-teaching" becomes a sloppy, redundant synonym for "education" and carries with it the assumption that "teaching" also is a synonym for "education." Such leads to the misleading, conventional equating of education and schooling and all sorts of consequential mischief.

Teaching, quite unlike education, is a process external to the self that the self assimilates, interprets, or ignores. We think of teaching as deliberate, but much of it is not; it is just there. The self is as likely to fix on the unintended as on the intended in sorting through the ubiquitous teaching of the daily surround. Definitions of education that exhort the deliberate cultivation of desired sensibilities and sensitivities are, more accurately, exhortations to the mission of teaching and schooling. When teaching becomes deliberate and takes on a mission, it becomes a moral act, with all the dilemmas associated with such.[3]

The most troubling phenomenon of teaching is the unpredictability, particularly in the moral consequences, of the interactions between self and surround. And one of the greatest errors in seeking attribution regarding the effects of teaching is looking only to the self for reasons and explanations for what occurs in the individual. The individual self cannot be held responsible for arranging all the contingencies of the educative surround.

> Definitions of education that exhort the deliberate cultivation of desired sensibilities and sensitivities are, more accurately, exhortations to the mission of teaching and schooling. Teaching then becomes a moral act, with all the dilemmas associated with such.

The whole of one's surround is the teacher—for better or for worse. The self is free to ignore or relate to, wittingly or unwittingly, anything in the ecosystem of which it is a part. These connections and interpretations shape individual values, beliefs, and dispositions. What is not in or encountered in the surround may stunt or deprive the development of certain dispositions—once again, for better or for worse. In a cosmic sense, what is not part of this whole teaches, too; the self is denied some of both the good and the bad.

DIVERSITY IN THE NARRATIVES OF TEACHING

The crowing of roosters soars clearly above the quiet of education, intensifying as dawn comes to the cathedrals of humankind. Their sounds are soon lost, however, to the rising decibels of teaching—that cacophony of telling, pleading, questioning, showing, promising, praising, condemning that courses through the streets and market-places.[4] We are all teachers, our lessons tied to narratives of incentives and consequences. The nearer the threat of doom, promise of redemption, expectation of gratification, or utopia envisioned, the more impact the teaching has. The more ubiquitous the message, the less likely the promulgation and reception of dissenting alternatives.

Over the centuries, several major narratives have dominated the human conversation: the narratives of salvation and everlasting life, of sectarian superiority, of gender privilege, of war and peace, of absolutism and relativism, of economic utility, of consumption and conservation. The struggle for dominance of ideology and belief has rarely been resolved on the basis of self-evident truth. Rather, it has been resolved on the basis of power in the political and physical combat arenas. After triumphing over their opposition, the despot's first actions are to exercise control over as much of the teaching cacophony as possible. The invention of the printing press and its rapidly expanding use changed the balance of power by ensuring that the local priest and soothsayer were not the only people with the book and the word. Likewise, superior invention and skill in the use of gunpowder reversed the economic fortunes of nations, superimposed new languages over the old, and made treasonous religious teachings previously unquestioned.

We are all born with the potential to develop a multiplicity of intelligences that together constitute the whole of our intelligence.[5] Although interrelated and intercontributory to this whole, each proceeds on its own trajectory. There is no assurance that an environment rich in musical contingencies will produce musical intelligence, but such an environment increases the probability of its development. As parents massage these contingencies, and musically inclined peers fill up the social surround, the education of musical intelligence in the self is more likely to blossom. There is no guarantee, however, that some other narrative will not prevail, perhaps turning one's attention more to the development of mathematical intelligence. Very often—not just rarely—it is a serendipitous encounter that triggers attention. The road to deliberate manipulation of the environment to foster in others an envisioned intelligence is marked by both successes and abysmal failures.

The combination of profound belief in the narrative, and the unpredictability of success in teaching it, is potentially explosive.

Nowhere is this more evident than in the history of what is arguably the most powerful and influential narrative genre: religion. Probe deeply and one finds an astonishing convergence of basic principles in the world's major religions, especially in regard to tolerance and love. It turns out, however, that these tenets of faith are not sufficiently grounded in the believers to risk the transcendence of love from sect to sect. And so the divine idiom is suspended for recourse to the terrestrial ground of the battlefield.

We see this two-headed model of contradiction today in every aspect of the human habitat. The concept of "family values" is so appealing to interpretation that it has become a tool of political manipulation. Yet, parental abuse is a leading cause of children's injury and death. The narrative of empathy for the poor and homeless is always at odds with the narrative of the poor as a lazy underclass, conjuring up a host of negative connotations. We know the educative power of modeling the narrative of kinesthetic intelligence but employ the pedagogical shortcut of resorting to linguistic teaching—"do as I say, not as I do." Observation tells us that the virtue of loyalty to clients, employees, and friends is always at risk to the appeal of self-serving narratives.

The competition for teaching time and space is as old as civilization. Rarely have the dominant narratives comprehensively encompassed the human condition. Few have been evolutionary in the sense of benefiting from use so as to reach more people. Most narratives have been advanced primarily to benefit those in command of rhetorical place and space. It should come as no surprise, then, that advancing the capabilities of technological place and space to accommodate those with the resources of command became a narrative in its own right, ready to serve any narrative, regardless of message. Today, communications is our most encompassing and ubiquitous industry, essential to the fortunes and accompanying power of other industries. The word of the warlord has been replaced by the corporate word. That Bill Gates said it carries more weight than what Bill Gates said. But what Bill Gates said has been incorporated into the lexicon of the narrative of economic utility anyway. The old power game is sustained and intensified; those controlling the medium control the messages that massage the populace.[6]

History argues that the less widely distributed the power, the less diverse the educative ecosystem of the surround; the less diverse this ecosystem, the less diverse the cultivation of intelligences; the less diverse the cultivation of intelligences, the fewer the narratives of possibilities and human sustainability; and the fewer of these narratives, the less the chances of survival. History provides an array of examples: the "ethnic cleansing" of jihad, the monopolies of cartels,[7] the subjugation of means to ends, the sacrifice of serendipity to narrowly focused purpose and assumed certainty, the divine mandate to control or master. The teaching of history is powerfully persuasive: our survival depends in large part on learning to let things be, on developing the ecological intelligence to know when we must be "leavers" and not mere victims of our passion for taking.[8]

But even as these words and thoughts take shape in my mind, I am awed by the complexity of what, on the surface, appears so obvious, necessary, and simple: We must take care of one another and the habitat of which we are a part. Two profound complications surface immediately. First, although the rhetoric of goodwill toward all takes up a sizable chunk of airtime, especially on nostalgic ceremonial occasions, other narratives, often appealing to divisiveness and personal aggrandizement, compete for our time, attention, and acceptance. What are the chances for a narrative of moral principle to be heard? Second, surely not all opinions, customs, choices, and dispositions are equally good. How does this moral principle become pervasive without the annihilation of those deeply committed to other narratives?

Through education, of course. But this is asking a great deal of a process that is invisible, never fully harnessed, personal, unpredictable, hardly ever linear, and heavily influenced by the narratives of the ecological surround. These narratives are not neutral and they are rarely for the common good. We depend largely on the rule of law to sustain the common good. Yet, when we refer to education as intended learning, the rhetoric is of the common good and soon turns to schools. Our assumption appears to be that we cannot expect much of the education we need from what transpires in the daily marketplace, and so we must count on the schools. My, what a burden to lay upon them!

> Desired student outcomes are determined through a political process by which an array of interests purported to be in the common good compete for attention and, ultimately, supremacy in both the ends and means of the schools.

NARRATIVES FOR SCHOOLS

Schools are political entities charged with carrying out teaching functions—functions, in turn, directed to deliberate student outcomes. These outcomes are determined through a political process by which an array of interests purported to be in the common good compete for attention and, ultimately, supremacy in both the ends and means of the schools.

Given the principles enunciated in the founding of the American Republic, we would assume that the process of setting the purposes for the deliberate teachings of the schools would be one of reaffirming the mission of developing democratic character in the young: an understanding and appreciation of liberal democracy, and a belief in the efficacy of upholding "a political system marked not only by free and fair elections, but also by the rule of law, a separation of powers, and the protection of basic liberties of speech, assembly, religion, and property."[9] In addition to these attributes of political citizenship, one might also anticipate the moral dispositions of fairness, equality, justice, freedom, caring, community, and relatedness.[10] We literally endorse, then, the symbiotics of both personal and community health and well-being: civility and civitas, respectively.

A major complaint of today's school-based educators is that there is no clear, agreed-upon mission for schooling; it changes after election time. But these changes provide no greater clarity and stability than existed before.

Given these liberal political and social democratic principles and concepts as the solid backdrop—the rhetorical fabric—of our discourse, we might also assume that all other persuasions would be granted only very tentative status, until discarded or incorporated into the design of this fabric. We might also assume that the school need pay little heed to the surrounding cacophony of interests and ideologies competing for attention while being steadfastly guided by the larger educative narrative, and would go about its business of developing democratic character in the young. As in the past, a new subject might be added, or an old one given a more prominent place in the curriculum, reflecting changes in the balance of expectations for effective citizenship. Today greater attention to ecology and technology might well be appropriate. But the mission of schooling would remain stable.

Not so. A major complaint of today's school-based educators is that there is no clear, agreed-upon mission for schooling; it changes after election time. But these changes provide no greater clarity and stability than existed before. The narrative of developing democratic character in the young enjoys no premier status among the diverse expectations of the marketplace. Further, there is no deep-grained professional ethos that grounds the educator in a teaching ethic of educational responsibility to the pupil, an ethic sufficient to transcend these expectations. There is little in the professional education of the teacher and the administrator to even suggest the possibility of such an ethic.[11] The empty cliché, "all children can learn," provides as little guidance as a street sign lying in a field, torn from its moorings by a windstorm.

What a marketing opportunity! With the presumably unassailable mission for schools largely unattended and little advocated, no real alternatives with a solid constituency, and the gates into teaching loosely latched to admit a body of school stewards lacking a common core of resolve and belief, the economic juggernaut that once regarded schools as off-limits simply expands the marketplace. The narrative of economic utility takes over.

The narrative of economic utility's appeal is straightforward and highly utilitarian: "Addressing the young," Neil Postman writes, "it offers a covenant of sorts with them: If you will pay attention in school, and do your homework, and score well on tests and behave yourself, you will be rewarded with a well-paying job when you are done." Postman continues: "Its driving idea is that the purpose of schooling is to prepare children for competent entry into the economic life of a community. It follows from this that any school not designed to further this end is seen as a frill or an ornament—which is to say, the waste of valuable time."[12]

It is this twisting and narrowing of school purpose that threatens development of the full, individual self and heightens the diabolical nature of this narrative of economic utility. There is nothing new or obscure in the hope that our young people will do well and feel good about their lives in school and, when adults, find satisfying jobs. Connecting the two has been and continues to be a motivating ploy used by parents and teachers alike. Even Mortimer Adler, no advocate for supremacy of the economic imperative in the mission of schooling, included "preparation for earning a living" with "preparation for duties of citizenship" and "preparation for discharging everyone's moral obligation to lead a good life and make as much of one's self as possible" as one of the three objectives of public schooling in our society.[13] Currently, however, we see not just the covenant with children regarding the jobs they will have, but a covenant to become the human capital for high-value-added industries fighting on the economic battlefields of the future for domination over "computers and software, robotics, civilian aviation, synthetic materials, microelectronics, biotechnology, and telecommunications"— to cite Professor Theodore Hershberg.[14]

This may be the battlefield you enthusiastically covet for your children's children, Professor, but when it comes to mine and theirs, I'm a conscientious objector. Your grandchildren and mine will assuredly have *that* option. But when you set the preparation for this fray as the mission of our schools, you know not what you do. You report answering queries about your earlier proposals for "radical school reform" with the response, "I don't have a clue."[15] This would be a more appropriate answer to questions about your proposed economic mission for schooling.

We should not be at all surprised or turned off by business interest in the schools as a market and a tool for ratcheting up the economy. To expect otherwise would be akin to expecting squirrels to eschew the bird feeder. And so my blood pressure rises only a little in response to the crassest exhortations of corporate leaders addressing educational conferences regarding the schools' responsibility to process student raw material for the nation's human-power needs. My body language suggests a little tension when still one more politician stages the tired ploy of severely blasting the schools in the hope that this sorry picture will be remembered a few years from now when he makes claims for improvement as a result of the efficient, bottom-line, corporate practices he was successful in injecting into state legislation for the schools. And I squirm only a little when one more school board, boasting last year about increased expenditures for computers (with no check on the availability of appropriate software), complains this year about the rising costs of instruction.

No, it is the reverence of so many educators for the god of Technology, now risen from the ashes of all previous gods of Technology,[16] that rouses my passion. Technology has become a religion. It is a religion that has no moral affinity with the great religions of the world, all of which "affirm and reverence life; . . . believe in the freedom and integrity of the person; . . . urge the existential self to seek self-transcendence in organic union with mankind and with mystical or divine ground of the cosmos. . . ."[17]

We have been promised educational salvation before by hucksters of previous gods of Technology. "Education for the Air Age" and "Education for the Space Age" are two puffballs of promised school reform that come to mind. But these and others were only weakly driven by the narrative of economic utility and soon drifted off to rest inconspicuously in that graveyard of educational fantasies marked, "Whatever happened to the future?" We need a *Journal of Educational Autopsy* to remind us of the common characteristics of the technologically related, hysterical follies of the past and their kinship with today's blunders.

Educators have had before them for decades creative proposals regarding the seemingly limitless possibilities for enriching both the educative surround and classroom instruction through the very technologies now available. Seymour Papert, for one, likened the child's future computer to her present pencil, the shaft wired to a technologically driven educative universe, with which she could interact any hour of the day, any day of the week.[18] The computer, teamed with the human teachers, would simply make it easier for the school to achieve its ideal goal of maximizing the abilities of every child encompassed by its stewardship. Neither Papert nor others of like vision had in mind a world, only speculated, where such a school mission would be replaced with goodness knows what. A handful of schools cautiously added a few computers to their arsenal of instructional aids and went about their usual business.

But, suddenly, Armageddon is just beyond the millennium. In the apocalyptic struggle to be waged, says the narrative, the implicit holiness of the god of Technology will triumph. Let us eschew the present and prepare for salvation in the glorious near-future. It comes to me as a surprise (as it most certainly would to all who know me well) that I am increasingly called upon to describe this future and what we must try to do in our schools to prepare their students for it. Unfortunately, I have yet to meet a person living in the future to turn to for a description of what it is like, how it feels to be there, and how to present myself to the then-incumbent god of Technology.

My life as a clairvoyant promises to be blessedly short. Unsought clients are monumentally disinterested in my answers to their questions. A recent group appeared to be about as nervous as those denizens of the woods who trembled at Chicken Little's dire predictions of the sky about to fall. Surrounded by the rhetoric of those most likely to profit from a technologically driven future and clothed in guilt by the words of those early-believing and early-using colleagues, they sought from me confirmation of what the work of tomorrow's schools and teachers would be.

I may not have removed the fear, but I certainly took away the fun of speculation when I asked about the present, "How was technology now changing or removing the mission of their schools?" There was silence; body language suggested some annoyance. The priorities of the school, I suggested, arise out of determining critical areas of educational need not being taken care of now by other institutions or not likely to be taken good care of elsewhere. Instead of endeavoring to hurtle to an assumed inevitable but unknown and, therefore, scary future, we began to enjoy the calm of contemplating what we should advocate in a relatively known present.

A reliable way to be unprepared for the future is to prepare for one confidently perceived. Predictions are far too much extrapolations from the present. B. C. Crandall quotes Ludwig Wittgenstein: "When we think about the future of the world, we always have in mind its being at the place it would be if it continued to move as we see it moving now. We do not realize that it moves not in a straight line, but in a curve, and that its direction constantly changes."[19] Some charts of the future, like the navigational charts of centuries ago, provide the general contours but, like those used by the early navigators, are useless for guiding one through the rocks and shoals.

We know that the future major domains of frontier exploration will be outer space, the oceans' depths, and the human mind, and that what we know now pales in the face of what is yet to be known. We also know that these domains will ensure trillion-dollar industries. Apple Computer, Inc., was one of the three sponsors of the first workshop on artificial life held in Los Alamos, New Mexico, in 1987; two years later, the Global Business Network was one of the sponsors of the first international conference on nanotechnology.[20] Hence, it follows that there will be jobs—good jobs—in these domains, but to make preparation for these jobs the mission of our schools is folly. Nonetheless, the narrative of economic utility will be alive and well, dominating rhetorical space with claims regarding the virtues of technology, exhortations regarding the schools' responsibility for ensuring the necessary human raw materials, while also ensuring that those who stand to profit most from venturing into the three major domains of exploration will be first to describe the wondrous benefits we will enjoy.

The more specific and exclusive we are about preparing the young for logico-mathematical and technological intelligence, for example, the less likely the future availability of the other intelligences. From a practical, economic perspective, it is dangerous to play god, be it the god of Technology or any other, and set for schools the development of precise abilities that rely on speculation. From a moral perspective, to hone the classroom environment so as to eschew those intelligences not deemed necessary to national economic welfare is a monstrous denial of the possibilities of the self. Whether we have in mind the best interests of the nation or of the individual, an ecumenical mission for the schools is the best guarantee of a present that ensures the diversity of human understandings, talents, and traits essential to a durable tomorrow—a mission with many open windows and doors to admit serendipity.[21]

SCHOOLS FOR ALL SEASONS

The school best prepared for tomorrow is the school best geared to today. It is a school for all seasons, engaging all of its students in as many domains of human experience as it is able to encompass. It is a school so committed to its comprehensive mission of preparing the young to participate broadly in the human conversation a democratic society seeks to sustain that it is not diverted into the narrowing of focus that devotion to some specific narrative requires. This is not easy.

> The school best prepared for tomorrow is the school best geared to today.

Creating and sustaining school programs that cultivate a wide range of human potential and simultaneously ensure the availability of the full range of abilities and dispositions a robust democratic society requires is not easy because the supporting narrative is so weakly sustained in the surrounding environment. Research shows that parents want a very broad range of educational goals for their children. Nonetheless, they are taught by the rhetoric of politically driven school reform to settle for what they are told are reliable surrogates—test scores. Teachers, with somewhat different weightings of the components, also opt for a comprehensive set of personal, social, economic, and academic goals. And they, too, are told to pay close attention to test scores. Those classroom activities that stress the intrapersonal and interpersonal are quite commonly regarded, as Postman points out, as frill and ornament. Nonetheless, it is difficult to come up with a domain of intelligence other than the personal that is more significant to individual development and the common welfare—and less reflected in test scores.

The loss felt by students because of a narrowing school focus extends beyond deprivation in the domains of intelligence left out of the environment in at least two significant ways. First, the various intelligences are part of a functioning whole; the emotional, for example, profoundly affects the academic. The latter suffers in an atmosphere insensitive to the emotional states of the learners. The time-worn emphasis on teaching the whole child has depths of meaning extending far beyond the platitudes so often attached to the concept.

The second loss is in the richness of pedagogy that teaching in schools productively requires. The narrowing of school expectations to a limited array of readily testable outcomes tends to restrict teaching to relatively uniform procedures that simply leave out some modes of learning. For example, the range of teaching methods used in most kindergarten classrooms is commonly cut in half by the fourth grade, where stress on testing increases significantly.

> The narrowing of school expectations to a limited array of readily testable outcomes tends to restrict teaching to relatively uniform procedures that simply leave out some modes of learning.

Often accompanying this dual narrowing of curricula and teaching is an intensification of teacher interest in finding "the method," an interest endlessly fed by an educational business conglomerate peddling instructional "how-to-do-its." One carrying considerable intellectual baggage has been particularly popular over the last two decades: brain science and its promise (not supported by neural scientists) of revolutionizing educational practice. In spite of the fact that "we do not know enough about brain development and neural function to link that understanding directly, in any meaningful, defensible way to instruction and educational practice,"[22] it has been rare that a conference for teachers lacks an ardent speaker exhorting the specifics of developing both the left and right hemispheres of the brain in daily classroom activities.

Another of the most serious concomitants of this narrow view of what constitutes human intelligence and the role of the school in its development is the continued failure of public policy to recognize the level of teacher education required to ensure a system of schooling essential to developing our citizenry as the wealth of the nation that far transcends mere economic functionality.

The necessary "school for all seasons" sustains a learning environment rich in sensory stimulation. One need not worry pedagogically about what stimulates the right or left side of the brain if the organizing centers selected by the teacher are broad in encompassing the domains of the kinesthetic, the aesthetic, the social, the linguistic, the mathematical, and so on. But arranging for such organizing centers is exceedingly demanding, and flies in the face of years of emphasizing the selection of relatively small, sharply focused organizing centers with individual subjects and specific grade levels in mind. The unit of selection designed to involve the entire class over a period of weeks, with accompanying teacher observation and diagnosis of individual learners, has largely disappeared in our schools, in part because of being associated in the public mind with "progressive education," and in part because such is highly demanding in the necessary pedagogy. Teacher education programs that sprinkle a few methods of teaching courses outside of and in between both the demands of general education and a major over four years of college simply do not suffice.

As a nation, we balk at ensuring for our teachers both the general and the professional education that the fostering of intelligence in the young requires. It should come as no surprise that the best guarantee of a broadly encompassing intelligence is to be born into a stimulating sensory environment, and subsequently, to attend a school in a community sufficiently affluent to provide the richest array of instructional resources—schools that attract and retain the teachers most favored in their own education. And, of course, there is a high correlation between these two sets of favorable circumstances,[23] both little affected by proposals for school reform. Schools for all our children and all our seasons await the ultimate impact of narratives designed to provide, if not the favorable circumstances of birth, the favoring circumstances of richly textured educational environments guided by caring, competent, professional teachers. Meanwhile, let us not be seduced by narratives offering covenants to our children that prescribe and limit their futures.

NOTES

1. For a fascinating analysis of the social origins of the necessarily individual mental functioning of the self, see S. Wineburg, T. S. Eliot,

Collaboration and the quandaries of assessment in a rapidly changing world. *Phi Delta Kappan,* September 1997, 59–65.

2. The connectedness of the self to the surround is compellingly portrayed by W. Berry. (1996). *The unsettling of America: Culture and agriculture.* San Francisco: Sierra Club Books. See especially Chapter 7.

3. G. Moran. (1997). *Showing how: The act of teaching.* Valley Forge, PA: Trinity Press International. See particularly Chapter 1.

4. The ubiquitous nature of this teaching is described by L. A. Cremin. (1990). *Popular education and its discontents.* New York: Harper & Row. Specifically, see p. viii for his introductory summary.

5. This paper is premised on the assumption that there are several different kinds of intelligence, and that the educative surround should embrace development of the full array. I rely significantly on the seminal work of Howard Gardner.

6. For groundbreaking insights into the medium as both the message and the massage, see M. McLuhan. (1994). *Understanding media: The extensions of man.* Cambridge, MA: The MIT Press; and M. McLuhan & Fiore, Q. (2005). *The medium is the massage.* Corte Madera: Gingko Press.

7. See B. R. Barber. (1996). *Jihad vs. McWorld.* New York: Ballantine Books, for two phenomena that threaten the world's future—religious fanaticism and global megacorporations.

8. See D. Quinn. (1995). *Ishmael.* New York: Bantam, for a fascinating description and analysis of the differences between the "takers" and the "leavers" in history.

9. F. Zakaria. (1997, November/December). The rise of illiberal democracy. *Foreign Affairs,* 22.

10. J. White. (1991). *Education and the good life: Autonomy, altruism, and the national curriculum.* New York: Teachers College Press.

11. See the findings in J. I. Goodlad. (1990). *Teachers for our nation's schools.* San Francisco: Jossey-Bass.

12. N. Postman. (1996). *The end of education.* New York: Vintage, pp. 27–28.

13. M. J. Adler. (1988). *We hold these truths.* New York: Scribner Paper Fiction, p. 20.

14, 15. T. Hershberg. (1997, December 10). The case for new standards. *Education Week,* 52.

16. I draw more heavily from Neil Postman here than my citations imply. On the worship of and disappointments from today's and earlier eras of technological innovation, see E. Tenner. (1997). *Why things bite back: Technology and the revenge of unintended consequences.* New York: Vintage.

17. W. W. Wagar. (1967). *The city of man: Prophecies of a world civilization in twentieth-century thought.* Boston: Houghton Mifflin, p. 171. For further explication of commonalities in both divine and secular idioms

of thought, see J. I. Goodlad. (1997). *In praise of education.* New York: Teachers College Press, Chapter 2.

18. S. Papert. (1993). *Mindstorms: Children, computers, and powerful ideas.* New York: Basic Books.

19. B. C. Crandall. (1996). *Nanotechnology: Molecular speculations on global abundance.* Cambridge, MA: MIT Press, p. 187.

20. Crandall, pp. 24 and 25.

21. Ted Gup writes of the sheer joy of finding treasures of thought not sought. See his "The end of serendipity," *Education Week,* November 21, 1997, A52.

22. J. T. Bruer. (1997, November). Education and the brain: A bridge too far. *Educational Researcher,* p. 4.

23. For a penetrating, data-based analysis, see B. J. Biddle. (1997, September). Foolishness, dangerous nonsense, and real correlates of state differences in achievement," *Phi Delta Kappan,* 78, 9–13.

Truth, Beauty, and Goodness

Education for All Human Beings

John Brockman interviews Howard Gardner

John Brockman is a literary and software agent and science author. He founded The Reality Club, a group of scientists who contemplate intellectual issues, and is the president of Edge Foundation, Inc., which provides a Web site that is an interactive forum for the sharing and expression of ideas among scientists and others. He is the author and editor of nineteen books, including By the Late John Brockman and The Third Culture: Beyond the Scientific Revolution.

Howard Gardner is the John H. and Elisabeth A. Hobbs Professor of Cognition and Education at the Harvard Graduate School of Education, adjunct professor of Neurology at the Boston University School of Medicine, and codirector of Harvard Project Zero. The recipient of many honors, including a MacArthur Prize Fellowship, Gardner is the author of twenty-two books, coauthor of four, and has written several hundred articles.

JB: How do you educate everybody?

Gardner: I want people at the end of their education to understand the world in ways that they couldn't have understood it before their education. In speaking of the world I mean the physical world, the biological world, the social world—their own world, their personal world as well as the broader social and cultural terrain. I believe that these are questions that every human being is interested in from a very young age. They're questions which kids ask all the time: who am I, where do I come from, what's this made out of, what's going to happen to me, why do people fight, why do they hate? Is there a higher power? Questions like that—children don't usually ask them in their words, they ask them in their play, in their stories, the myths they like to listen to and so on.

These are also the questions that historically have been explored in religion, philosophy, science. While it's great for people to ask these questions on their own, and to make use of their own experience, it's crazy for people not to take advantage of the other attempts to answer those questions over the millennia. And the disciplines represent to me the most concerted efforts to provide answers to those questions. History tells us where we come from. Biology talks about what it means to be alive. Physics talks about the world of objects, alive or not.

It's important to emphasize the role of disciplines when you're talking about precollegiate education. Some people think the disciplines are irrelevant, and others think all the interesting work is interdisciplinary so you can kind of jump right into that. I reject both of these claims. Disciplines are what separate us from the barbarians; I don't think you can do interdisciplinary work unless you've done disciplinary work.

The people who defend disciplines often go to the opposite extreme; there's a joke in my field which is—in elementary school we love the kids, in high school we love the disciplines, in college we love ourselves. I don't think disciplines ought to be loved for their own sake; they ought to be seen as the best way to answer questions that human beings are interested in. Therefore I see the purpose of education as helping people understand the best answers that cultures and societies have come up with to basic questions, what I would call essential questions. So at the end we can form our own personal answers to those questions, which will be based to a significant extent on how other people have approached them, and will at the same time allow us to make our own syntheses.

The word *understanding* is very important here because I would say the overwhelming part of what we do in schools has nothing to do with understanding. It has to do with memorizing material and feeding it back in the form of short-answer tests. Understanding for me, on the other hand, is taking something that you've learned—a skill, a bit of knowledge, a concept—and applying it appropriately in a new situation. We very rarely ask students to do that. The most interesting finding of cognitive science for education is that when we ask even the best students in the best schools to make use of the knowledge in a new situation, they don't typically know how to do it.

> Understanding for me, on the other hand, is taking something that you've learned—a skill, a bit of knowledge, a concept—and applying it appropriately in a new situation. We very rarely ask students to do that.

JB: Maybe the premise of schools should be how to take tests. I became very good at it—I'm not being ironic.

Gardner: What you're saying is more true than you may realize. By and large throughout history, schools have not known exactly what it is that they want to do, but those who fund and operate schools have known that they want to have people who are responsible, and show up, and can master a task. So over the years they have developed what we might call ersatzes. If you wanted to go to Harvard College a hundred years ago, you had to be able to read Latin, Greek and Hebrew. Nobody went out and did a job where they had to read Latin, Greek and Hebrew. Nowadays, it's mastering a certain amount of mathematics, even though almost nobody will be using that mathematics when they go on. They are hurdles which we set up to discover whether somebody has—the Yiddish word is *yechas,* the German word is *sitzfleisch*—the ability to sit down and do something they don't really want to do.

Suddenly, the notion of seeing whether people can memorize lots of stuff and are able to sit down and study becomes irrelevant because we can get computers and other kinds of instrumentation to do that work for us. We don't need to remember the capital of Montana because it is likely to be at our fingertips. When I talk about being able to understand the discipline so that we can approach essential questions, I mean that we need to be able to train ways of thinking, so when new stuff comes along, people will be able to say, "Gee, I know how to approach that because of some ways of thinking that I've learned"; or if not, at least I have some recourse where I can go to figure out what to do. And this can be other people, books, or some kind of training that you do yourself or with a simulation—there are many options.

The notion of coverage—of going through a bunch of disciplines, and learning facts and concepts—is assessed by schools all over the world. It's never been a very good idea, but now it's really irrelevant. I would throw away 95 percent of the coverage that we do, figure out really important questions and issues, and give people lots and lots of time to learn about how disciplined minds think about those issues, and then allow them to practice those disciplines themselves.

JB: Let's get more concrete about your present initiatives.

Gardner: I'm a progressive in education—a follower of Dewey and people like that—but I want to essentially seize the initiative from the conservatives who have dominated the educational discussion in this country to its detriment. I'm selecting as my examples things which no conservative could possibly shake a fist at, but which would drive postmodernists nuts: truth, beauty, and goodness. When I talk about truth, I'm talking about science but also folk knowledge; when I talk about beauty, I'm talking about the arts, but it could be nature as well; and when I'm talking about goodness and evil, I'm talking about morality.

My specimen topic in truth is the theory of evolution; my topic in beauty is the music of Mozart; my topic in morality is the Holocaust. Getting even more specific than that, my example in evolution is Darwin's finches; within the music of Mozart my example is a trio in *The Marriage of Figaro*—it's the 13th performed set piece in the first act; and in the Holocaust, my example, the Wannsee Conference, is the place where the Nazis actually launched the Final Solution. These three things—the finches, the trio, and the Wannsee Conference—actually respond to questions that kids are interested in. (For example, why are there so many different kinds of birds on a little island?) They are what I call entry points to topics which are crucial if you want to think scientifically, aesthetically, or historically. What I would do as a teacher would be to spend weeks, months, even years really going into these things so that people will develop the habits of mind so they can think about topics like that.

If you asked me if people should be studying physics or chemistry or biology or geology in high school, I would say it doesn't make the slightest bit of difference. They should study some topics, of course, but the choice is wide open—I'm interested in depth, not breadth. I'm not talking about college education; I'm just taking on K to 12. What I want when kids get through a K to 12 education is for them to have a sense of what their society thinks is true, beautiful and good; false, ugly and evil; how to think about these things and how to act on the basis of your thoughts.

JB: Where is the Howard Gardner of multiple intelligences in all of this? Isn't this what you're known for in education?

Gardner: There have been literally hundreds and perhaps thousands of applications of my ideas educationally, both in this country and in the world. I say that with as much mystification and embarrassment as pride, because I have had almost nothing to do with it; these are things other people have done. But one thing that struck me is how incredibly superficial most of the applications have been, and one obsessive thought that's stimulating me through this current work in education is this: I don't want to be part of the trivialization of education. What I'm arguing is that if you decide which things are important and which things are worth spending time on, like evolution and the music of Mozart, then you can approach such a topic in many different ways. Multiple intelligences can be useful in three quite interesting ways in dealing with important topics that are worth spending time on.

First of all, by providing what I call *entry points.* Any topic that's worth spending time on can be approached in many different ways. I, in fact, have seven different entry points which roughly relate to my intelligences, but that's neither here nor there.

Secondly, by providing powerful *analogies* or *metaphors* for what you're trying to understand. Again, we don't know if there are seven analogies for anything you want us to understand, but there is always more than one analogy or metaphor.

And third, by providing what I call different *model languages* for understanding a concept. Let's take evolution. You can learn about evolution in ordinary language; you can learn about it through logical propositions; you can draw diagrams with the branching tree of evolution; you can do taxonomic classifications of various kinds of species. Many people, including experts, make the mistake of thinking that one of these languages is, so to speak, a privileged representation of a topic. I would say on the contrary that our understanding of a topic is rich to the extent that we have a number of different ways of representing it, and we can go pretty readily from one representation to the other.

> We need to take what we know about the different ways in which children think, the different ways in which people make sense of the world, and build that into the teaching of important topics.

Here I become Howard Gardner the progressive. We need to take what we know about the different ways in which children think, the different ways in which people can make sense of the world, and really build that into the teaching of important topics. First of all, we reach more kids, because some kids learn from stories, some kids learn from works of art, some kids learn from hands-on kinds of things. We also give kids a sense of what it's like to be an expert, because experts will think about something in lots of different ways. If you can only think about a topic in one way, your understanding is tenuous at best.

JB: What will parents think of this?

Gardner: It's going to confuse some of them, because in a sense I'm trying to have the best of a progressive and traditional perspective. When we talk about the true, the beautiful, and the good, that's very classical. Then you have multiple intelligences. I went on radio and talked about how you could teach the Civil War through dance. I received the most outraged correspondence from people on that topic, even though I just heard about a wonderful dance about the Holocaust that's really quite amazing and powerful; and many of us understand the Spanish Civil War through Picasso's paintings or Andre Malraux's novels. So, it's really going to confuse people.

JB: Is this approach for everybody? Have you tried it out on local boards of inner-city public schools, for instance?

Gardner: I am not saying that everybody should study evolution, Mozart, and the Holocaust. I'm saying that each educator needs to work in his or her culture to figure out what the important truths, beauties, falsities, and moralities are, and spend time with those. In the sciences there are hundreds of them. And if you don't believe in the sciences, then there are hundreds of them in folk knowledge. But the important point is to spend a lot of time on something, rather than just superficially sampling a lot of things. People say, well, you've got to read 500 books before you get through high school—I say bull! You've got to read a small number of good books very carefully, and learn how to think about books. You have the rest of your life to read *Moby Dick, Silas Marner,* or *The Color Purple.*

At the "Gardner school," we're going to interest your son, Max Brockman, and my son, Benjamin Gardner, in these really interesting questions, which are human questions—what life's all about? Then you encounter these funny squiggles and you've got to make sense out of the literacies. Why? Because we can't read those books and listen to those works of art and understand those machines unless we pick up some of those literacies. But the literacies are not ends in themselves. President Clinton said we want to have every kid reading by third grade. I say, we know how to teach kids how to read; the problem is that kids *don't* read. Literacies have to be a *means* to get to the disciplines. The disciplines are the handmaidens to help us come up with reasonable first answers to all these essential questions. We can't do it on our own. But there are only three or four basic disciplines that we should worry about before college. One, how to think scientifically. Most people in America still believe in astrology; they're clueless about how to make sense of an experiment. They don't know what a hypothesis is. Two, they need to know something about the history of their country, something about their background, maybe a little about the rest of the world too. But again, people don't know how to do this historically. They think the Punic Wars occurred about the same time as the Truman administration. They don't understand the ways in which we are like and

> There are only four basic disciplines that we should worry about before college: how to think scientifically, the history of their country and the larger world, how to make sense of works of art, and mathematical thinking—the language of science.

unlike other cultures or other historical eras; they tend to think the past was all different and all bad, the present is all good, and that history is progress—they're filled with misconceptions. So you need to know something about history. Three, people need to know something about how to make sense of works of art, because those are treasures of the culture, and four, they have to know something about mathematics because it's the language of science, and they're going to be stuck if they don't know. The particular books they read and the particular science they learn are completely irrelevant until you get to college. You're picking up some tools so you can enter into the conversations of the centuries on these and other important questions.

So what happens in this ideal school? Students have learned a lot about some very important topics that the culture cherishes. And they've secured some tools so if they want to know about something besides the things they've focused on, they can study it in college or read about it on their own; they've got the rest of their life to pursue it.

How do we find out what they've learned? We ask them to issue performances of understanding. We give them materials that they haven't encountered before, and ask, how can you make sense of it? For instance, say you just studied the Holocaust. I'm going to tell you about Bosnia. Or about what happened in Armenia in the First World War. And I want you to talk about that, or write about it, or enact it—do a play about it. Help me understand what's going on and tell me in what ways Bosnia or Armenia is like what happened in Germany and in what ways it's different.

You've been studying evolution? I'm going to tell you something about virtual reality, if you're interested in that. I'm going to tell you about computers. Stretch—use that knowledge in a new situation.

You've read and understood this George Eliot book? I'm going to give you a book by Jane Austen. I don't care which book it is, it's simply not relevant. And the students who get to go on scholarship to private universities are not the ones who can tell me when every battle occurred, or who can memorize every chemical formula. I'm going to admit those students who can show me how to think about issues in those areas. I'll give them a hundred choices. They have to perform their understanding on something which matters in the culture.

JB: What about resistance from people who are in the education industry—teachers, among others?

Gardner: For one thing, I'm calling on people to change what they do. For another, coverage is very comforting. One of the reasons why E. D. Hirsch is so popular is that you can say your students knew 300 things last year, and now they know 600. Now they know 300 things more. But I say facts are completely discipline-neutral. If you don't learn how to think and speak differently about things then you really haven't been schooled at all. You remember the old *$64,000 Question? Jeopardy* and the *$64,000 Question* form the American consciousness about what it is to know things. Other countries aren't much better, but international studies bear me out. The kids in East Asia and Western Europe who do better in science and math are the ones who attend schools where they actually do more "uncovering" and less covering. They go more deeply into topics and they build up more habits of thinking; they don't worry about spending ten seconds on many different things.

In fact, a lot of my ideas have been less confusing to people in other countries than they have been in the United States. Our education discourse is so primitive. If you compare, for example, writing about science in our newspapers to writing about education, writing about science has really improved over the last 20 years—if you read *Science Times* and the science pages of other papers, you learn something in areas where you are not an expert.

In writing about education, everything is about test scores, and every six months there's a piece about some cute place where they're teaching kids something in the arts—but there's no cumulative knowledge there, there's no *Wall Street Journal* for people who are interested in education. Yet in the rest of the world nearly everybody realizes that education is what it's all about.

The irony is that in countries that are very resource-rich, like the United States, Argentina, maybe Russia to a certain extent, one is able to get away with an education system that has just been okay for a small percentage of the population, because there are so many resources. That's not going to be true forever. It's individuals who will be better at problem finding as well as problem solving who will be better at working together in groups, who'll be able to be very good at troubleshooting, who will be able to take these disciplines and bring them to bear in new areas. They're the ones that will be in power 50 years from now. While there are some aspects of our society which are very benevolent with reference to those things, our schools aren't one of them. Our schools are behind except for a very few schools which the elite get the chance to send their kids to, but that's not where the future's going to be cast. What's going to happen to the 75 percent of our population that doesn't have high-quality education? That's the question.

> If you don't learn how to think and speak differently about things then you really haven't been schooled at all.

JB: How do you see these ideas playing out over the next years—the implications of book [*The Disciplined Mind,* by Howard Gardner, Penguin, 2000] in terms of what you might do with it, or how other people might use it?

Gardner: I've already given part of the answer to this; these ideas will fall on more receptive ears in other parts of the world, where not only is education taken more seriously, but where it's possible to have a more unified kind of national conversation. We may not like the French system, but when they make a decision, it gets implemented very widely. There are many countries which no longer are part French colonies which still run their schools the way the French ran their schools 50 or a hundred years ago.

JB: We're too patchy for that.

Gardner: The interesting thing will be to see whether individuals who are traditionally oriented, whether scholars or lay people, who like the goal of a traditional orientation will be drawn to the notion of this deep uncovering, rather than covering superficially, and of being very imaginative and flexible in how you present such a curriculum to a very diverse population. That's what the issue is going to hang on. It could be that it'll serve as a meeting ground for people who have hitherto thought they were at each other's necks—but it could also elicit a "plague on both your houses" reaction. The people who are more liberal/progressive will say that Gardner's really lost it, because he's talking about "pale stale males," whereas the people on the right will say, well, granted he wants to talk about some things that are worth talking about, but first of all there are thousands of other things that the kids have to know as well. He won't tell us what those things are, and second of all, what is all this nonsense about teaching things in different ways? There's one way to teach, the right way, and either the kids will learn it or it's too bad.

JB: You're right. People might think you're losing it.

Gardner: Maybe I am!

JB: It's a departure.

Gardner: I probably feel more of a personal commitment to this than anything else I've ever undertaken—it really comes from my soul. I have been deeply involved in school reform for at least 15 years. I've been very frustrated by the superficiality of the discussion, and by my perception that people don't really get down to the basic of what an ordinary citizen ought to be able to know so that he can cope with a world that's changing very quickly and is very confusing.

JB: Ideas like this don't have a prayer of getting adopted by a typical school board—but they certainly can seep into the culture, in a very almost clandestine way.

Gardner: It will take 50 years to see whether the ideas I've developed have an impact. One of the things I've pushed very much is the idea of individual-centered education. Up to now, everybody's taught the same thing, the same way, they're tested in the same way, if you do well fine, if not, too bad—it's seen as being very fair. My argument, which contradicts any argument ever made in history, is it's the most unfair method in the world. It privileges one kind of mind, which I call the language-logic mind, or sometimes the Al Dershowitz mind (which I admire), this view that says, the more you're like that, the better you'll do, and the more rewards we'll give you, and the more you're different from that, tough *nuggies.* (A technical term in Cambridge—Ed. Note)

With the advent of the new technologies, individual-centered education is only a matter of time. People in 50 years will laugh at the notion that we thought everybody had to be taught the same thing in the same way. Already, with anything that's worth teaching, we know dozens of ways of teaching it; we can make available technologically these things to any individual. Moreover, because we have smart machines, they can record what the child learned well, what he learned poorly, how he learned well, how he learned poorly; and make use of that knowledge. So that's an idea that I know is right.

Understanding—that's a much bigger enchilada, so to speak. We've been content to see whether kids can sit on their duffs and do what they don't particularly want to do; that's been the operational definition of "making it," and that just isn't going to be enough any more. That might take a hundred years, so our grandchildren will know whether the world has become more receptive to an education-centered understanding.

> It's malpractice to expose kids to things for a week or two and go on to something else. We know that doesn't work.

The evidence that students do not even understand what we're teaching them is legion now. It's malpractice to expose kids to things for a week or two and go on to something else. We know that doesn't work. The work of Project Zero in this arena, where I've worked for over 30 years both in multiple intelligences and in teaching understanding, is promising. That's exactly the right word to use. If I had to go to a congressional committee and make the best case, I could give numbers, but that would be a best case rather than the most accurate description. It's promising, it's tough work, and because education is not a science, it's an art. It's very hard when something goes well to know why.

Everybody in this country who knows about education, including me, admires Debbie Meier. The school that she founded is in New York City: Central Park East, secondary school and elementary school. Those are schools in very tough areas, East Harlem, and they really turn out kids who get through, go on to four-year colleges, and do decently. But nobody really understands whether it's one thing, two things, or twenty things there. It's too hard to figure out what the variables are; you can't do a controlled experiment.

The important thing for someone like me is to do no harm. For the first ten years of work in multiple intelligences I kept my mouth shut and let people do what they wanted to do, and then I finally came to the conclusion that that was a mistake, because some of the things people were doing were harmful. So I began to speak up about it, and I began to take a more active role. In Project Zero, we're actually studying schools around the country that claim to be doing well in cultivating the intelligences, and we are trying to separate the wheat from the chaff. And I assume the same sense of responsibility for these new ideas.

Art, Imagination, and School Renewal

Toward a Common Language

Maxine Greene

Maxine Greene is Professor Emerata at Teachers College, Columbia University, where she has taught courses in aesthetics, educational philosophy, the arts and American education, and social philosophy. As the founder and director of the Center for Social Imagination, the Arts, and Education, she has long served as a leader in the effort to infuse education with views of imaginative possibility.

Confronting the problem of a common language—accessible to diverse artists, teachers, members of communities, and administrators—I recall the title of an Adrienne Rich collection called *The Dream of a Common Language* (1993). To think of it as a dream, of course, is to imagine it as something still out of reach, something sought for, something (at least for Rich) in some manner extraordinary. She wrote:

> But there come times—perhaps this is one of them—when we have to take ourselves more seriously or die; when we have to pull back from the incantations, rhythms we've moved to

thoughtlessly, and disenthrall ourselves, bestow ourselves to silence, or a severer listening, cleansed of oratory, formulas, choruses, laments, static crowding of the wires. (1993, pp. 74–75)

No one, she said, who survives to speak a new language can avoid a cutting of the wires, a kind of "free fall." Surely we know what she meant. She was calling on us to break with bureaucratic talk, pious talk, media talk, with what John Dewey called the "crust of conventionalized and routine consciousness" (1954, p. 183). He was, as many of you know, always critical of fixities, of the routine, the thoughtless, the mechanical, and what he sometimes called the "anesthetic," meaning the banal, the repetitive, the static. In *The Public and Its Problems* (1954), he pointed to the superficial plane on which so many people formed their opinions and made their judgments and went on to say that our lives reach a deeper level that only art can touch. It is, after all, one of the functions of art to break through that crust of "routine consciousness," to awaken us, I would say (along with Virginia Woolf and Albert Camus), and enhance our being in the world. "Common things," Dewey said, "a flower, a gleam of moonlight, the wing of a bird, not things rare and remote, are means with which the deeper levels of life are touched so that they spring up as desire and thought. Poetry, the drama, the novel, are proofs that the process of presentation is not insoluble. Artists have always been the real purveyors of the news, for it is not the outward happening in itself which is new, but the kindling by it of emotion, perception and appreciation" (1954, pp. 183–184). Virginia Woolf called what he was trying to describe "moments of being" (1985, p. 71). Albert Camus wrote about the break with deadly routine, and how "one day the 'why' arises and everything begins in that weariness tinged with amazement. 'Begins'—this is important. Weariness comes at the end of the acts of a mechanical life, but at the same time it inaugurates the impulse of consciousness" (1991, p. 13). It is my view that encounters with certain art forms from either the creative or the appreciative point of view (I would hope from both) are what make such awakenings, such beginnings possible. And I believe that it is only after such awakenings, such moments of what have been called unconcealment, that young people as well as older people are enabled to see, feel, hear what Dewey called "the common things" that touch the deeper levels of life.

I want to believe that it is the release of imagination that makes these moments more likely and more frequent. In a book entitled *Imagination,* Mary Warnock links imagination to the belief that "there is more in our experience of the world than can possibly meet the unreflecting eye, that our experience is significant for us, and worth the attempt to understand it . . . this kind of belief may be referred to as the feeling of infinity" (1978, p. 202). Oddly or not, I associate that with what Adrienne Rich, in quite another mood, called a "free fall." Warnock goes on:

It is a sense . . . that there is always more to experience, and more in what we experience than we can predict. Without some such sense, even at the quite human level of there being something which deeply absorbs our interest, human life becomes perhaps not actually futile or pointless, but experienced as if it were. It becomes, that is to say, boring. In my opinion, it is the main purpose of education to give people the opportunity of not ever being, in this sense, bored; of not ever succumbing to a feeling of futility, or to the belief that they have come to the end of what is worth having. It may be that some people do not need education to save them from this; my claim is only that, if education has a justification, this salvation for those who do need it must be its justification. (1978, pp. 202–203)

I have looked into (yes, and read about) the dead and empty eyes of children who think they have nothing to hope for. Some, when asked what they want to be when they grow up, cannot respond, or they tell us (as I have heard in several schools) that all depends on whether they live that long. We have seen the ways in which poor, neglected, or homeless children inscribe their pain when they are given crayons or pastels or pieces of chalk, and when their teachers or visiting artists give them clues about translating thoughts or feelings into objects or movements or shapes or sound. I think of the poetry young people are writing and what it can mean when they are moved (as I was) to explore the work of those called "real poets" for suggestions when it comes to rhythm and image and even (although they may not know the word) metaphor.

One of the significant changes in what many conceive of as dark times in the public schools seems to me a growing acknowledgment of the richness, the complexity, often the darkness of young people's experience. It is not so long ago that schoolchildren, for all the efforts of progressive educators, were thought of as empty vessels, there to be filled with officially sanctioned knowledge, if not (as in the case of Dickens' Mr. Gradgrind) "facts, Sissy, facts." Teachers, asked to keep their own journals, to come in touch with their own life stories, are far more likely to recognize that young people too can be seekers of meaning, makers of meaning. Many teachers have begun to view themselves as coaches, concerned for children's active sense-making, active learning. Much depends on their imaginations being aroused, on their feelings infusing their thinking, their perceptions grounding what they come to know and understand.

It is in encounters with the arts, informed encounters, that their capacities are activated in ways traditionally ignored. Their understanding, like their interest in bringing paintings and dance performance and musical pieces and poems to life in their experience, surely is enriched by whatever experiences we can make available in exploring media, the materials with which artists work. It is not only that they are provided a means of expression and symbolization, an unexpected way of making imprints on the world. They are enabled to comprehend the efforts that must be exerted, the discipline that must be grasped, if what they perceive and feel and remember is to be given form— meaning to which others might respond.

> It is in encounters with the arts, informed encounters, that children's capacities are activated in ways traditionally ignored. Their understanding and interests are enriched by whatever experiences we can make available in exploring media.

I remember a young man, a teenager, who had learned to work with others to make video renderings of his neighborhood and his friends. One that I saw had to do with boys in Harlem talking about why they needed guns. The youngsters who chose to capture that conversation told us how learning the skills required in making these videos gave them a sense of purpose, even freed them to look at other people's videos and even television programs with a more critical understanding. They discovered, among other things, that they had a right to interpret what they saw against their own lived experience. Not only did they seem to recognize what Mary Warnock (1978) said—that their experience held more than they might have predicted, that there were openings, spaces they might never have suspected—but the adventure (and it was an adventure), like the work required, gave them a feeling of dignity they had never known.

Surely, many of us have seen the same kinds of awakenings in poetry workshops or when youngsters are coached in the writing of stories. We have seen it when studios, as it were, are opened in schools where painters can work with students and visual transformations are made part of the curriculum and part of their lives.

I am very aware, as we all are, of the enjoyment and excitement that can envelop a school when artists come to perform, after (if time and budget allow) involving students in the preparation, in the making of a dance, say, or a Shakespearean work, or a Gilbert and Sullivan piece. And I am aware of the pleasures of working with papier-mâché in homage, say, to Red Grooms, or of gathering to listen to Midori's violin when she visits a school. Like all of you, I hope we can keep alive the excitement, the pure pleasure, the break in routine arts in school bring with them. The breaking of the old lockstep scheduling, the surprise that is so much a part of involvement with art forms (at least those appropriate to different stages of development) cannot but lighten the atmosphere, even in the grim old buildings where so many young people are compelled to spend their days or (and I have seen this too) to hang out (once they check in) in the hallways or at the doors.

I have a recollection of going to one of those schools, a high school in the Bronx, and finding a group of boys on the steps in front of the door. One of them had written "school sucks" on the doors, and I stopped for a minute to stare, unsure of the expression on my face. One of the boys looked questioningly at me and, suddenly, free associating a bit mindlessly, I asked whether they had ever read *Catcher in the Rye* (Salinger, 1957). And then I told them that in that book, Holden Caulfield, the young hero, had talked about cleaning all the dirty words off the walls of the school—and that I wondered how he would have handled that door. One of the boys scoffed and said that no one could wipe off all the walls in their school; the writing would only come back again. And then a small voice asked me, what was this book I was talking about anyway? Suddenly, this elderly lady from downtown was sitting on the step telling them—and I must say I had a hushed and attentive audience for a while—about Holden Caulfield, particularly about the fantasy having to do with keeping children from falling off the cliff from the field of rye into what I always thought of, and think Holden thought of too, as the adult world. Perhaps you remember Holden misreading the Robert Burns poem. Instead of "If a body meet a body coming through the rye," he thought it was "If a body catch a body." Then he says, "Anyway, I keep picturing all these little kids playing some game in this big field of rye and all. Thousands of little kids, and nobody's around,—nobody big, I mean—except me. And I'm standing on the edge of some crazy cliff. What I have to do, I have to catch everybody if they start to go over the cliff—I mean if they're running and they don't look where they're going I have to come out from somewhere and *catch* them. That's all I'd do all day. I'd just be the catcher in the rye and all. I know it's crazy but that's the only thing I'd really like to be. I know it's crazy." His sister finally tells him, "Daddy's going to kill you." And Holden says, "I don't give a damn if he does" (Salinger, 1957, pp. 224–225). I am not sure if I remembered to tell my auditors that right after that Holden wants to "phone up this guy that was my English teacher" (Salinger, 1957, pp. 224–225), now teaching English at NYU.

I think the kids listened to me because they were bored, but also because I was opening a kind of door for them, a door through which they could look into an as/if world, a created world, but one that might (at least for the moment) make their world a little more intelligible. If I had had time, if I could have kept their attention and taken them with me, I would have told them about Huckleberry Finn and maybe Bartleby, the scrivener, and Gatsby (you may remember that Holden was crazy about *The Great Gatsby*—"Old Gatsby. Old sport. That killed me" [Salinger, 1957, p. 183]). I would have liked to provoke them to match their stories against the stories of those who pursued stubbornly and hopelessly the American dream, who "preferred not to" in the end, or who, refusing to be all cramped up and have people try to "civilize them," lit out for the territory ahead—unaware that it was closed.

> Most of us involved in any way with the arts know very well the interrogative role they play or ought to play in life.

No, I do not believe I was offering any solution for them or any promise of sanctuary. I know, as most of you know, that it is not the function of art to offer answers, nor the function of teachers to come in with comfortable certainties. Novels, and for me great plays (I keep thinking of *The Doll's House,* a year or two ago, of *The Chairs,* of *The Beauty Queen of Leonane,* even certain paintings—Franz Hals's, as John Berger has taught me, Rembrandt's, Cezanne's, van Gogh's, Monet's, Goya's, even—and I keep seeing that dark cloud over the city of Delft—Vermeer's), open question after question, questions that sharpen the questions, and make me—as Rilke (1993) told his young poet to do—love the questions because they make me reach in so many directions, because they make me feel alive. And I believe, wrongly or rightly, that the kinds of questions that make me so uneasy, that make me feel so alive, so eager to keep on in the face of meaninglessness, are questions I share with other human beings, young ones included, once they are awakened, once they are helped to see. That suggests for me one of the sources of a common language—perhaps what Dewey meant when he talked about "deeper levels of life" (1954, p. 183).

In any case, most of us involved in any way with the arts know very well the interrogative role they play or ought to play in life, the power (according to Denis Donoghue [1984]) to defamiliarize the taken for granted, to shed a new light, sometimes a light of unwanted exposure on our lived lives. (I cannot thrust away a closing scene in the recent production of Ionescu's *The Chairs* when a fierce light suddenly is lit on the back of the stage, making members of the audience rear back and cover their eyes—and perhaps, breathing hard at the end, manage to say, "I see.") I appreciate Donoghue's reminding us that the arts may be useless in the sense they cannot cure toothaches, but in another way are momentous "because they provide for spaces in which we can live in total freedom. Think of it as a page. The main text is central, it is the text of need, of food and shelter, of daily preoccupations and jobs, keeping things going. This text is negotiated mostly by convention, routine, habit, duty; we have very little choice in it. So long as we are in this text, we merely coincide with our ordinary selves. If the entire page were taken with the text, we would have to live according to its conventional rhythms, even in our leisure hour, because they too are subject to conventions" (1984, p. 129).

Donoghue goes on to say that, for him, the arts are on the margins of most of our lives, the margin being the place for those feelings and intuitions that daily life doesn't have a place for and mostly seems to suppress. "Yet those," he writes, "who choose to live within the arts can make a space for themselves and fill it with intimations of freedom and presence" (1984, p. 129). The idea of making spaces for ourselves, experiencing ourselves in our tension and connectedness, and taking initiatives to move through those spaces seem to me to be of the first importance—for learning, for teaching, for feeling alive. As the philosopher Martin Heidegger said, things happen now and then beyond what is when an open place suddenly appears. There is a clearing, a lighting, a reaching beyond what we are sure we know.

There are, I must say, a number of people who are beginning to point out the relevance of social class to all of this. Not only is it still affirmed that our choices of what we choose to call "art" are still influenced by our Western traditions and by elitist conception of quality. Granted, we are allowing for multiculturalism; everyone recognizes the significance of major artists like Toni Morrison, Alice Walker, Maya Angelou, August Wilson, Audre Lorde, Ralph Ellison, James Baldwin, as well as major thinkers like Cornel West, Henry Louis Gates, and Patricia Williams. But we tend to forget, time and time again, that many of the questions educators foster, many of the critiques that find expression, are not those raised by newcomers to our country, immigrants, outsiders eager, above all, to join the mainstream and to assure not only requisite skills for their children but an acceptance of the prevailing value system as well. Talk of spaces and intuitions of freedom, talk of the unpredictable, while understandable, are not what many of such people want from schools. As we learn from African American scholar and teacher Lisa Delpit and others, many people want structure, they want a kind of humane process of socialization, they want recognition, they want technological training for their young, as they want security and the ability to survive. And some people become convinced that the freedom, the perceptive acuity, the consciousness of possibility we stress when we argue for the arts deserve a priority in the curricula of so-called reformed schools.

Seeking a common language, as we do, hoping for an emancipatory role for the several arts (when reflected upon, when made accessible), we still need to think of the multiple realities now represented in our cities and our schools. With New York's centennial celebration, we were reminded of the rich fabrics of different art forms and different cultures, some of which have been, deliberately or not, ignored. There is the Korean tradition, there is the Puerto Rican tradition, there are the multiple Caribbean traditions—French, English, Creole. There are Arabic and other Middle Eastern traditions; today, there are Russian colonies, Haitian colonies.

Think of the challenge to those of us in search of a common language. Think, even more importantly, of classrooms where most of the students are still caught up in the symbol systems of cultures that do not view "art" as individual creation or a phenomenon depending for its realization on individual percipients' seeing or listening or constructing as meaningful.

Clifford Geertz, the anthropologist, writes about the gap most of us feel between the amount of talk about art that proceeds all around us and our ability to define or understand it. Because people perceive something important in the arts in general or in particular works, they talk or write about it endlessly. He writes that "we describe, analyze, compare, judge, classify; we erect theories about creativity, form, perception, social function; we characterize art as a language, a structure, a system, an act, a symbol, a pattern of feeling; we reach for scientific metaphors, spiritual ones, technological ones, political ones: and if all else fails, we string dark sayings together and hope someone will elucidate them for us" (2000, p. 95). Geertz views art in its multiple contexts as one of the several ways in which people participate in the general systems of symbolic forms we call cultures. Art, whatever its form, must be seen as part of the life of signs in a society, and Geertz asks his readers to move toward a consideration of them in their natural habitat—the "common world" in which we look, name, make things, and listen. "If there is a commonality, it lies in the fact that certain activities everywhere seem specifically designed to demonstrate that ideas are visible, audible, and tactile, that they can be cast in forms where the senses and through the senses, the emotions, can reflectively address them. The variety of artistic expression stems from the variety of conceptions we have about the way things are and is indeed the same variety" (2000, pp. 118–119). Signs, Geertz says, are modes of thought as much as they are modes of communication, and we need still to concern ourselves with what they tell us about the changing life around them—life in its fullness and deficiency, in its wonder and disillusionment, in its hopes and broken promises. They feed into what Jerome Bruner (1987) describes as the mode of knowing called storytelling; they orient us to the horizons and to the surrounding world.

In most of the cultures represented in today's classrooms, there is relatively little interest in what reflective engagement with art forms can mean when it comes to self-knowledge, to being in the world as a conscious being who is in most ways unduplicable. Children who come from non-Western cultures are more than likely to conceive of art as something incorporated into the textures of a

> Art, whatever its form, must be seen as part of the life of signs in a society.

shared social life, if they think of the arts at all. The "margin" of which Donoghue speaks, like the moments of freedom and presence, cannot have more meaning for Islamic or Buddhist or Guyanese children than a description of art forms in terms of formal relationships. The more we honor the traditions and expectations of such children and young people, the more complex becomes the problem of arguing for the arts in education. It may be that certain of their parents may view an acknowledgment of individuality and point of view as an aspect of the socialization process, but neither they nor their children are likely to think of the Western view of aesthetic power as the authoritative view. To visit an exhibition of Islamic or Byzantine art, to read novels like *The God of Small Things, Lucy, Ceremony, Jasmine, A Pale View of Hills,* or another postcolonial text is to recognize that the center has shifted and that we can no longer refer to the same norms in arguing for our conceptions of the artistic-aesthetic, or what represents, what presents, what is beautiful, what moves us to aspire. Patrick Chamoiseau, a writer from Martinique and the author of *Texaco* (1997), wrote a small and revealing note at the start of an earlier book called *School Days* (1997), which ought to also be taken into account as we seek a common language:

Youngster,
    Of the West Indies, of French Guyana, of New Caledonia, of Reunion, of Mauritius, of Rodriques and other Mascarenes, of Corsica, of Brittany, of Normandy, of Alsace, of the Basque country, of Provence, of Africa, of the four corners of the Orient, of all national territories, of all far-flung dominions, of all outlying posts of empires or federations, you who have had to face a colonial school, yes, you who in other ways are still confronting one today, and you who will face this challenge tomorrow in some other guise: This voice of bitter laughter at the One and Only—a firmly centered voice challenging all centers, a voice beyond all home countries and peacefully diversal in opposition to the universal—is raised in your name.
    In Creole friendship,
    PC (Chamoiseau, 1997, epigraph, n.p.)

As we search, it is that voice, I believe, that name to hold in mind.

There must be dialogue, particularly between teachers and artists, or so I believe. Democracy, Dewey (1944) told us, is a community in the making, and so, I would suggest, is a common language. If it ever solidified and became in some way absolute, it would begin resembling Chamoiseau's "One and Only" and give rise to the same bitter response. When I think of partnership, in any event, I do not think of institutions coming together. I think of individuals, live persons coming together. Again I turn to poetry, this time to a Muriel Rukeyser poem called "Effort at Speech Between Two People." Each verse begins with a variation "Speak to me. Take my hand. Where are you now?" (1992, p. 2). And this is the final verse:

What are you now? If we could touch one another, If these our separate entities could come to grips, Clenched like a Chinese puzzle. . . . yesterday I stood in a crowded street that was alive with people, And no one spoke a word, and the morning shone, Everyone silent, moving. . . . Take my hand. Speak to me. (Rukeyser, 1992, p. 4)

Yes, I know partnerships have emerged and whom they are intended to include, as schools reach out to arts organizations that are willing to support and to sustain in the name of and hope for renewal or reform. At once, I know that collaboration and partnership can only be realized through personal encounters, which often begin where people are silent because they do not, at first, know what to say. It is not only that so many of the words are encapsulated in formulas, choruses, laments, as Adrienne Rich (1978) suggested. It is that, once we reach below the surface of spontaneity and entertainment, we discover contradictions, differences we never anticipated. What of the young, bathing in popular culture, defining the performances that make it to the screens as unquestionably art? What of the distances that still appear to yawn between theater (either Broadway this year or off-Broadway) and the films and concerts young people choose to attend, the videos they buy, the CDs in the countless music stores? What of the teachers who still dread the "free fall," even as they dread the openings the unpredictable imagination makes possible? What of those teachers who teach to the test in order to ensure predictability, the ones who need to measure in order to justify what they do? What of the teachers who have scarcely known the arts in the course of their lives, who think of them as frivolous, purely affective, at best, motivational? What of those who conceive standards as predefined, fixed, and to be imposed from above? What of those immersed in instrumental rationality, seeing themselves as molding the young, treating them as resources for the state, for the business community, for the new technology, not as existing persons in process, seeking their own ways?

There are at least three approaches to school reform in these times. There is one connected to "Goals 2000," centered on increasing general literacy for the sake of readying the new generation in a millennium governed by new technologies, linked by more and more complicated interests, an age respondent to free market ideologies. There is the approach connected to the Christian Right, ostensibly preoccupied with virtue and character education, with abstinence and chastity, with the family, with prayer in schools, with school choice, and with campaigning against abortion and homosexuality. (I am reminded of Dewey again, writing about what he called "social pathology" in 1927, finding its symptoms in "idealization of long established, in a facile optimism assumes as a cloak, in riotous glorifications of things 'as they are,' in intimidation of all dissenters— ways which depress and dissipate through all the more effectual because they operate with subtle and unconscious persuasiveness" [Dewey, 1954, p. 170].)

Then there is the reform that purportedly continues the progressive or the experiential tradition, stemming from Rousseau, Pestalozzi, Emerson, Froebel, Dewey, Bruner, Gardner, Duckworth, and others familiar to any of you in touch with that stream in American history running in the direction of personal liberation, awareness, and (in time) humane face-to-face community. Its watchwords today are active learning, critical questions, and the construction of meaning, what Deborah Meier (1996) calls "the power of ideas." It involves efforts to release long silenced voices, to treat learners as situated persons speaking from their own locations as "who they are," to quote Hannah Arendt, "not what they are" (1998, p. 183). Collaborative learning, classroom communities, engagement with parents, outreach to neighborhoods, evolution by portfolio and exhibition, concern for the qualitative rather than the quantitative, a commitment to care and connectedness, as women's ways of knowing supplement and complement the autonomous rationality so long considered the source of standards as well as the goal of human development: all these mark many of the schools that see themselves involved in reform.

In the event of partnership between such schools and art organizations that are concerned for the health of children and in forging creative responses to their needs, the meaning of "art" and of "aesthetic experience" needs to be continually explored. It is not a matter of transforming teachers into artists or artists into public school teachers. Artists in the several domains themselves often reach for a common language, so that dancers may work in workshops with composers, poets with theater people, and painters with musicians. In an atmosphere where dialogue is welcomed, teachers and artists may come together to articulate what they understand to be the meaning and ends in view of their distinctive projects. And they are distinctive. Teachers who reflect upon their projects (the projects by which they have defined themselves over the years) may think about their own thinking when it comes to devising situations in which young people are provoked to learn and teach themselves. Artists, taking the initiative in an ongoing conversation, may consider the differences between teaching future practitioners of their own art forms and communicating to classroom teachers the languages of those art forms. The point in the classroom, as I see it, is to open spaces for the use of those languages to complement and extend what is understood through verbal and mathematical literacy. There are issues, however, having to do with how the concept of art is to be understood. (I can imagine, for instance, a dialogue generated by the play called Art, with all its hidden questions about representation, monochromatic paintings, price, elitism, and human friendship before and behind the painting on the wall. Or, thinking back to the play entitled *Six Degrees of Separation,* I can recall a mystery about a Kandinsky painting, which also gives rise to questions and talk. And then there are the purported moral issues related to certain works of art in the debates surrounding the declining support for the National Arts Endowment. Teachers, too, might be involved in an exploration of Robert Mapplethorpe exhibitions, the performances of Karen Finley, the work of Robert Serrano. It may still be that dialogue among persons differently situated in the culture can advance the search for a common language.)

Nelson Goodman in the book *Languages of Art* (1976) treats the arts as symbol systems that are invented, applied, transformed, and

> The point in the classroom is to open spaces for the use of artistic languages to complement and extend what is understood through verbal and mathematical literacy.

manipulated in a variety of ways—and that cannot be translated into one another. He makes what to me is a significant and relevant point when he challenges the notion that the aesthetic attitude is a kind of passive contemplation of the immediately given, uncontaminated by conceptualization, isolated from echoes of the past. He views it entirely differently (and compares old views of the disinterested and passive aesthetic attitude with gazing at a poem on a printed page without reading it). He goes on:

> I have held, on the contrary, that we have to read the painting as well as the poem, and that aesthetic experience is dynamic rather than static. It involves making delicate discrimination and discerning subtle relationships, identifying symbol systems and characters within these systems and that these characters denote and exemplify, interpreting works and reorganizing the world in terms of works and works in terms of the world. Much of our experience and many of our skills are brought to bear and may be transformed by the encounter. The aesthetic 'attitude' is restless, searching, testing—is less attitude than action: creation and recreation. (1976, p. 242)

Not everyone will share Goodman's philosophy nor be willing to understand the different arts in terms of symbol systems or languages. Nonetheless, there is something in this paragraph suggesting active transaction between human beings and the world that brings it close to the spirit of what we think of as school reform. When I ponder the problem of a common language, words like *interpreting* and *reorganizing* and *restless, searching,* and *testing* seem somehow essential to it and essential to our thinking about art.

It happens that Goodman is impatient with judgments of merit and an over-concentration on the question of excellence, which leads to distortion of aesthetic inquiry, he believes.

> To say that a work of art is good or even to say how good it is does not after all provide much information, does not tell us whether the work is evocative, robust, vibrant or exquisitely designed, and still less what are its alien specific qualities of color, shape, or sound . . . judging the excellence of works of art or the goodness of people is not the best way of understanding them. (1976, p. 261)

Holding that in mind, I would suggest that the standards we affirm ought not to be imposed from without; they ought to be in some manner emergent as people work together, trying to discover how they ought to work together, reaching somehow beyond themselves with a sense of ought-ness—a desire to appear before others as the best they can possibly be.

Surely, the common language we work toward can be infused—should be infused—with a sense of what both process and product ought to be. Quantification, the habitual ways of determining merit, the preoccupation with the measurable and the predictable: all must be cast aside as we concern ourselves with action and new beginnings, with imagination opening windows, allowing visions of what is not yet. I choose to conclude with an evocation of Toni Morrison's Nobel address. She was thinking primarily of literature, but what she says applies, I think, to the several arts and certainly to the dream we are nurturing with so many others, "the dream of a common language."

Be it grand or slender, burrowing, blasting or refusing to sanctify; whether it laugh out loud or is a cry without an alphabet, the choice word or the chosen silence, unmolested language surges toward knowledge, not its destruction. But who does not know of literature banned because it is interrogative; discredited because it is critical; erased because alternate? And how many are outraged by the thought of a self-ravaged tongue? Word-work is sublime because it is generative; it makes meaning that secures our difference, our human difference—the way in which we are like no other life. We die. That may be the meaning of life. But we do language. That may be the measure of our lives (1994, pp. 21–22).

We can dream and we can yearn and we can act. And we can say, as Muriel Rukeyser did in still another poem, "Something again is beginning to be born. A dance is dancing in me" (1992, p. 154).

REFERENCES

Arendt, H. (1998). *The human condition*. Chicago: University of Chicago Press.

Bruner, J. (1987). *Actual minds, possible worlds.* Cambridge, MA: Harvard University Press.

Camus, A. (1991). *The myth of Sisyphus and other essays.* New York: Vintage.

Chamoiseau, P. (1997). *School days.* Lincoln: University of Nebraska Press.

Chamoiseau, P. (1997). *Texaco.* New York: Pantheon Books.

Delpit, L. (2006). *Other people's children.* New York: The New Press.

Dewey, J. (1944). *Democracy and education.* New York: Macmillan Company.

Dewey. J. (1954). *The public and its problems.* Athens, OH: Swallow Press. (Original work published 1927)

Donoghue, D. (1984). *The arts without mystery.* Boston: Little Brown and Company.

Geertz, C. (2000). *Local knowledge: Further essays in interpretive anthropology.* New York: Basic Books.

Goodman, N. (1976). *Languages of art.* Indianapolis, IN: Hachett Publishing Company.

Heidegger, M. (2001). *Poetry, language, and thought.* New York: Harper Perennial Modern Classics.

Meier, D. (1996). *The power of their ideas.* Boston: Beacon Press.

Morrison, T. (1994). *Nobel lecture.* New York: Alfred A. Knopf.

Rich, A. (1993). *The dream of a common language: Poems 1974–1978.* New York: W. W. Norton and Company.

Rilke, R. M. (1993). *Letters to a young poet.* New York: W. W. Norton and Company.

Rukeyser, M. (1992). Effort at speech between two people. In M. Rukeseyer, *Out of silence.* Evanston, IL: Northwestern University Press. "Effort at speech between two people" first published in *Theory of flight,* 1935.

Rukeyser, Muriel. (1992). Recovering. In M. Rukeyser, *Out of silence.* Evanston, IL: Northwestern University Press.

Salinger, J. D. (1957). *Catcher in the rye.* New York: Grosset and Dunlap.

Warnock, M. (1978). *Imagination.* Berkeley: University of California Press.

Woolf, V. (1985). *Moments of being: Unpublished autobiographical writings.* New York: Harvest Books.

Schools Should Nurture Wisdom

Robert J. Sternberg

Robert J. Sternberg *is the dean of Tufts' School of Arts and Sciences, professor of psychology, and director of the PACE (Psychology of Abilities, Competencies and Expertise) Center. Before coming to Tufts, he was the IBM Professor of Psychology and Education in the Department of Psychology at Yale University. Sternberg is the author of more than 1,000 publications. He has won numerous awards from various educational organizations and is Fellow of the American Academy of the Arts and Sciences, American Association for the Advancement of Sciences, American Psychological Association, and American Psychological Society.*

I n the United States and more than a dozen other countries for which records have been available, IQ scores have been rising roughly at a rate of 18 points per generation (thirty years) (Flynn, 1987). This increase has been going on for at least several generations (see also Neisser, 1998).

Given that IQs have been rising, what does our world have to show for it? Judging by the amount, seriousness, and sheer scale of global conflict, perhaps not much. There has been no apparent corresponding increase in peace and, in many countries, prosperity has not done so well either. Certainly there is no reason to believe that increasing IQs have improved people's relations with each other.

In the United States, the increase in IQ scores has been accompanied by another trend: increasing use of standardized test scores to determine people's place in society. Herrnstein and Murray (1996) suggested that our society is creating what they referred to as a "cognitive elite"—a socioeconomic upper class dominated by people of high cognitive ability. Universities heavily weigh standardized test scores for admissions, both at the undergraduate and graduate levels. It is difficult to gain admission to prestigious institutions without high test scores. Moreover, surveys such as that of *U.S. News and World Report,* which rank undergraduate and graduate programs using, in part, standardized test scores, place increasing pressure on institutions to weigh those scores heavily in admission. Institutions want to rank highly in these ratings and one method is admitting students with high test scores. It is easier for an institution to raise its test scores than to raise, say, faculty productivity or visibility in research.

> Education is currently seen more as an access route to the best jobs rather than as an end in itself.

So with IQs going up and IQ-related abilities counting more and more for success in society, one can only conclude that the IQ-like abilities of those at the top of the socioeconomic spectrum are higher than ever before—even higher than would be predicted merely by the Flynn effect, because IQs have become more important for gaining access to premium jobs. But again, the rise in IQs among the socioeconomic elite does not seem to have created a happier or more harmonious society, and one only has to read the daily newspapers to see the poor uses to which high IQ can be put.

The rise in IQ scores and their increasing importance has been accompanied by another trend—the increasing use of education as a means of credentialing rather than of learning (Labaree, 1999). Education is seen more as an access route than as an end in itself, and parents and children alike scramble for admission of the children to elite colleges not so much to obtain the best possible education but to obtain the best possible job later on. The result is that the IQs of both parents and children are directed not so much toward the enhancement of their learning and thinking as toward obtaining through education the best possible credentials for individual socioeconomic advancement. Education is seen not so much as a means of helping society but of helping one obtain the best that society has to offer socially, economically, and culturally.

This trend is likely to be amplified by the individualistic norms of U.S. society. Americans typically learn how to live on their own, succeed on their own, and watch out for themselves. Few developed societies invest as little in helping the elderly, the poor, and the ill as does the United States. In short, we turn the increase in IQ not toward collective advantage but instead toward individual advantage. Although there is nothing wrong with such a trend, per se, it is driving us toward a tragedy of the commons. People are now looking out so well for themselves that it results in their collective loss. Consider cows grazing on a common green. As each cow eats more grass, the total available grass decreases. In our society, the total available resources are being sucked up in the service of those who can use their cognitive abilities and skills to maximize their own gains. What exactly are these cognitive abilities and skills, and how are they nurtured?

What Skills Do Schools Currently Nurture?

Memory

Memory is probably essential to all other higher-level cognitive skills. One cannot analyze, create, or apply knowledge without first having the knowledge to analyze, create, or use. But memory for an impressive knowledge base seems like a beginning rather than an end, as illustrated by "walking encyclopedias" who do not seem to be able to effectively use much of what they know. Even people with less impressive knowledge bases often seem to be stuck with inert knowledge that they are unable to use. Many teachers and professors encounter students who get A's in courses but seem unable to use their knowledge in research projects or other types of applications.

Our research suggests that schools overemphasize the development and use of memory-based learning. We have found, for example, that students whom we taught in a way that matches their triarchic (analytical, creative, and practical) pattern of abilities learn more and perform better than do children simply taught for memory (Sternberg, Ferrari, Clinkenbeard, & Grigorenko, 1996; Sternberg, Grigorenko, Ferrari, & Clinkenbeard, 1998). We have also found that children taught triarchically outperform children taught for memory, even on memory-based tests of achievement (Sternberg, Torff, & Grigorenko, 1998a, 1998b).

Cognitive psychologists, like teachers in school, seem to devote a great share of their attention to memory, but one may wonder whether both are not seduced by the greater ease of studying and assessing memory than of studying and assessing other cognitive phenomena, such as creativity or wisdom. There is, of course, a large body of evidence suggesting the importance of a large and well-organized knowledge base for expertise (Chi, Glaser, & Farr, 1988; Ericsson, 1996; Ericsson & Smith, 1991). But such knowledge seems to be more of a necessary than sufficient condition for expertise (Sternberg, 1996). Great thinkers like Descartes, Picasso, Mozart, Dante, Einstein, and Pasteur were clearly knowledgeable, but it seems implausible that it was solely their knowledge that led to their amazing contributions. So perhaps these abilities alone are not enough.

Analytical Abilities

Analytical abilities are the kinds of abilities most frequently measured by conventional tests of abilities (Sternberg, 1997b). Scores on such tests are predictive of grades in school as well as other scholastic criteria (Jensen, 1998). At the same time, one cannot help but wonder whether if these tests measure what distinguishes highly creative leaders of a field from their less creative counterparts. It also seems unlikely that world leaders who are viewed as wise (Nelson Mandela, perhaps, or Abraham Lincoln or Winston Churchill) and those viewed as unwise (Adolf Hitler, Joseph Stalin, or Mobutu Sese Seko) were distinguished cognitively primarily by IQ. As noted earlier, the rise in IQs over the generations has not been matched by any obvious increase in world peace or world order.

Herrnstein and Murray (1996) have argued for the importance of IQ-like analytical abilities in one's attainment of socioeconomic success, but as I have argued elsewhere, the correlation between IQ and societal success seems in large part a societal creation (Sternberg, 1995). By requiring high ability test scores, achievement test scores, or grades for access to the routes to societal success, a society takes a large step toward ensuring that only those who score at high levels on measures of analytical abilities will achieve success, whether or not these particular abilities are actually instrumental for success in the jobs for which they are required. Caste, race, and gender have also been used to create distinctions among groups in their attained socioeconomic levels, a procedure that also creates an artificial correlation between an individual attribute and attainments. The predictor variable "predicts" largely because we force it to. Again, perhaps these abilities are not enough.

Creative Abilities

Creative abilities are attractive as a set of abilities schools should develop and nurture, if only because they seem so important to success in the complex and rapidly changing world in which we live (Sternberg & Lubart, 2002). These abilities also seem important in distinguishing major contributors from minor contributors to a field (Simonton, 1994; see also essays in Sternberg, 1988).

According to Gardner (1993), however, many creative contributors are extremely hard on those around them, making life miserable for others. They also may make life miserable for themselves, as is clear from the lives of people like Mozart, van Gogh, and Hemingway. Others may use their creativity toward the worst possible ends, like the notorious Joseph Mengele. Creativity is not enough either.

> It seems unlikely that world leaders who are viewed as wise and those who are viewed as unwise are primarily distinguished by their IQ scores.

Practical Intelligence

Practical intelligence would seem to be a good candidate for something schools should value and nurture, perhaps more than they do. Research shows the relative independence of practical intelligence from academic intelligence (e.g., Ceci & Liker, 1986; Nuñes, 1994; Sternberg, Wagner, Williams, & Horvath, 1995; see essays in Sternberg & Wagner, 1986). Practical intelligence complements memory and academic intelligence in that it concerns not just what one knows but how one uses it in one's everyday life. Yet practical intelligence, too, even on top of everything else I have discussed, may not be enough.

For one thing, some of the most cunning business people and even world leaders use their practical intelligence to advance themselves and perhaps their close associates, at the same time leaving their businesses or countries (as in the case of Mobutu or Suharto or

Abacha) close to or in bankruptcy. For another thing, some of these individuals not only look out for themselves and their families or close associates, but further use their wiles to destroy anyone who seems like the slightest threat, real or imagined.

Memory, analytical, creative, and practical skills are all important, but they are not enough. What else is there? One additional skill we will explore in depth is wisdom.

MAJOR APPROACHES TO UNDERSTANDING WISDOM

Wisdom has been defined as the "power of judging rightly and following the soundest course of action, based on knowledge, experience, understanding, etc." (*Webster's New World College Dictionary*, 1997, p. 1533). Such a power would seem to be of vast importance in a world that at times seems bent on destroying itself.

A number of psychologists have attempted to understand wisdom in different ways. The approaches underlying some of these attempts are summarized in Sternberg (2003). These approaches might be classified as philosophical, implicit-theoretical, and developmental.

Philosophical approaches have been reviewed by Robinson (2003; see also Robinson, 1999, with regard to the Aristotelian approach in particular, and Labouvie-Vief, 2003, for a further review). Robinson notes that the study of wisdom long predates psychological study, with the Platonic dialogues offering the first intensive analysis of the concept of wisdom. In these dialogues, there are three different senses of wisdom: wisdom as (a) *sophia,* which is found in those who seek a contemplative life in search of truth; (b) *phronesis,* which is the kind of practical wisdom shown by statesmen and legislators; and (c) *episteme,* which is found in those who understand things from a scientific point of view.

Implicit-theoretical approaches to wisdom have in common the search for an understanding of people's conceptions of what wisdom is. Thus, the goal is not to provide a "psychologically true" account of wisdom but rather an account with respect to people's beliefs, whether these beliefs are right or wrong. Some of the earliest work of this kind was done by Clayton (1975, 1976, 1982; Clayton & Birren, 1980), who multidimensionally scaled ratings of pairs of words potentially related to wisdom for three samples of adults differing in age (younger, middle-aged, older). In her earliest study, the terms that were scaled were ones such as *experienced, pragmatic, understanding,* and *knowledgeable* (Clayton, 1975).

Holliday and Chandler (1986) also used an implicit-theories approach to understanding wisdom. Approximately 500 participants were studied across a series of experiments. The investigators were interested in determining whether the concept of wisdom could be understood as a prototype or central concept (Rosch, 1975). Principal-components analysis of one of their studies revealed five underlying factors: exceptional understanding, judgment and communication skills, general competence, interpersonal skills, and social unobtrusiveness.

Sternberg (1985b, 2003) has reported a series of studies investigating implicit theories of wisdom. Six components of wisdom emerged from ratings of behaviors by college students: reasoning ability, sagacity, learning from ideas and environment, judgment, expeditious use of information, and perspicacity.

Explicit theories are constructions of theorists and researchers rather than of laypeople. In the study of wisdom, most explicit-theoretical approaches are based on constructs from the psychology of human development. The most extensive program of research has been that conducted by Baltes and his colleagues. For example, Baltes and Smith (1987, 1990) gave adult participants life-management problems, such as "A fourteen-year-old girl is pregnant. What should she, what should one, consider and do?" and "A fifteen-year-old girl wants to marry soon. What should she, what should one, consider and do?" Baltes and Smith tested a five-component model on participants' protocols in answering these and other questions. The five components in the model are (a) rich factual knowledge (general and specific knowledge about the conditions of life and its variations), (b) rich procedural knowledge (general and specific knowledge about strategies of judgment and advice concerning matters of life), (c) life-span contextualism (knowledge about the contexts of life and their temporal or developmental relationships), (d) relativism (knowledge about differences in values, goals, and priorities), and (e) uncertainty (knowledge about the relative indeterminacy and unpredictability of life and the ways to manage it). An expert answer should reflect more of these components, whereas a novice answer should reflect fewer of them. The data were generally supportive of their model.

> Environmental support for the acquisition of tacit knowledge is minimal—organizations sometimes actually suppress its acquisition.

Some theorists have viewed wisdom in terms of postformal-operational thinking, thereby viewing wisdom as extending beyond the Piagetian stages of intelligence (Piaget, 2001). Thus, wisdom might be a stage of thought beyond Piagetian formal operations. For example, some authors have argued that wise individuals are those who can think reflectively or dialectically, in the latter case with the individuals realizing that truth is not always absolute but rather evolves in a historical context of theses, antitheses, and syntheses (e.g., Basseches, 1984; Kitchener, 1983, 1986; Kitchener & Brenner, 2003; Kitchener & Kitchener, 1981; Labouvie-Vief, 1980, 1982, 2003; Pascual-Leone, 2003; Riegel, 1973). Other theorists have viewed wisdom in terms of finding important problems to solve (Arlin, 2003).

Although most developmental approaches to wisdom are ontogenetic (that is, pertaining to the development of specific individuals), Csikszentmihalyi and Rathunde (2003) have taken a phylogenetic or evolutionary approach, arguing that constructs such as wisdom must have been selected for over time, at least in a cultural sense. They define wisdom as having three basic dimensions of meaning: (a) that of a cognitive process, or a particular way of obtaining and processing information; (b) that of a virtue, or socially valued pattern of behavior; and (c) that of a good, or a personally desirable state or condition.

A Tacit-Knowledge Approach to Understanding Wisdom

The view of wisdom proposed here has at its core the notion of tacit knowledge (Polanyi, 1976). Tacit knowledge is action-oriented knowledge, typically acquired without direct help from others, that allows individuals to achieve goals they personally value (Sternberg et al., 1995). Tacit knowledge has three main features: (a) it is procedural; (b) it is relevant to the attainment of goals people value; and (c) it typically is acquired with little help from others.

When we refer to tacit knowledge as being both procedural and intimately related to action, we are viewing it as a form of "knowing how" rather than of "knowing that" (Ryle, 2000). In our work, we view condition-action sequences (production systems) as a useful formalism for understanding the mental representation of tacit knowledge.

For example, if one needs to deliver bad news to one's boss and if it is Monday morning and if the boss's golf game was rained out the day before and if the boss's staff seems to be "walking on eggshells," then it is better to wait until later to deliver the news. Note that tacit knowledge is always wedded to particular uses in particular situations or classes of situations.

Tacit knowledge also is practically useful. It is instrumental to the attainment of goals people value. Thus, people use this knowledge in order to achieve success in life, however they may define success. Abstract academic knowledge about procedures for solving problems with no relevance to life would not be viewed as constituting tacit knowledge.

Finally, tacit knowledge typically is acquired without direct help from others. At best, others can guide one to acquire this knowledge. Often, environmental support for the acquisition of this knowledge is minimal, and sometimes organizations actually suppress the acquisition of tacit knowledge. For example, a school system might not want its teachers to know how high-level decisions are really made, as opposed to how they are supposed to be made. From a developmental standpoint, this view suggests that wisdom is not taught so much as indirectly acquired. One can provide for the circumstances and case studies to help students develop wisdom, but one cannot teach general courses of action that would be considered wise regardless of circumstances. Indeed, tacit knowledge is wedded to contexts, so that particular knowledge that would apply in one context would not necessarily apply in another context. To help someone develop tacit knowledge, one would provide mediated learning experiences rather than direct instruction as to what to do, and when.

Measurement of Tacit Knowledge

In a series of studies (summarized in Sternberg, Wagner, & Okagaki, 1993; Sternberg et al., 1995), we have sought to develop assessments of tacit knowledge in real-world pursuits. The methodology for constructing assessments is rather complex but involves interviewing individuals for how they have handled critical situations on their jobs (Horvath et al., 1996). We then extract the tacit knowledge implicit in these interviews. Assessments are then constructed that ask people to solve the kinds of problems they find in managing themselves, others, and tasks on the job. Each of these problems typically presents a scenario about a job-related problem along with possible options for dealing with that problem. Test takers are asked to evaluate the quality of the problems on a Likert scale. Their response profiles for all items are then typically scored against the averaged profile of a nominated expert group.

Tacit Knowledge as an Aspect of Practical Intelligence

We have argued that tacit knowledge is a key aspect of practical intelligence (Sternberg, 1985b, 1997b; Sternberg & Wagner, 1993; Sternberg et al., 1993, 1995), or the ability to apply various kinds of information-processing components of intelligence to experience for the purposes of the adaptation to, the shaping of, and the selection of environments. Practical intelligence requires a balance of adaptation, shaping, and selection, because different kinds of environments and environmental situations require different kinds of responses.

In a series of studies (see review in Sternberg et al., 1995), we have shown that tacit knowledge tends to increase with experience on a job but that it is what one learns from the experience rather than the experience itself that seems to matter. Measures of tacit knowledge tend to be correlated with each other, both within and across measures for different occupations. Our measures of tacit knowledge also predict actual performance in jobs such as sales, management, and college teaching. Not only is this prediction statistically significant and fairly substantial in magnitude (with correlations typically at about the 0.3 level), but this prediction is largely independent of the prediction provided by conventional tests of academic intelligence. This is true within a fairly broad range of academic abilities (Eddy, 1988). But the prediction is not always independent. In one study among Kenyan schoolchildren, we have actually found a significant negative correlation between tacit knowledge relevant to environmental adaptation (knowledge of natural herbal medicines believed to fight infections) and performance on measures of fluid and crystallized abilities (see Sternberg & Grigorenko, 1997).

> It is what one learns from an experience, rather than the experience itself, that seems to matter.

THE BALANCE THEORY OF WISDOM

Several of the theories described above emphasize the importance of various kinds of integrations, or balances, in wisdom. At least three major kinds of balances have been proposed: among various kinds of thinking (e.g., Labouvie-Vief, 2003), among various self systems, such as the cognitive, conative, and affective (e.g., Kramer, 2003), and among various points of view (e.g., Kitchener & Brenner, 2003). Baltes has also argued for the importance of balance (Baltes, 1993, 1994; Baltes & Staudinger, 2004; Staudinger, Lopez, & Baltes, 1997). The view presented here expands on but also differs from these kinds of notions in providing for particular kinds of balance in wisdom.

Wisdom as Tacit Knowledge Balancing Interests

The definition of wisdom proposed here draws both upon the notion of tacit knowledge, as described above, and on the notion of balance (Sternberg, in press). Wisdom is thus viewed as a kind of practical intelligence, but not the kind that is applied simply to benefit oneself or an individual one cares about. In particular, wisdom is defined as the application of tacit knowledge as mediated by values toward the achievement of a common good through a balance among (a) intrapersonal, (b) interpersonal, and (c) extrapersonal interests in order to achieve a balance among (a) adaptation to existing environments, (b) shaping of existing environments, and (c) selection of new environments as shown in Figure 1.

Thus, wisdom is a kind of practical intelligence in that it draws upon tacit knowledge, but it is not just a kind of practical intelligence. Wisdom is not just about maximizing one's own or someone else's self-interest, but about balancing of various self-interests (intrapersonal) with the interests of others (interpersonal) and of other aspects of the context in which one lives (extrapersonal), such as one's city, country, environment, or even God.

An implication of this view is that when one applies practical intelligence, one may deliberately seek outcomes that are good for oneself and bad for others. In wisdom, one certainly may seek good ends for oneself, but one also seeks common good outcomes for others. If one's motivations are to maximize certain people's interests and minimize other people's, wisdom is not involved. In wisdom, one seeks a common good, realizing that this common good may be better

Figure 1.1   Wisdom as Tacit Knowledge Balancing Goals, Responses, and Interests

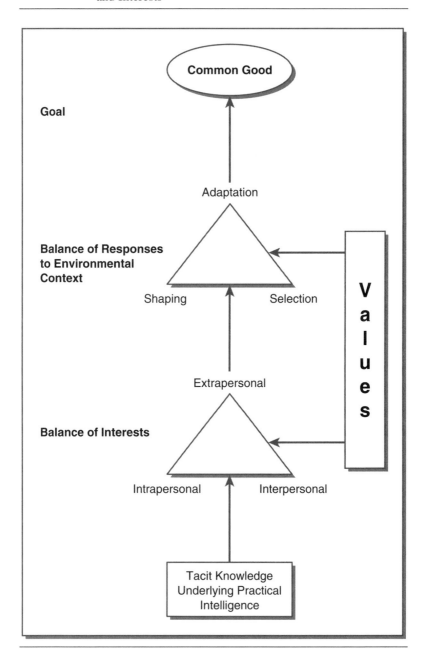

for some than for others. An evil genius may be academically intelligent; he may be practically intelligent; he cannot be wise.

I refer here to "interests," which are related to the multiple points of view that are a common feature of many theories of wisdom (as reviewed in Sternberg, 2003). Diverse interests encompass multiple points of view, and thus the use of the term "interests" is intended to include "points of view." Interests go beyond points of view, however, in that they include not only cognitive aspects of divergences but affective and motivational divergences as well. Sometimes differences in points of view derive not so much from differences in cognitions as from differences in motivations, as when teachers and boards of education have different ideas about how scarce budget dollars should be spent.

> If one's motivations are to maximize certain people's interests and minimize other people's, wisdom is not involved. In wisdom, one seeks a common good, realizing that this common good may be better for some than for others.

Problems requiring wisdom always involve at least some element of each of intrapersonal, interpersonal, and extrapersonal interests. For example, one might decide that it is wise to take a particular teaching position, a decision that seemingly involves only one person. But many people are typically affected by an individual's decision to take a job—significant others, children, perhaps parents and friends. And the decision always has to be made in the context of what the whole range of available options is. Similarly, a decision about whether to have an abortion requires wisdom because it involves not only oneself but the baby who would be born, others to whom one is close such as the father, and the rules and customs of the society.

As is true with all forms of practical intelligence, wisdom involves a balancing of not only the three kinds of interests but also of three possible courses of action in response to this balancing: adaptation of oneself or others to existing environments; shaping of environments in order to render them more compatible with oneself or others; and selection of new environments (Sternberg, 1985a, 1997b). In adaptation, the individual tries to find ways to conform to the existing environment that forms his or her context. Sometimes adaptation is the best course of action under a given set of circumstances. But typically, one seeks a balance between adaptation and shaping, realizing that to fit to an environment requires not only changing oneself but changing the environment as well. When an individual finds it impossible or at least implausible to attain such a fit, he or she may decide to select a new environment altogether, leaving, for example, a job, a community, or a marriage.

Wisdom manifests itself as a series of processes, which are typically cyclical and can occur in a variety of orders. These processes are related to what I have referred to as "metacomponents" of thought, including (a) recognizing the existence of a problem, (b) defining the nature of the problem, (c) representing information about the problem, (d) formulating a strategy for solving the problem, (e) allocating resources to the solution of a problem, (f) monitoring one's solution of the problem, and (g) evaluating feedback regarding that solution (Sternberg, 1985a). In deciding about a teaching job, for example, one first has to see both taking the position and not taking it as viable options (problem recognition), then figure out exactly what taking or not taking the position would mean for oneself (defining the problem), then consider the costs and benefits to oneself and others of taking the position (representing information about the problem), and so forth.

The balance theory suggests that wisdom is at least partially domain specific in that tacit knowledge is acquired within a given context or set of contexts. It is typically acquired by selectively encoding new information that is relevant for one's purposes in learning about that context, selectively comparing this information to old information in order to see how the new fits with the old, and selectively combining pieces of information in order to make them fit together into an orderly whole (Sternberg et al., 1993).

As noted above, however, our research has found significant correlations on scores of tacit knowledge across domains. For example, we have found that scores on tests of tacit knowledge for academic psychology and management correlate significantly (Wagner & Sternberg, 1985), as do scores on tests of tacit knowledge for management and military leadership (Hedlund et al., 2002). Thus, although one's development of wisdom might be domain specific, the tacit knowledge one learns in one domain might well extend to other domains. At the same time, the wise individual necessarily would have to know the limits of his or her own tacit knowledge. Wisdom may also correlate across domains, although such correlations have yet to be shown empirically.

Although tacit knowledge is acquired within a domain, it more typically applies to a field, following a distinction made by Csikszentmihalyi (1988, 1996). Csikszentmihalyi refers to the domain as the formal knowledge of a socially defined field. So, for example, knowing how to construct, conduct, or analyze the results of experiments would be knowledge important to the domain of experimental psychology. But knowing how to speak about the results persuasively, how to get the results published, or how to report the results in a grant proposal would constitute knowledge of the field. Thus, academic intelligence would seem to apply primarily in the domain, practical intelligence and wisdom in the field. Because the field represents the social organization of the domain, it primarily is in the field that intrapersonal, interpersonal, and extrapersonal interactions take place.

Problems Measuring (and Not Measuring) Wisdom

If one looks at the kinds of problems that have been used to measure wisdom in empirical work, one can evaluate the degree to which they measure wisdom, at least according to this balance theory. Life-planning tasks are excellent tasks for measuring wisdom because they involve one's own interests but inevitably must take into account the interests of others about whom one cares deeply, as well as the context in which one lives and may live in the future (Baltes, Staudinger, Maercker, & Smith, 1995). A task in which one must decide what to do when a good friend calls and says he or she wants to commit suicide also involves the interests of the other, one's own interest in getting involved and possibly failing to convince the person not to commit suicide, and also the difficulty of acting in the context of an unexpected telephone call (Staudinger & Baltes, 1996). Similarly, counseling a fourteen-year-old girl who is pregnant or a sixteen-year-old boy who wants to marry soon both involve balancing the interests of the individuals to be counseled, the other people in their lives, and the costs of giving the wrong advice (Baltes & Smith, 2003).

Perhaps the ideal problems for measuring wisdom, in light of the balance theory proposed here, are complex real-world dilemmas—especially conflict-resolution problems involving multiple competing interests and no clear resolution of how these interests can be reconciled (see Sternberg & Dobson, 1987; Sternberg & Soriano, 1984). For example, one might be asked to resolve a conflict between a board of education and teachers' unions. Given the relevance of such problems, it makes sense that research has found that clinical psychologists do particularly well on wisdom-related tasks (Smith, Staudinger, & Baltes, 1994). Another group who might be expected to do well would be experienced mediators and other negotiators who have helped school boards and teachers' unions in conflict reach resolutions.

The tacit-knowledge approach to measurement described above might present a useful way of measuring wisdom. The exact problems would differ, however, from those we have used to measure practical intelligence. In particular, the problems would involve solutions that maximize not just one's own self-interest, but a variety of intrapersonal, interpersonal, and extrapersonal interests. The stakes, therefore, would be higher and more complex because so many different interests would be involved. In our current work, we are using tacit-knowledge problems of these kinds to assess wisdom and its relation to other constructs.

In contrast to problems such as the ones we have explored thus far, typical problems found on conventional tests of intelligence, such as the Stanford-Binet (Thorndike, Hagen, & Sattler, 1986) or the Wechsler (Wechsler, 1991), measure wisdom minimally or not at all, according to the balance theory. There is no obvious similarity between these problems and the kinds of problems described above that would measure wisdom. Even when they measure thinking in a variety of domains, they typically do not involve judgments about intrapersonal, interpersonal, and extrapersonal interests for purposes of adapting to, shaping, and selecting environments. Similarly, there is little apparent similarity between problems measuring wisdom and those measuring creativity, whether from a psychometric point of view (e.g., Torrance, 1974) or from a systems point of view (e.g., Sternberg & Lubart, 2002). For example, wisdom-related problems seem remote from finding unusual uses of a paper clip, writing creative short stories, drawing creative pictures, or devising creative scientific experiments or explanations.

SOURCES OF DEVELOPMENTAL AND INDIVIDUAL DIFFERENCES IN WISDOM

The balance theory suggests a number of sources of developmental and individual differences in wisdom. In particular, there are two kinds of sources, those directly affecting the balance processes and those that are antecedent.

Individual and Developmental Differences Directly Affecting the Balance Processes

There are five sources that directly affect the balance process:

1. *Goals.* People may differ in terms of the extent to which they seek a common good, and thus in the extent to which they aim for the essential goal of wisdom.

2. *Balancing of responses to environmental contexts.* People may differ in their balance of responses to environmental contexts. Responses always reflect the interaction of the individual making the judgment and the environment, and people can interact with contexts in myriad ways.

3. *Balancing of interests.* People may balance interests in different ways.

4. *Tacit knowledge.* People bring different kinds and levels of tacit knowledge to judgmental situations, which are likely to affect their responses.

5. *Values.* People have different values mediating their utilization of tacit knowledge in the balancing of interests and responses.

These sources of differences produce variation in how wise people are and in how well they can apply their wisdom in different kinds of situations. To the extent that wisdom typically is associated with greater intellectual and even physical maturity, it is presumably because the development of tacit knowledge and of values is something that unfolds over the course of the life span and not just in childhood or even in early years of adulthood. While the above sources of individual differences pertain to the balancing processes, other sources are antecedent to these processes.

Developmental and Individual Differences in Antecedent Variables

Antecedent variables leading to developmental and individual differences are those specified by my earlier theory (Sternberg, 2003). They include (a) knowledge, (b) analytical and creative as well as practical thinking (Sternberg, 1997b), (c) a judicial thinking style (Sternberg, 1999), (d) personality variables, (e) motivation to think wisely, and (f) environmental variables.

Relations of Wisdom to Knowledge and to Analytical, Creative, and Practical Abilities

Wisdom is related to other psychological constructs but is not identical to any of them.

First, wisdom requires knowledge, but the heart of wisdom is tacit, informal knowledge of the kind learned in the school of life, not the kind of explicit formal knowledge taught in schools. One could be a "walking encyclopedia" and show little or no wisdom because the knowledge one needs to be wise is not to be found in encyclopedias or even, generally, in the type of teaching found in most schools (with the possible exception of those that teach Socratically).

> Wisdom requires analytical thinking, but not the kind of analytical thinking typically emphasized in schools or measured on tests of academic abilities and achievements.

Second, wisdom requires analytical thinking, but not the kind of analytical thinking typically emphasized in schools or measured on tests of academic abilities and achievements (discussed in Sternberg, 1980). Rather, it is analysis of real-world dilemmas in which clean and neat abstractions often give way to messy and disorderly concrete interests. The kind of abstract analytical thinking that may lead to outstanding performance on a test such as the Raven Matrices, which presents figural reasoning items, will be of some but not much use in complex real-world dilemmas such as how to defuse the conflict between India and Pakistan.

Third, wise solutions are often creative ones, as King Solomon demonstrated in cleverly determining which of two women was the true mother of a child. But the kind of crowd-defying, buy-low, sell-high attitude that leads to creative contributions does not in itself lead to wisdom (Sternberg, 2000). Creative people often tend toward extremes, although their later contributions may be more integrative (Gardner, 1993). Creative thinking is often brash whereas wise thinking is balanced. This is not to say that the same people cannot be both creative and wise. It is to say, however, that the kinds of thinking required to be creative and wise are different and thus will not necessarily be found in the same person. Moreover, teaching people to think creatively will not teach them to think wisely (see Sternberg & Williams, 1996).

Practical thinking is closer to wisdom than are analytical and creative thinking, but again, it is not the same. Wisdom is a particular kind of practical thinking. It is practical thinking that (a) balances competing intrapersonal, interpersonal, and extrapersonal interests, (b) balances adaptation to, shaping of, and selection of environments, in (c) the service of a common good. Thus, people can be good practical thinkers without being wise but they cannot be wise without being good practical thinkers. Good practical thinking is necessary but not sufficient for the manifestation of wisdom.

Wise thinking will not develop simply by teaching for other kinds of thinking. How might it be developed? And why is it so scarce?

IMPLICATIONS FOR EDUCATION

My speculation is that increases in intelligence—at least as measured by IQ—have not been matched by comparable increases in wisdom. Indeed, to the extent that our society has increasingly stressed the use of IQ to maximize one's own chances of admission to and success in the "cognitive elite" posited by Herrnstein and Murray (1996), increases in IQ may have actually been concomitant with decreases in wisdom. High IQ has brought us a world on the brink of destruction with the power to finish itself off many times over.

Teaching for wisdom might bring us a world that sought instead to better itself and the conditions of all the people in it. At some level, we as a society have a choice. What do we wish to maximize through our schooling? Is it knowledge? Is it intelligence? Or is it wisdom? If it is wisdom, then we need to put our students on a much different course. We need to value not only how they use their outstanding individual abilities to maximize their attainments, but how they use their individual abilities to maximize the attainments of others as well. We need, in short, to value wisdom. What would education that valued wisdom look like?

First, students would be reading classic works of literature and philosophy (whether Western or otherwise) to learn and reflect upon the wisdom of the sages. The rush to dump classic works in favor of modern works would make sense only if the wisdom these modern works had to impart equaled or exceeded that of the classic works.

Second, students would be engaged in class discussions, projects, and essays that encouraged them to discuss the lessons they have learned from these works and how they can be applied to their own lives and the lives of others. A particular emphasis would be placed on the development of dialectical thinking. Such thinking, carried out over space, involves thinkers understanding significant problems from multiple points of view and understanding how others legitimately could conceive of things in a way that is quite different from one's own. Carried out over time, dialectical thinking involves thinkers' understanding that ideas and the paradigms under which they fall evolve and keep evolving, not only from the past to the present, but from the present to the future (Hegel, 1931; see also Sternberg, 1998).

Third, students would need to study not only "truth," as we know it, but values. The idea would not be to force-feed a set of values but to encourage students to reflectively develop their own.

Fourth, such instruction would place an increased emphasis on critical, creative, and practical thinking in the service of good ends—ends that benefit not only the individual doing the thinking but others as well. All of these types of thinking would be valued, not just critical thinking.

Fifth, students would be encouraged to think about how almost everything they study might be used for better or worse ends and to realize that the ends to which knowledge are put do matter.

Finally, teachers would realize that the only way they could develop wisdom in their students would be to serve as role models of wisdom themselves. A role model of wisdom will, I believe, take a much more Socratic approach to teaching than teachers customarily do. Students often want large quantities of information spoon-fed to them. They then attempt to memorize this material for exams, only to forget it soon thereafter. In a wisdom-based approach to teaching, students take a more active role in constructing their learning. But a wisdom-based approach is not, in my view, tantamount to a constructivist approach to learning. Students have not achieved or even come close to achieving wisdom when they merely have constructed their own learning. Rather, they must be able to not only construct knowledge from their own point of view but be able to construct or reconstruct knowledge from the point of view of others. Constructivism from only a single point of view can lead to an egocentric, rather than a balanced, understanding.

Lessons taught to emphasize wisdom would have a rather different character from lessons as they often are taught today. Consider the following examples.

First, social studies and especially history lessons would look very different. For example, high school American history books typically teach American history from only one point of view, that of the new Americans. Thus, Columbus is referred to as having "discovered" America, a ridiculous notion from the standpoint of the many occupants who already lived there when it was "discovered." The conquests of the southwest and the Alamo are also only presented from the point of view of the new settlers, not from the standpoint of, say, the Mexicans who lost roughly half their territory to the invaders. This kind of ethnocentric and frankly propagandistic teaching would have no place in a curriculum that sought to develop wisdom and an appreciation of the need to balance interests.

Lessons taught to emphasize wisdom would have a rather different character from lessons as they often are taught today.

Second, science teaching would no longer be about facts presented as though they are the final word. Psychology, for example, is often presented as though it represents the end of a process of evolution of thought rather than one of many midpoints (Sternberg, 1998). Students could scarcely realize from this kind of teaching that the paradigms of today—and thus the theories and findings that emanate from them—will eventually be superseded, much as the paradigms, theories, and findings of yesterday were replaced by those of today. Students further would need to learn that, contrary to the way many textbooks are written, the classical "scientific method" is largely a fantasy rather than a reality and scientists are as susceptible to fads as are members of other groups (Sternberg, 1995).

Third, teaching of literature would need to reflect a kind of balance that right now often is absent. Literature often is taught in terms of the standards and context of the contemporary U.S. scene. Characters are often judged in terms of our contemporary thought rather than in terms of the standards of the time and place in which the events took place. From the proposed standpoint, the study of literature must, to some extent, be done in the context of the study of history. The banning of books often reflects the application of certain contemporary standards to literature, standards of which an author from the past never could have been aware.

Many people will not see the value of teaching something that shows no promise of raising conventional test scores.

Fourth, foreign languages would always be taught in the cultural context in which they are embedded. I suggest that American students have so much more difficulty learning foreign languages than do children in much of Europe not because they lack the ability, but because they lack the motivation. They do not see the need to learn another language whereas, say, a Flemish-speaking child in Belgium does. Americans would be better off if they made more of an attempt to understand other cultures, rather than simply expecting people from other cultures to understand them. And learning the language of a culture is a key to understanding. Americans might be less quick to impose their cultural values on others if they understood others' cultural values.

Culture cannot be taught, in the context of foreign-language learning, in the way it now often is—as an aside divorced from the actual learning of the language. It should be taught as an integral part of the language—as a primary context in which the language is embedded. The vituperative fights we see about bilingual education and about the use of Spanish in the United States or French in Canada are not just or even primarily fights about language. They are fights about culture, in need of wise resolutions.

Finally, as implied throughout these examples, the curriculum needs to be far more integrated. Literature needs to be integrated with history, science with history and social-policy studies, and foreign language with culture. Even within disciplines, far more integration is needed. Different approaches to psychology, for example, are often taught as competing when in fact they are totally compatible. Thus, biological, cognitive, developmental, social, and clinical psychology, for instance, provide complementary viewpoints on human beings. They do not compete with each other as being the "right approach." The study of the brain is important, for example, but most of the insights about learning and memory that have been applied to instruction have come from behavioral and cognitive approaches, not from the biological approach. And some of the insights that have supposedly come from the biological approach—such as "left-brain" and "right-brain" learning—are based on ignorant or outdated caricatures of research in this area rather than on actual findings.

The road to this new approach is bound to be a rocky one. First, entrenched structures are difficult to change, and wisdom is neither taught in schools nor is it generally even discussed. Second, many people will not see the value of teaching something that shows no promise of raising conventional test scores. These scores, which formerly were predictors of more interesting criteria, have now become ends in themselves. Society has lost track of why these scores ever mattered in the first place, and they have engendered the same kind of mindless competition we see in people who relentlessly compare their economic achievements with those of others. Third, wisdom is much more difficult to develop than is the kind of achievement that can be developed and then readily tested via multiple-choice tests. Finally, people who have gained influence and power in a society via one means are unlikely to want either to give up that power or to see a new criterion be established on which they do not rank as favorably. Thus, there is no easy path to wisdom. There never was and probably never will be.

―――――――――

Author Note: Preparation of this article was supported by a government grant under the Javits Act Program (Grant No. R206R50001) as administered by the Office of Educational Research and Improvement, U.S. Department of Education. Grantees undertaking such projects are encouraged to express freely their professional judgment. This article, therefore, does not necessarily represent the positions or the policies of the U.S. government, and no official endorsement should be inferred.

References

Arlin, P. K. (2003). Wisdom: The art of problem finding. In R. J. Sternberg (Ed.), *Wisdom: Its nature, origins, and development* (pp. 230–243). New York: Cambridge University Press.

Baltes, P. B. (1993). The aging mind: Potential and limits. *The Gerontologist, 33,* 580–594.

Baltes, P. B. (1994). Wisdom. Unpublished manuscript, Max-Planck-Institut für Bildungsforschung, Berlin.

Baltes, P. B., & Staudinger, U. M. (2004). *Wisdom: The orchestration of mind and virtue.* Max Planck Institute for Human Development, Berlin, 2004.

Baltes, P. B., & Smith, J. (1987, August). *Toward a psychology of wisdom and its ontogenesis.* Paper presented at the Ninety-Fifth Annual Convention of the American Psychological Association. New York City.

Baltes, P. B., & Smith, J. (2003). Toward a psychology of wisdom and its ontogenesis. In R. J. Sternberg (Ed.), *Wisdom: Its nature, origins, and development* (pp. 87–120). New York: Cambridge University Press.

Baltes, P. B., Staudinger, U. M., Maercker, A., & Smith, J. (1995). People nominated as wise: A comparative study of wisdom-related knowledge. *Psychology and Aging, 10,* 155–166.

Basseches, J. (1984). *Dialectical thinking and adult development.* Norwood, NJ: Ablex.

Ceci, S. J., & Liker, J. (1986). Academic and nonacademic intelligence: An experimental separation. In R. J. Sternberg & R. K. Wagner (Eds.), *Practical intelligence: Nature and origins of competence in the everyday world* (pp. 119–142). New York: Cambridge University Press.

Chi, M. T. H., Glaser, R., & Farr, M. J. (Eds.). (1988). *The nature of expertise.* Hillsdale, NJ: Erlbaum.

Clayton, V. (1975). Erickson's theory of human development as it applies to the aged: Wisdom as contradictory cognition. *Human Development, 18,* 119–128.

Clayton, V. (1976). *A multidimensional scaling analysis of the concept of wisdom.* Unpublished doctoral dissertation, University of Southern California.

Clayton, V. (1982). Wisdom and intelligence: The nature and function of knowledge in the later years. *International Journal of Aging and Development, 15,* 315–321.

Clayton, V., & Birren, J. E. (1980). The development of wisdom across the life-span: A reexamination of an ancient topic. In P. B. Baltes & O. G. Brim (Eds.), *Life-span development and behavior* (Vol. 3, pp. 103–135). New York: Academic Press.

Csikszentmihalyi, M. (1988). Society, culture, and person: A systems view of creativity. In R. J. Sternberg (Ed.), *The nature of creativity: Contemporary psychological perspectives* (pp. 325–339). New York: Cambridge University Press.

Csikszentmihalyi, M. (1996). *Creativity.* New York: HarperCollins.

Csikszentmihalyi, M., & Rathunde, K. (2003). The psychology of wisdom: An evolutionary interpretation. In R. J. Sternberg (Ed.), *Wisdom: Its nature, origins, and development* (pp. 25–51). New York: Cambridge University Press.

Eddy, A. S. (1988). *The relationship between the Tacit Knowledge Inventory for Managers and the Armed Services Vocational Aptitude Battery.* Unpublished master's thesis, St. Mary's University, San Antonio, TX.

Ericsson, K. A. (Ed.). (1996). *The road to excellence.* Mahwah, NJ: Lawrence Erlbaum Associates.

Ericsson, K. A., & Smith, J. (Eds.). (1991). *Toward a general theory of expertise: Prospects and limits.* Cambridge, England: Cambridge University Press.

Flynn, J. R. (1987). Massive IQ gains in 14 nations. *Psychological Bulletin, 101,* 171–191.

Gardner, H. (1993). *Creating minds.* New York: HarperCollins.

Hedlund, J., Horvath, J. A., Forsythe, G. B., Snook, S., Williams, W. M., Dennis, M., & Sternberg, R. J. (2002). *The acquisition of tacit knowledge for military leadership.* Yale University.

Hegel, G. W. F. (1931). *The phenomenology of the mind* (2nd ed.). (J. D. Baillie, Trans.). London: Allen and Unwin. (Original work published 1807)

Herrnstein, R. J., & Murray, C. (1996). *The bell curve: Intelligence and class structure in American life.* New York: Free Press.

Herrnstein, R. J., Nickerson, R. S., de Sanches, M., & Swets, J. A. (1986). Teaching thinking skills. *American Psychologist, 41,* 1279–1289.

Hofstede, G. (1980). *Culture's consequences: International differences in work-related values.* Thousand Oaks, CA: SAGE.

Holliday, S. G., & Chandler, M. J. (1986). *Wisdom: Explorations in adult competence.* Basel, Switzerland: Karger.

Horvath, J. A., Sternberg, R. J., Forsythe, G. B., Sweeney, P. J., Bullis, R. C., Williams, W. M., & Dennis, M. (1996). *Tacit knowledge in military leadership: Supporting instrument development* (Technical Report 1042). Alexandria, VA: U.S. Army Research Institute for Behavioral and Social Sciences.

Jensen, A. R. (1998). The g factor: The science of mental ability. Westport, CT: Praeger.

Kitchener, K. S. (1983). Cognition, metacognition, and epistemic cognition: A three-level model of cognitive processing. *Human Development, 4,* 222–232.

Kitchener, K. S. (1986). Formal reasoning in adults: A review and critique. In R. A. Mines and K. S. Kitchener (Eds.), *Adult cognitive development.* New York: Praeger.

Kitchener, K. S., & Brenner, H. G. (2003). Wisdom and reflective judgment: Knowing in the face of uncertainty. In R. J. Sternberg (Ed.), *Wisdom: Its nature, origins, and development* (pp. 212–229). New York: Cambridge University Press.

Kitchener, K. S., & Kitchener, R. F. (1981). The development of natural rationality: Can formal operations account for it? In J. Meacham & N. R. Santilli (Eds.), *Social development in youth: Structure and content.* Basel, Switzerland: Karger.

Kramer, D. A. (2003). Conceptualizing wisdom: The primacy of affect-cognition relations. In R. J. Sternberg (Ed.), *Wisdom: Its nature, origins, and development* (pp. 279–313). New York: Cambridge University Press.

Labaree, D. F. (1999). *How to succeed in school without really learning: The credentials race in American education.* New Haven, CT: Yale University Press.

Labouvie-Vief, G. (1980). Beyond formal operations: Uses and limits of pure logic in life span development. *Human Development, 23,* 141–161.

Labouvie-Vief, G. (1982). Dynamic development and mature autonomy. *Human Development, 25,* 161–191.

Labouvie-Vief, G. (2003). Wisdom as integrated thought: Historical and developmental perspectives. In R. J. Sternberg (Ed.), Wisdom: *Its nature, origins, and development* (pp. 52–83). New York: Cambridge University Press.

Machado, L. A. (1980). *The right to be intelligent.* (M. C. Wheeler, Trans.). New York: Pergamon Press.

Neisser, U. (Ed.). (1998). *The rising curve.* Washington, DC: American Psychological Association.

Nuñes, T. (1994). Street intelligence. In R. J. Sternberg (Ed.), *Encyclopedia of human intelligence* (Vol. 2, pp. 1045–1049). New York: Macmillan.

Pascual-Leone, J. (2003). An essay on wisdom: Toward organismic processes that make it possible. In R. J. Sternberg (Ed.), *Wisdom: Its nature, origins, and development* (pp. 244–278). New York: Cambridge University Press.

Piaget, J. (2001). *The psychology of intelligence.* New York: Routledge.

Polanyi, M. (1976). Tacit knowledge. In M. Marx and F. Goodson (Eds.), *Theories in contemporary psychology* (pp. 330–344). New York: Macmillan.

Riegel, K. F. (1973). *Dialectical operations: The final period of cognitive development.* Human Development, *16,* 346–370.

Robinson, D. N. (1999). *Aristotle's psychology.* New York: DNMRobinson.

Robinson, D. N. (2003). Wisdom through the ages. In R. J. Sternberg (Ed.), *Wisdom: Its nature, origins, and development* (pp. 13–24). New York: Cambridge University Press.

Rosch, E. (1975). Cognitive representations of semantic categories. *Journal of Experimental Psychology: General, 104,* 192–233.

Ryle, G. (2000). *The concept of mind.* Chicago: University of Chicago Press.

Simonton, D. K. (1994). *Greatness: Who makes history and why?* New York: Guilford.

Smith, J., Staudinger, U. M., & Baltes, P. B. (1994). Occupational settings facilitating wisdom-related knowledge: The sample case of clinical psychologists. *Journal of Consulting and Clinical Psychology, 66,* 989–999.

Staudinger, U. M., & Baltes, P. B. (1996). Interactive minds: A facilitative setting for wisdom-related performance? *Journal of Personality and Social Psychology, 71,* 746–762.

Staudinger, U. M., Lopez, D. F., & Baltes, P. B. (1997). The psychometric location of wisdom-related performance: Intelligence, personality, and more? *Personality and Social Psychology Bulletin, 23,* 1200–1214.

Sternberg, R. J. (1980). Sketch of a componential subtheory of human intelligence. *Behavioral and Brain Sciences, 3,* 573–614.

Sternberg, R. J. (1985a). *Beyond IQ: A triarchic theory of human intelligence.* New York: Cambridge University Press.

Sternberg, R. J. (1985b). Implicit theories of intelligence, creativity, and wisdom. *Journal of Personality and Social Psychology, 49,* 607–627.

Sternberg, R. J. (Ed.). (1988). *The nature of creativity: Contemporary psychological perspectives.* New York: Cambridge University Press.

Sternberg, R. J. (1995). For whom the bell curve tolls: A review of the bell curve. *Psychological Science, 6,* 257–261.

Sternberg, R. J. (1996). Costs of expertise. In K. A. Ericsson (Ed.), *The road to excellence* (pp. 347–354). Mahwah, NJ: Lawrence Erlbaum Associates.

Sternberg, R. J. (1997a). Fads in psychology: What we can do. *APA Monitor, 28,* 7–19.

Sternberg, R. J. (1997b). *Successful intelligence.* New York: Plume.

Sternberg, R. J. (1998). The dialectic as a tool for teaching psychology. *Teaching of Psychology, 25,* 177–180.

Sternberg, R. J. (1999). *Thinking styles.* New York: Cambridge University Press.

Sternberg, R. J. (2000). *Psychology: In search of the human mind.* Orlando, FL: Harcourt College Publishers.

Sternberg, R. J. (2003). Wisdom and its relations to intelligence and creativity. In R. J. Sternberg (Ed.), *Wisdom: Its nature, origins, and development* (pp. 142–159). New York: Cambridge University Press.

Sternberg, R. J. (Ed.). (2003). *Wisdom: Its nature, origins, and development.* New York: Cambridge University Press.

Sternberg, R. J. (in press). A balance theory of wisdom. *Review of General Psychology.*

Sternberg, R. J., & Dobson, D. M. (1987). Resolving interpersonal conflicts: An analysis of stylistic consistency. *Journal of Personality and Social Psychology, 52,* 794–812.

Sternberg, R. J., Ferrari, M., Clinkenbeard, P., & Grigorenko, E. L. (1996). Identification, instruction, and assessment of gifted children: A construct validation of a triarchic model. *Gifted Child Quarterly, 40,* 129–137.

Sternberg, R. J., & Grigorenko, E. L., (1997). The cognitive costs of physical and mental ill-health: Applying the psychology of the developed world to the problems of the developing world. *Eye on Psi Chi 2, 1,* 20–27.

Sternberg, R. J., Grigorenko, E. L., Ferrari, M., & Clinkenbeard, P. (1998). A triarchic analysis of an aptitude interaction. *European Journal of Psychological Assessment, 15,* 3–13.

Sternberg, R. J., & Lubart, T. I. (2002). *Defying the crowd: Cultivating creativity in a culture of conformity.* New York: Free Press.

Sternberg, R. J., & Soriano, L. J. (1984). Styles of conflict resolution. *Journal of Personality and Social Psychology, 47,* 115–126.

Sternberg, R. J., Torff, B., & Grigorenko, E. L. (1998a). Teaching for successful intelligence raises school achievement. *Phi Delta Kappan, 79,* 667–669.

Sternberg, R. J., Torff, B., & Grigorenko, E. L. (1998b). Teaching triarchically improves school achievement. *Journal of Educational Psychology,* *90,* 374–384.

Sternberg, R. J., & Wagner, R. K. (Eds.). (1986). *Practical intelligence: Nature and origins of competence in the everyday world.* New York: Cambridge University Press.

Sternberg, R. J., & Wagner, R. K. (1993). The g-ocentric view of intelligence and job performance is wrong. *Current Directions in Psychological Science, 2,* 1–5.

Sternberg, R. J., Wagner, R. K., & Okagaki, L. (1993). Practical intelligence: The nature and role of tacit knowledge in work and at school. In H. Reese & J. Puckett (Eds.), *Advances in lifespan development* (pp. 205–227). Hillsdale, NJ: Erlbaum.

Sternberg, R. J., Wagner, R. K., Williams, W. M., & Horvath, J. A. (1995). Testing common sense. *American Psychologist, 50,* 912–927.

Sternberg, R. J., & Williams, W. M. (1996). *How to develop student creativity.* Alexandria, VA: Association for Supervision and Curriculum Development.

Thorndike, R. L., Hagen, E. P., & Sattler, J. M. (1986). *Stanford-Binet Intelligence Scale* (4th ed.). Itasca, IL: Riverside.

Torrance, E. P. (1974). *Torrance tests of creative thinking: Technical-norms manual.* Bensenville, IL: Scholastic Testing Services.

Wagner, R. K., & Sternberg, R. J. (1985). Practical intelligence in real-world pursuits: The role of tacit knowledge. *Journal of Personality and Social Psychology, 49,* 436–458.

Webster's New World College Dictionary (3rd ed.). (1997). New York: Simon & Schuster.

Wechsler, D. (1991). *Wechsler intelligence scale for children* (3rd ed.). San Antonio, TX: The Psychological Corporation.

The Intelligent Learner

The meaning and concept of who is a learner are key concerns of teaching for intelligence. Many particular characteristics about learners are suggested in the second section of this volume. Writers come at the topic from various levels of teaching and with different assumptions in mind, but they all address many of the factors noted by the theorists in the first section.

Barell focuses on the significance of the inquisitiveness of students, on their inherent motivation to learn, and on the importance of developing the abilities required to ask good questions about whatever content is being studied. Darling-Hammond reminds us that teachers need to be learners as well. Beyond the ability to ask important questions, she says, a teacher must raise for every student the issue of what makes learning accessible to the student's immediate skills for crafting knowledge. While there is no one formula for who is a potentially successful learner, the teacher responsible for the educational program needs to take into account the individual learner's particular condition and background in their becoming an inquiring student. What other insights about learners do the writers of this section uncover about the important concerns of being and becoming a serious thinker?

First, there seems to be a process to be mastered in learning to learn. According to the writers of this section, there are many paths that can be traveled in developing that process. Posing problems or asking meaningful questions are challenging tasks for the teacher and student alike. Darling-Hammond emphasizes the importance of language in the thinking classroom. While Eisner acknowledges that important cognitive functions may indeed include language development, he somewhat counters Darling-Hammond's position and suggests there is much more to be learned than a linguistic approach to the development of full, imaginative thought. Eisner stresses the essential role of learning the various arts in a developing cognitive curriculum. There are key discriminations involved in mastering aesthetic intelligence, and these critical means or standards provide a foundation—an enriched sense of the whole, of human experience. Eisner presents a conception of the mind that encompasses perceptual as well as logical thought, enables learners to deal with greater diversity in the world, and fosters the development of complex patterns of interpretation. If we are to become true learners and not mere mimics of others' knowledge, he says, the arts provides essential tools toward developing this type of thoughtfulness. How troubling is the world of schooling, then, that cuts the arts from the school program as though they are a frivolous concern.

Allington deals with the importance of reading ability as a cornerstone of developing intelligence in elementary school. Classrooms need to be rich environments that encourage reading, provide many varied reading experiences, and enable students to master reading skills with confidence and fluency. While Allington underlines the inherent educability of every youngster to read the language he or she speaks, he is keen to point out that learners need to have access to an environment that engages their interest and commands their attention. These assumptions are not that distant from Eisner's estimate of the classroom of the arts.

Schools are living systems. This section raises the continuous development of both learning teachers and learning students as the *raison d'être* of education itself. Looking inside the system, the first focus has been on the key actors and the dramatic parts they play. The next challenge is to examine the pedagogical act itself, to look at instruction under a magnifying glass. That is the substance of the next section of this book.

Teacher Learning That Supports Student Learning

Linda Darling-Hammond

Linda Darling-Hammond is Charles E. Ducommun Professor of Education in the School of Education at Stanford, California. She also is executive director of the National Commission for Teaching and America's Future. She is actively engaged in research, teaching, and policy work on issues of school restructuring, teacher education reform, and the enhancement of educational equity.

Today's schools face enormous challenges. In response to an increasingly complex society and a rapidly changing, technology-based economy, schools are being asked to educate the most diverse student body in our history to higher academic standards than ever before. This task is one that cannot be "teacher-proofed" through management systems, testing mandates, or curriculum packages. At its root, achieving high levels of student understanding requires immensely skillful teaching—and schools that are organized to support teachers' continuous learning.

What do teachers need to know to teach all students according to today's standards? What kinds of preservice training and ongoing professional development will make teacher success more likely?

WHAT TEACHERS NEED TO KNOW

First, teachers need to understand subject matter deeply and flexibly, so that they can help students create useful cognitive maps, relate ideas to one another, and address misconceptions. Teachers need to see how ideas connect across fields and to everyday life. This kind of understanding provides a foundation for pedagogical content knowledge (Shulman, 1987), which enables teachers to make ideas accessible to others. The audience is also key: A skillful teacher figures out what students know and believe about a topic and how learners are likely to "hook into" new ideas.

Interpreting learners' statements and actions and shaping productive experiences for them require knowledge of child and adolescent development and an understanding of how to support growth in various domains—cognitive, social, physical, and emotional. Teaching in ways that connect with students also requires an understanding of differences that may arise from culture, family experiences, developed intelligences, and approaches to learning. Teachers need to be able to inquire sensitively, listen carefully, and look thoughtfully at student work, as well as to structure situations in which students write and talk about their experiences. This builds a foundation of pedagogical learner knowledge (Grimmett & MacKinnon, 1992). Motivating students requires an understanding of what individual students believe about themselves, what they care about, and what tasks are likely to give them enough success to encourage them to work hard to learn.

Teachers need several kinds of knowledge about learning. Teachers need to think about what it means to learn different kinds of material for different purposes and how to decide which kinds of learning are most necessary in different contexts. Teachers must be able to use different teaching strategies to accomplish various goals and many means for evaluating students' knowledge and assessing students' approaches to learning. Teachers must be able to identify the strengths of different learners while addressing their weaknesses. In addition, all teachers need tools to work with students who have specific learning disabilities or needs. And because language is the gateway to learning, teachers must understand how students acquire language, so that they can build language skills and create accessible learning experiences.

Teachers need to know about curriculum resources and technologies to connect their students with sources of information and knowledge that allow them to explore ideas, acquire and synthesize information, and frame and solve problems. And teachers need to know about collaboration—how to structure interactions among students so that more powerful shared learning can occur, how to collaborate with other teachers, and how to work with parents to learn more about their children and to shape supportive experiences at school and home.

Finally, teachers need to be able to analyze and reflect on their practice, to assess the effects of their teaching, and to refine and improve their instruction. They must continuously evaluate what students are thinking and understanding and reshape their plans to take account of what they've discovered.

> Teachers need to be able to analyze and reflect on their practice, assess the effects of their teaching, and then refine and improve their instruction.

NEW STRATEGIES FOR TEACHER LEARNING

Acquiring this sophisticated knowledge and developing a practice that is different from what teachers themselves experienced as students requires learning opportunities for teachers that are more powerful than simply reading and talking about new pedagogical ideas (Ball & Cohen, 1999). Teachers learn best by studying, doing, and reflecting; by collaborating with other teachers; by looking closely at students and their work; and by sharing what they see.

This kind of learning cannot occur in college classrooms divorced from practice or in school classrooms without knowledge about how to interpret practice. Good settings for teacher learning—in both colleges of education and schools—provide lots of opportunities for research and inquiry, for trying and testing, for talking about and evaluating the results of learning and teaching. The "rub between theory and practice" (Miller & Silvernail, 1994) occurs most productively when questions arise in the context of real students and work in progress, and where research and disciplined inquiry are also at hand.

Better settings for such learning are appearing. More than 300 schools of education in the United States have created programs that extend beyond the traditional four-year bachelor's degree program, providing both education and subject-matter coursework that is integrated with clinical training in schools. Some are one- or two-year graduate programs for recent graduates or mid-career recruits. Others are five-year models for prospective teachers who enter teacher education as undergraduates. In either case, the fifth year allows students to focus exclusively on the task of preparing to teach, with yearlong, school-based internships linked to coursework on learning and teaching. Studies have found that graduates of these extended programs are more satisfied with their preparation, and their colleagues, principals, and cooperating teachers view them as better prepared. Extended program graduates are as effective with students as are much more experienced teachers and are much more likely to enter and stay in teaching than their peers prepared in traditional four-year programs (Andrew & Schwab, 1995; Denton & Peters, 1988; Shin, 1994).

Many of these programs have joined with local school districts to create Professional Development Schools. Like teaching hospitals, these schools aim to provide sites for state-of-the-art practice that are organized to support the training of new professionals, extend the professional development of veteran teachers, and sponsor collaborative research and inquiry. Both university and school faculty plan and teach in these programs. Beginning teachers get a more coherent learning experience when they are organized in teams with more experienced faculty and with one another. Senior teachers deepen their knowledge by serving as mentors, adjunct faculty, co-researchers, and teacher leaders. Thus, these schools can help create the rub between theory and practice, while creating more professional roles for teachers and constructing knowledge that is more useful for both practice and ongoing theory building (Darling-Hammond, 1994).

These new programs typically engage prospective teachers in studying research and conducting their own inquiries through cases, action research, and structured reflections about practice. They envision the professional teacher as one who learns from teaching rather than as one who has finished learning how to teach, and the job of teacher education as developing the capacity to inquire systematically and sensitively into the nature of learning and the effects of teaching. This is like the approach to knowledge production John Dewey (1929) sought—one that empowers teachers with greater understanding of complex situations rather than seeking to control them with simplistic formulas or cookie-cutter routines.

If teachers investigate the effects of their teaching on students' learning, and if they read about what others have learned, they become sensitive to variation and more aware of what works for what purposes in what situations. Training in inquiry also helps teachers learn how to look at the world from multiple perspectives and to use this knowledge to reach diverse learners. As Lisa Delpit (1996) notes,

We all interpret behaviors, information, and situations through our own cultural lenses; these lenses operate involuntarily, below the level of conscious awareness, making it seem that our own view is simply "the way it is." (p. 151)

Teachers concerned with democratic education must develop an awareness of their own perspectives in the classroom and out to avoid a "communicentric bias" (Gordon, Miller, & Rollock, 1990) that limits understanding of students as well as of different areas of study.

These goals suggest a new relationship between research and practice. For most of this century, policymakers sought knowledge to aid in the remote control of teaching—generalizable dictums that could shape teaching via texts, curriculum packages, and teacher manuals. When these proved inadequate, teachers were left with the knowledge they'd managed to accumulate on their own. By contrast, the kind of learning found in rich professional development settings has several key features (Ball & Cohen, 1999):

> The professional teacher is one who learns from teaching, rather than one who has finished learning how to teach.

- Development is centered around the critical activities of teaching and learning—planning lessons, evaluating student work, developing curriculum—rather than in abstractions and generalities;
- Teacher knowledge grows from investigations of practice through cases, questions, analysis, and criticism; and
- Learning is built on substantial professional discourse that fosters analysis and communication about practices and values in ways that build colleagueship and standards of practice.

These elements need to be part of a seamless process of professional learning that begins in preservice education, continues through the early years of induction, and extends through years of developing accomplished practice. This approach is common elsewhere around the world and in a growing number of schools in the United States.

PROFESSIONAL LEARNING IN PRACTICE

Countries like Germany, Belgium, and Luxembourg have long required two to three years of graduate-level study for prospective teachers on top of an undergraduate degree in the subject(s) to be taught. Education courses include the study of child development and learning, pedagogy, and teaching methods, plus an intensively supervised internship in a school affiliated with the university. In 1989 both France and Japan undertook major teacher education reforms to extend both university- and school-based training. In France, all candidates now complete a graduate program in newly created University Institutes for the Preparation of Teachers that are connected to nearby schools. In Japan and Chinese Taipei, new teachers complete a year-long supervised internship with a reduced teaching load that allows for mentoring and additional study. By Japanese law, first-year teachers receive at least 20 days of inservice training and 60 days of professional development. Master teachers are released from their classrooms to advise and counsel them. In both Japan and China, new teachers watch other teachers at length, discuss problems of practice, present and critique demonstration lessons, and, with groups of colleagues, imagine and act out how students might respond to certain presentations of material. In their study of mathematics teaching in Japan, Taiwan, and the United States, Stigler and Stevenson (1991) note

[One of the] reasons Asian class lessons are so well crafted is that there is a very systematic effort to pass on the accumulated wisdom of teaching practice to each new generation of teachers and to keep perfecting that practice by providing teachers the opportunities to continually learn from each other. (p. 46)

Because schools in other countries provide for this kind of regular collegial exchange, teachers share knowledge and refine their practice throughout their careers.

Without these supports, learning to teach well is extremely difficult. Most U.S. teachers start their careers in disadvantaged schools where turnover is highest, are assigned the most educationally needy students whom no one else wants to teach, are given the most demanding teaching loads with the greatest number of extra duties, and receive few curriculum materials and no mentoring. After this hazing, many leave the profession. Others learn merely to cope rather than to teach well. After entry, teachers are expected to know everything they will need for a career, or to learn through workshops mostly on their own, with few structured opportunities to observe and analyze teaching with others. As one high school teacher who has spent 25 years in the classroom once told me: "I have taught 20,000 classes; I have been 'evaluated' 30 times; but I have never seen another teacher teach." With this degree of isolation so common, is it any wonder that shared knowledge and standards of practice are so difficult to forge?

Some school districts have begun to create new models of induction and ongoing professional development for teachers and principals. These feature mentoring for beginners and veterans; peer observation and coaching; local study groups and networks for specific subject matter areas; teacher academies that provide ongoing seminars and courses of study tied to practice; and school-university partnerships that sponsor collaborative research, interschool visitations, and learning opportunities developed in response to teachers' and principals' felt needs.

For example, at Wells Junior High, a Professional Development School working with the University of Southern Maine,

> The whole notion of staff development was turned on its head. The emphasis shifted from outside consultants to in-house experts. Collaborative learning groups replaced the traditional lecture/demonstration format. Problem posing and problem solving supplanted the recipes and prescriptions for effective schools that teachers had heard for years and never managed to implement.
>
> "Using the knowledge" became the starting point for developing a new view of staff development. . . . [Allocated workshop days] were used for teachers' review of research and for critical discussion and reflection. On one such day teachers spent two hours individually reading research about grouping.

During another day, they worked in cooperative groups to share their perceptions on the research they had read. On yet another day, the staff met to engage in the process of consensus building with the goal of reaching a decision about grouping practices in the school. (Miller & Silvernail, 1994, pp. 30–31)

Similarly, at Fairdale High School in Louisville, Kentucky, teachers' research coupled with shared decision making produced major changes:

As part of a self-study, 10 teachers followed 10 children through a school day. When it was over, teachers said things like, "It was boring," or, "You know, this isn't a very humane place to be." Teachers read and began to trade articles from the *Kappan, Educational Leadership,* and *Education Week.* . . . Even before participative management was initiated at Fairdale, the teachers started changing things. . . ."Make no mistake about it," [the principal] said, "We are building a professional culture." (Kerchner, 1993, p. 9)

In other schools, teachers have organized their learning around the development of standards and assessments of student work, evaluating both student learning and the effectiveness of their own teaching in the process. The result is a greater appreciation for what matters and what works, as well as what needs to change to promote student success.

Professional development strategies that succeed in improving teaching share several features (Darling-Hammond & McLaughlin, 1995). These strategies tend to be

- experiential, engaging teachers in concrete tasks of teaching, assessment, and observation that illuminate the processes of learning and development;
- grounded in participants' questions, inquiry, and experimentation as well as profession-wide research;
- collaborative, involving a sharing of knowledge among educators;
- connected to and derived from teachers' work with their students as well as to examinations of subject matter and teaching methods;

- sustained and intensive, supported by modeling, coaching, and problem solving around specific problems of practice; and
- connected to other aspects of school change.

These approaches shift from old models of "teacher training" or "inservicing" to a model in which teachers confront research and theory directly, are regularly engaged in evaluating their practice, and use their colleagues for mutual assistance.

THE BENEFIT FOR STUDENTS

Growing evidence suggests that this kind of professional development not only makes teachers feel better about their practice, but it also reaps learning gains for students, especially in the kinds of more challenging learning that new standards demand (Darling-Hammond, 2000; NFIE, 1996). Creating a profession of teaching in which teachers have the opportunity for continual learning is the likeliest way to inspire greater achievement for children, especially those for whom education is the only pathway to survival and success.

Author's Note: This article draws in substantial part on the author's recently published book *The Right to Learn* (San Francisco: Jossey-Bass, 2001).

REFERENCES

Andrew, M. D., & Schwab, R. L. (1995, Fall). Has reform in teacher education influenced teacher performance? An outcome assessment of graduates of eleven teacher education programs. *Action in Teacher Education, 17*(3), 43–53.

Ball, D., & Cohen, D. (1999). Developing practice, developing practitioners: Toward a practice-based theory of professional education. In L. Darling-Hammond & L. Sykes (Eds.), *The heart of the matter: Teaching as the learning profession.* San Francisco: Jossey-Bass.

Darling-Hammond, L. (2000). *Doing what matters most: Investing in quality teaching.* New York: The National Commission on Teaching and America's Future.

Darling-Hammond, L., (Ed.). (1994). *Professional development schools: Schools for developing a profession.* New York: Teachers College Press.

Darling-Hammond, L., & McLaughlin, M. W. (1995). Policies that support professional development in an era of reform. *Phi Delta Kappan, 76*(8), 597–604.

Delpit, L. (1996). *Other people's children: Cultural conflict in the classroom.* New York: New Press.

Denton, J. J., & Peters, W. H. (1988). Program assessment report: Curriculum evaluation of a non-traditional program for certifying teachers. Unpublished report. College Station: Texas A&M University.

Dewey, J. (1929). *The sources of a science of education.* New York: Horace Liveright.

Gordon, E. W., Miller, F., & Rollock, D. (1990). Coping with communicentric bias in knowledge production in the social sciences. *Educational Researcher, 19,* 14–19.

Grimmett, P., and A. MacKinnon. (1992). Craft knowledge and the education of teachers. In G. Grant (Ed.), *Review of Research in Education, 18.* Washington, D.C.: American Educational Research Association.

Kerchner, C. T. (1993). Building the airplane as it rolls down the runway. *School Administrator, 50*(10), 8–15.

Miller, L., & Silvernail, D. L. (1994). Wells Junior High School: Evolution of a professional development school. In L. Darling-Hammond (Ed.), *Professional development schools: Schools for developing a profession.* New York: Teachers College Press.

National Foundation for the Improvement of Education. (1996). *Teachers take charge of their learning: Transforming professional development for student success.* Washington, D.C.: Author.

Shin, H. (1994). *Estimating future teacher supply: An application of survival analysis.* Paper presented at the annual meeting of the American Educational Research Association, New Orleans.

Shulman, L. (1987). Knowledge and teaching: Foundations of the New Reform. *Harvard Educational Review, 57*(1), 1–22.

Stigler, J. W., & Stevenson, H. W. (1991, Spring). How Asian teachers polish each lesson to perfection. *American Educator, 15*(1), 12–21, 43–47.

Did You Ask a
Good Question Today?

John Barell

John Barell is Professor Emeritus of Curriculum and Teaching and Adjunct Professor of English Literature at Montclair State University. Past Director of the Association for Supervision and Curriculum Development (ASCD) Network on Teaching Thinking, he currently is conducting pilot experiences in field-based teacher education in the development of a Professional Development High School. He is continuing research on how to help students ask better questions in the classroom.

OUR NATURAL CURIOSITIES

Have you ever wondered what goes on inside the head of a baby, as physicist Freeman Dyson has? Or like psychologist Nicholas Humphrey, have you ever asked yourself, "Why is music such a pleasure?"[1]

Have you ever speculated about the size of the sun as it sets upon the horizon, where it always looks so much bigger than when it is at the high noon position? But is it? My grandfather had fun asking me about this seeming incongruity when I was a child, leading me to consider how the sun's rays might be affected by shining through Earth's atmosphere.

We are always posing questions such as these and have since the dawn of time when Homo sapiens first began to walk upright on east African savannahs. As a species, we wouldn't be here were it not for our ability to use language and, with this incomparable tool, to communicate our sense of wonder at the natural world. As Ian Tattersall noted, Homo sapiens came upon the world as a new creature, a new concept far different from existing Neanderthals. We were able to use language and create symbols and artistic products, such as drawings in the caves at Lascaux and Venus figurines, and we buried our dead with artifacts for an afterlife.[2]

I imagine Cro-Magnons asked themselves a lot of questions: What is that brilliant orange ball that grows into the sky? What is fire? How shall we capture that woolly creature, and can we eat it when we do? Where shall we live? What happens when one of us no longer can walk or talk? Where do we go?

Our development and our destiny are structured by questions such as these.

THE MEANING OF QUESTIONING

What does it mean, "to question"? It means an ability to think beyond what we see, touch, and hear with our senses. For example, to see the sunset and to imagine, to reason, to wonder, to speculate on what the sun might be composed of, to ask ourselves how it originated. To see the possibility of there being a creator of that heavenly body.

It means to recognize that we are confronted with a mystery, a puzzle. There is that bright yellow-orange object and every day it seems to rise above the horizon and move. What makes it move across the skies and then disappear?

Richard Feynman, a Nobel Prize–winning physicist and member of the *Challenger* space shuttle disaster investigating committee, once noted that science flourishes within a free, democratic society where we have the freedom to doubt, to wonder:

> I feel a responsibility to proclaim the value of this freedom and to teach that doubt is not to be feared, but that it is to be welcomed as the possibility of a new potential for human beings. If you know that you are not sure, you have a chance to improve the situation.[3]

THE SIGNIFICANCE OF QUESTIONING AND WONDERING

First, questioning represents our humanity. To ask a question reflects our human ability to think beyond the immediate present, to speculate beyond the concrete realities confronting us at this very moment. When we have doubts about governmental policies toward China, about the inflation rate, about our relationships with loved ones, we are challenging the status quo, questioning the realities we perceive. We are developing our potential for continuous intellectual, social, and emotional growth when we recognize incongruities and follow our curiosities.

Second, curiosity is a road to success. The best example of this comes from scientist Isidore I. Rabi. Someone once asked him, "Why did you become a scientist, rather than a doctor or lawyer or businessman, like other immigrant kids in your neighborhood?"[4]

Dr. Rabi's response is very revealing and instructive:

> My mother made me a scientist without ever intending it. Every other Jewish mother in Brooklyn would ask her child after school, "So? Did you learn anything today?" But not my mother. She always asked me a different question. "Izzy," she would say, "did you ask a good question today?" That difference—asking good questions—made me become a scientist.[5]

Without young Izzy's mother encouraging him to follow up on his curiosities, perhaps he would not have gone on to graduate from MIT, to work on the Manhattan Project, or to conduct Nobel Prize–winning research on the electron.

So, questioning is one road to becoming more fully the human beings we are capable of being.

WHAT IS A "GOOD QUESTION"?

What do you suppose mother Rabi knew about such questions that she asked her son, Izzy, if he asked not just a question but a "good question"? She must have had some ideas in her mind about the characteristics of good questions; it's unfortunate that we can't ask her or her son!

To gain some insight into what a good question might contain, let's consider a well-known example from another scientist, Albert Einstein. One of his questions as a young man was the following: "What would happen if I rode along a ray of light and looked back? What would I see?"[6]

This was an amazing question! As astronomer Carl Sagan observed, Einstein noted that "something strange happens at the speed of light. The more Einstein thought about such questions, the more troubling they became. Paradoxes seemed to emerge everywhere. . . ."[7]

This question led Einstein to determine that Newton's way was not the only way to see the universe. His special theory of relativity, proposed in 1905, changed the "glasses" through which we view the world of subatomic particles, outer space, and time travel. Einstein's imaginative curiosity produced a good question because it challenged our underlying assumptions about the universe.

But you do not need to be an Einstein to pose a good question!

A MOTHER'S SKEPTICISM

Recently I was showing my mother a spectacular picture of towering brownish and yellow images of hydrogen gas in the Eagle Nebula on the Hubble Space Telescope (HST) Web site. I was amazed that these towers of hydrogen gas some 7,300 light-years from Earth depicted stars in formation. When I told my mother this, she looked at the bright white images at the head of these towers of hydrogen, then looked at me and asked, "Well, how do they know that these are stars being created?"

I fumbled around for a few minutes talking about data gathering and she kept countering with, "How did astronomers figure this out before the launching and perfecting of the HST?" I couldn't answer fully. I had to seek out the university astronomer.

Had my mother asked a good question? Yes! She is just like the mother of Pulitzer Prize–winning Annie Dillard, who used to ask her young daughter, "How do you know?" when Annie would make a claim about politics she had picked up around the neighborhood.[8] Both mothers wanted to know the sources of their children's information. They are challenging the credibility of our sources and our unquestioning acceptance of what we are told, in print, on the Internet, and in person.

Questioning involves, as philosopher John McPeck asserted, a "certain skepticism" about what we are told to do or believe.[9] When someone asserts that the dinosaurs died out because of a huge meteor falling onto what is now Latin America, we most certainly will pose a few questions about the evidence that supports this conclusion, what assumptions it might be based upon, and what we know about the biases or special interests of the source of the claim.

Good questions do all of the following:

- Reflect our genuine curiosities, our wonderings about mysteries, ambiguities, and puzzling situations that we do not understand.
- May uncover assumptions, biases, new sources of evidence, and challenge the reliability of sources.
- Lead us to investigate, to inquire, and to search for answers.
- Help us reflect on our ways of knowing.

WHY AREN'T WE MORE CURIOUS IN SCHOOLS?

Educational researcher J. T. Dillon conducted research on questioning in high school history classrooms where he found that during twenty-seven discussions in six schools students posed only eleven questions, most of which had to do with management of the classroom and lower levels of intellectual challenge! Ninety-nine percent of students asked nothing.[10] Why might this be so?

Recently *The New York Times* printed a story about the U.S. State Department's chief spokesperson James P. Rubin. When [former] Secretary of State Madeline K. Albright was ambassador to the United Nations, she brought Rubin along to handle her public relations. In this position he was asked many, many questions about the United States' position on various conflicts. Occasionally, he responded in a fashion that might have had an effect on whether or not a particular reporter ever asked him a question again: "He was known to demean reporters from less prestigious news organizations with put-downs like, 'That question bespeaks incredible ignorance!'"[11]

> Good questions reflect our curiosities, uncover our assumptions and biases, lead us to investigate and inquire, and help us reflect on our ways of knowing.

Imagine how you would feel, as a reporter trying to get a story for a hometown paper about the United States' position on the Bosnian conflict, for example, and being slapped with that remark. How likely is it you would approach Mr. Rubin again, at least in a public forum?

Do you think these kinds of comments do anything to foster the kind of curiosity we are speaking about? Do you suppose such put-downs ever occur at home? In the school?

My own informal survey of students in a university genetics class suggested that students quite often encounter these kinds of remarks when they ask a question to resolve a doubt or difficulty they are having. Some professors responded to questions with comments such as "I ask the questions here!" "See me after class for that one," "Let's not bother with those kinds of speculations [in response to a student's what if question]. We have enough to do to figure out what the facts are," and "I'm not sure. Why don't you look it up?"

These kinds of responses, according to the students, led them to think, "Well, this guy's not interested in my thinking here! So I'll just shut up."

Our inability to create an invitational environment that encourages students to take risks and to adventure into the unknown with their questioning is undoubtedly one reason why students do not ask more questions in our classes.

WHAT CAN WE DO IN OUR CLASSROOMS?

Model Inquiry

If we want our students to become curious about the world, we need to model our own curiosities within an invitational environment.[12] We need to take situations from our own daily lives and to think aloud before our students, for example, relating how we confront the situation of getting into a jam with our laptop computers. We model our inquiry process and then invite participants to analyze our thoughts and feelings in these kinds of complex and challenging situations.

> If we want our students to become curious about the world, we need to model our own curiosities within an invitational environment.

Another approach is to present the models of several of the nation's foremost scientists and researchers and their questions. For example, astronomer John Barrow posed this question to himself: "Is the universe a great mechanism, a great computation, a great symmetry, a great accident, or a great thought?"[13]

Author Duncan Steel asked: "Why are most individuals and all human societies grossly underachieving their potentials?"[14]

The New York Times recently published an article on some of the nation's foremost intellectuals posing these questions for themselves, and their questions were posted on the Internet Web site organized by John Brockman, a literary agent and author. Brockman's question, "What is the question you are asking yourself [now]?"[15] might help us consider what we can learn from others who pose meaningful, good questions.

Make Questioning Part of Every Day's Lessons

One way of making inquiry a part of every classroom is to develop our students' abilities to pose meaningful questions about content. After modeling our own curiosities about, for example, why an author begins his short story with a specific line or paragraph, we encourage our students to develop their own questions about content. One easy way to do this is through a thinking journal.

Biology teacher Dorothy Lozauskas modeled inquiry for her students and then assigned them to develop questions from their own readings and lab experiments using a thinking journal. The students' questions would become the topics for discussion the following day. She assisted her students' inquiry by suggesting lead-in statements such as "What I do not understand is . . . , I wonder why . . . , What I want to know is . . . , Suppose . . . , and What if . . . ?"

These lead-in statements resulted in questions such as "In lab we are making models of molecules with different bonds, and have just made a butane molecule that has free bond rotation. Even though they have the capability of doing so, why would they? I wonder what the world would be like if there was no free bond rotation—really cold?"[16]

Peg Murray, a third-grade teacher, experimented with students posing their own questions about their immediate surroundings— "Why are school buses always yellow?"—and about science—"Why do sun flares shoot out into space?"[17]

Create Problem-Based Units That Focus on Inquiry

Problem-based learning is a way of organizing whole units of instruction around students' interest in figuring out complex phenomena.[18] If, for example, students are studying the Appalachian region, the nature of bacteria in public places, how to create a geometric patio adjacent to a house, or the issue of censorship in public education, they can engage in an inquiry process that facilitates their identifying the problematic situations worthy of investigation. Rather than having the teacher identify the problem, which is what is likely to occur most often, the students' questions can structure the inquiry if they use the following strategy:

K   What do we think we **know** about the subject?

W   **What** do we need and/or want to find out?

H   **How** will we go about finding answers?

Then after investigation:

L   What have we **learned** and how does it compare with our expectations?

A   How might we **apply** our findings to this subject, to other subjects, and to our lives?

Q   What are our **questions** now?

This process is designed to shift the balance of power and control within the classroom from the teacher toward the students so they can take more responsibility for their own learning.[19] Teachers are creating problem-based units for kindergarten through grade twelve that put students into situations requiring them to think productively and gain authentic assessment and feedback; for example, "You are members of the mayor's ecology team charged with investigating the status of the water supply in our town. . . ."

Make Metacognitive Self-Questioning
Part of the Learning Process

As educational researcher Barbara McCombs noted, self-reflection is one avenue toward enhancing students' self-direction, sense of efficacy, and "inherent motivation to learn."[20] Metacognitive reflections engage us in a process of planning, monitoring, and evaluating.[21] This process involves questioning ourselves in this fashion: What is my task and how do I intend to accomplish it? How well am I doing? How well do I think I have done? What might I do differently next time?

Sixth graders in Regina Kamlet's classroom reflected on their learning in science and one student noted: "I work better when there is a task and I ask questions and make a plan. . . ."[22]

CONCLUSION

When my grandfather asked me about the sun, he knew I probably hadn't thought about this incongruity. But he posed the questions because we both loved the game of it. Consequently, I grew up with a certain amount of curiosity about the world. Now, I realize that he was my model; he introduced me to a process of questioning that I now value more than any answers I might discover. As with problem solving, it may be that the process of inquiry is more important for brain development than any one answer.[23]

Monsignor Richard Mohan, prior of St. Patrick's Purgatory, a shrine in Station Island, Ireland, recently noted: "I don't go around with answers. I hear people's questions. It's far more important to have questions than answers. The people who have all the answers have stopped living."[24]

Yes.

NOTES

1. In an on-line salon, scientists sit back and ponder: "What is the question you are asking yourself?" (1997, December 30) *The New York Times,* p. F4.

2. Tattersall, I. (1998). *Becoming human: Evolution and human uniqueness.* New York: Harcourt Brace and Co.

3. Feynman, R. (1998). *Thoughts of a citizen scientist.* Reading, MA: Addison-Wesley.

4., 5. Sheff, D. (1988, January 19). Letters to the editor, *The New York Times.*

6. Sagan, C. (1980). *Cosmos* (p. 199). New York: Random House.

7. Sagan, C. (1980). *Cosmos* (p. 80). New York: Random House.

8. Dillard, A. (1988). *An American childhood.* New York: Harper and Row.

9. McPeck, J. (1984). *Critical thinking and education.* Oxford, England: Martin Robertson.

10. Dillon, J. T. (1988). *Questioning and teaching: A manual of practice.* New York: Teachers College Press.

11. Henneberger, M. (1998, January 10). Albright right-hand man finds spotlight's on him. *The New York Times,* p. 1.

12. Barell, J. (1995). *Teaching for thoughtfulness* (2nd ed.). White Plains, NY: Longman.

13, 14, 15. In an on-line salon, scientists sit back and ponder: "What is the question you are asking yourself?" (1997, December 30) *The New York Times,* p. F4.

16. Lozauskas, D., & Barell, J. (1992, November). Reflective reading: A journal for inquiring minds. *The Science Teacher,* 42–45.

17. Barell, J. (1992). . . . *Ever Wonder . . . ?* Columbus, OH: Zaner Bloser.

18. Barell, J. (2006). *Problem-based learning: An inquiry approach.* Thousand Oaks, CA: Corwin Press.

19. McLaren, P. (1998). *Life in schools: An introduction to critical pedagogy in the foundations of education* (3rd ed.). New York: Addison Wesley Longman.

20. McCombs, B. (1991). Metacognition and motivation for higher level thinking. Paper presented at the annual meeting of the American Educational Research Association, Chicago.

21, 22. Barell, J. (1995). *Teaching for thoughtfulness* (2nd ed.), p. 267. New York: Longman.

23. Jensen, E. (1998). *Teaching with the brain in mind.* Alexandria, VA: Association for Supervision and Curriculum Development.

24. Clarity, J. (1996, August 5). Finding faith the hard way: The pluck of the Irish. *The New York Times,* p. A4.

The Misunderstood Role of the Arts in Human Development

Elliot W. Eisner

Elliot W. Eisner is Professor of Education and Art at Stanford University. He was trained as a painter at the School of the Art Institute of Chicago and later studied design at Illinois Institute of Technology's Institute of Design. He works in three fields: arts education, curriculum studies, and educational evaluation. Professor Eisner's research interests focus on the development of aesthetic intelligence and on the use of critical methods from the arts for studying and improving educational practice. He has lectured on these topics throughout the world and is widely considered one of the leading scholars in arts education today.

Providing a decent place for the arts in our schools may be one of the most important first steps we can take to bring about genuine school reform, Dr. Eisner maintains.

In twenty-first-century America, the American people are presented with a reform agenda for their schools in which the arts are virtually absent. Should they be? To provide an intelligent answer, one needs a concept of the arts and a view of the functions of education. What conception of the arts do people who shape education policy have? What image do they have of the aims of education? What kind of culture do they prize? What do they feel contributes to a life worth living? I believe that prevailing conceptions of the arts are based on a massive misunderstanding of the role of the arts in human development and education. This misunderstanding is rooted in ancient conceptions of mind, knowledge, and intelligence. Collectively, these conceptions impoverish the programs of schools and the education of the young.

Make no mistake, the curriculum we prescribe for schools and the time we allocate to different subjects show children what adults believe is important for them to learn. There is no more telling indicator of the importance of the subjects students study than the amount of time allocated to them.[1] In American schools, the arts receive about two hours of instructional time per week at the elementary level and are generally not a required subject of study at the secondary level. The allocation of time to what we teach has other consequences as well. The amount of time allocated to a field of study influences the kinds of mental skills children have the opportunity to acquire.

Thus time represents both value and opportunity: value, because it indicates what is considered significant; opportunity, because the school can be thought of as a culture of opportunity. A culture in the biological sense is a place for growing things. Schools, too, are cultures. They are cultures for growing minds, and the direction this growth takes is influenced by the opportunities the school provides. These opportunities are defined by the school's program—its curriculum—and by the artistry with which teachers mediate that program. A school in which the arts are absent or poorly taught is unlikely to provide the genuine opportunities children need to use the arts in the service of their own development.

To speak of mind as developed or, even more pointedly, as grown may seem strange. Yet, in a basic sense, mind is a form of cultural achievement. We are born with brains, but our minds are made, and the shape they take is influenced by the culture in which that development occurs. For children, the school constitutes a primary culture for the development of mind. Therefore, decisions that are made about the school's priorities are also fundamental decisions about the kinds of minds children will have the opportunity to develop.

COMMON MISCONCEPTIONS ABOUT INTELLIGENCE

Since our educational priorities are significantly influenced by our conceptions of mind, knowledge, and intelligence and since I believe that prevailing conceptions of the arts misconceive their primary features, I will briefly identify five widely held but fundamentally flawed beliefs about mind, knowledge, and intelligence that give direction to our schools. I will then describe what the arts can contribute to the educational development of the young.

1. *Human conceptual thinking requires the use of language.* Perhaps no belief shapes our understanding of cognition more than the conviction that language plays a necessary role in its operation. Indeed, thinking itself has sometimes been thought of as a kind of subvocalizing, a physical process that accompanies the chain of language activity that best represents the higher mental processes. Language and thought are inseparable.

There are many reasons why this belief will not stand scrutiny. First, to argue that language is a necessary condition for cognition is to conclude that children cannot think until they are able to speak. Yet anyone who has lived with a child knows firsthand how inquisitive a child can be before speech has developed and how intelligent such a child can be in solving problems: a child who cannot think cannot survive.

Second, language as we normally use it is a symbolic device, and symbolic devices that do not have referents do not symbolize. To symbolize, a symbol must be connected to a referent—that is, to an array of qualities one can experience, or that one has experienced, or that one has imagined. To speak meaningfully of baroque music—or of an oak tree or of a jet airplane—requires a conception of these objects and events, and these objects and events exist as qualities in our experience prior to the labels we assign to them. Contrary to popular opinion, in the beginning there was the image. It is the image that gives meaning to the label. The information the image provides is a cognitive event.

> Decisions that are made about a school's priorities are also fundamental decisions about the kinds of minds its children will have the opportunity to develop.

2. *Sensory experience is low on the hierarchy of intellectual functioning.* The genesis of this belief can be found in Plato's ideas

about the nature of human understanding. In the sixth book of *The Republic,* Socrates asks Glaucon to imagine a single, vertical line divided unequally into an upper and a lower segment. The longer upper half of the line represents the intelligible world; the bottom portion, the visible world. The intelligible world is grasped through rational procedures; the visible world, through perception. Rationality is high; perception is low. Plato's hierarchy was not diluted by the expansion of the Roman Empire. It is alive and well in the schools and universities of modern America.

But is it true that the perception of qualities is a low-level cognitive activity? When those qualities are complex and subtle, as they are in the arts, the perception of their relationships and nuances can be daunting. To put this matter in context, listen to Rudolf Arnheim:

> By "cognitive" I mean all mental operations involved in the receiving, storing, and processing of information: sensory perception, memory, thinking, learning. This use of the term conflicts with one to which many psychologists are accustomed and which excludes the activity of the senses from cognition. It reflects the distinction I am trying to eliminate; therefore I must extend the meaning of the terms "cognitive" and "cognition" to include perception. Similarly, I see no way of withholding the name of "thinking" from what goes on in perception. No thought processes seem to exist that cannot be found to operate, at least in principle, in perception. Visual perception is visual thinking.[2]

Ironically, indifference to the refinement of perception and inattention to the development of imagination have limited children's cognitive growth. Since no teacher has direct access to a child's mind, it is the child's ability to see the connections between the example the teacher uses, what the child already knows, and what the teacher hopes he or she will understand that makes the example instrumental to new meaning. In short, understanding depends on the child's ability to think by analogy and to grasp, often through metaphor, what needs to be understood. Poetry may indeed be closer to the most sophisticated forms of cognition than many people suspect.

3. *Intelligence requires the use of logic.* The importance of logic in the exercise of intelligence is clear if the form that is to be used to speak to the world is one in which the literal use of propositions is

necessary. Mathematics and the sciences place a premium on a certain form of precision: literal statement. Logical consistency in such forms of representation is a condition for meaning. But to regard logic as a necessary condition for the exercise of intelligence is to restrict intelligence to those forms of representation that require its use.[3] The result of such a conception is to banish from the domain of intelligence those forms of representation whose meanings are not conveyed by and do not depend upon the use of logic. Poetry, for example, achieves meaning by employing language in ways that do not depend solely on logic; poetic meaning is often "extra-logical." The meanings conveyed by this extra-logical feature of poetry are what might better be thought of as the product of human rationality, and the same point pertains to the other arts.

Although rationality and logicality have been closely associated, rationality is a broader and more fundamental concept. Logic is one of the ways in which rationality is expressed, but it is not the only way. Individuals who manage human relationships well, those who draw or paint well, those who dance well, or those who sing well all do their thinking *within* the medium in which they work. Writing in 1934, John Dewey recognized that intelligence is usually regarded as the sole property of those whom we regard as intellectuals— especially, but not exclusively, in the academy. For those holding such a view, Dewey said:

Any idea that ignores the necessary role of intelligence in the production of the works of art is based upon identification of thinking with use of one special kind of material, verbal signs and words. To think effectively in terms of relations of qualities is as severe a demand upon thought as to think in terms of symbols, verbal and mathematical. Indeed, since words are easily manipulated in mechanical ways, the production of a work of genuine art probably demands more intelligence than does most of the so-called thinking that goes on among those who pride themselves on being "intellectuals."[4]

4. *Detachment and distance are necessary for true understanding.* Emotion has long been regarded as the enemy of reflective thought: the more we feel, the less we know. Now there certainly is a case to be made that such emotions as rage can radically influence one's perception and judgment. When running rampant, emotions can cloud vision, impair thought, and lead to trouble of all kinds.

But perception without feeling can do the same. Not to be able to feel, say, a human relationship is to miss what may very well be its most critical features. To be unable to get a sense of history, to not be able to stand with Columbus on the deck of the *Santa Maria* and experience the pounding of the vessel by the relentless sea and the excitement of his first sighting of land is to miss—and perhaps even misunderstand—that aspect of history. And in failing to experience the emotion of such moments, we miss out on an aspect of life that has the potential to inform. Detachment and distance have their virtues, but they are limited resources for understanding, and any conception that assigns them dominion in cognition misconceives the ways in which understanding is fostered.

5. *Scientific method is the only legitimate way to generalize about the world.* The traditional, flawed conception of the arts claims that, when they are about anything, the arts are only about particulars: they yield no generalizations. Their virtues reside in delight rather than insight. They provide nothing that can reasonably be regarded as knowledge or understanding. Since the instrumental value of the products of science is considered greater than the delight derived from the arts (which in any case is usually thought to be merely a matter of personal taste), the value of the arts in comparison to the sciences is set low.

This conception of generalization defines much too narrowly the sources through which generalizations are actually made. The need to generalize is fundamental. Human beings generalized long before either science or statistics were invented. Generalizations are not only scientific and naturalistic; they also emerge from those intense forms of experience that we call the arts. They are sometimes called concrete universals.

Consider the paintings of Francis Bacon, Velásquez, or Picasso, or consider the novels of John Steinbeck or Cervantes. Even fiction—perhaps especially fiction—can help us grasp the meaning not only of Don Quixote, the particular man, but of what we all

> The last thing a modern teacher of the arts in America wants is a class full of standardized performances on a given task.

share with him as we tilt at our own windmills, struggling to overcome seemingly insurmountable obstacles.[5] Cervantes helps us understand such travails, and, because he succeeds so well, we come away from his work with a new view, a view that enables us to recognize and reflect on one of the important features of our own lives. Through his work, we are also able to recognize these features elsewhere.

EDUCATIONAL CONTRIBUTIONS CENTRAL TO THE ARTS

My argument thus far has focused on beliefs that have given direction to the educational enterprise. I have contended that the five beliefs I have described—that thought requires language, that sensory experience is a low-level function, that logic is necessary for intelligence, that detachment and distance foster understanding, and that science is the only legitimate way to generalize—create an intellectual climate that marginalizes the arts because what these beliefs celebrate seems to have little to do with what the arts provide. I will now focus on four contributions that I believe are central to all the arts. In doing so, I will not describe the specific contributions that each individual art makes to children of different ages. Instead, my aim is to identify the common, core contributions of the arts and their potential role in furthering the aims of education.

1. *Not all problems have single, correct answers.* One of the important lessons the arts teach is that solutions to problems can take many forms. This lesson from the arts would not be so important were it not for the fact that so much of what is taught in school teaches just the opposite lesson. Almost all of the basic skills taught in the primary grades teach children that there is only one correct answer to any question and only one correct solution to any problem. Spelling, arithmetic, writing, and even reading are pervaded by conventions and rules that, in effect, teach children to follow rules well.

The arts teach a different lesson. They celebrate imagination, multiple perspectives, and the importance of personal interpretation. The last thing a modern teacher of the arts in America wants is a class full of standardized performances on a given task. The last thing an English teacher wants are idiosyncratic interpretations of how words are spelled. This is as it should be. Creativity in spelling is no virtue. But when the curriculum as a whole is so heavily saturated with tasks and expectations that demand fealty to rule, opportunities to think in unique ways are diminished. When carried to an extreme, the school's program becomes intellectually debilitating.

2. *The form of a thing is part of its content.* We have a tendency in our schools to separate form from content. Form is regarded as the shape something takes, and content is the meaning something conveys. In notational systems, we can live with such a dichotomy. In such systems, attention to form as such is largely irrelevant. For example, the number six can be symbolized in many ways, but its meaning is the same as long as one recognizes it as a six. The task is one of categorization. Early reading also emphasizes categorization. And when children learn to assign a form—say, a particular tree—to its category rather than to explore its distinctive features, perception is aborted. As Dewey pointed out, perception ceases when recognition begins. Assigning a label to an entity is an act of categorization, and when entities are assigned to categories, the exploration of their uniqueness stops.

The arts, however, teach the child that the grass is not simply green; it is lavender, gray, gold. And when it is green, its varieties are endless. Furthermore, in the arts and in much of life, the form something takes is very much a part of its content. In fact, what the content is often depends on the form it takes. The arts are prime examples of how this marriage of form and content is created and of the effect that it has on our experience.

I have made a special point here of emphasizing the function of the arts in human development. The arts are neglected resources and deserve attention in our schools. But I do not want to give the impression that at least some of the features that the arts possess are not also to be found in the sciences. The products of science have their own aesthetic features: the parsimony of theory, the beauty of conceptual models, the elegance of experiments, and the imagination and insight of interpretation. Indeed, the qualities for which a work of science is cherished are often related as much to its aesthetic appeal as to its explanatory power. A theory, after all, is a perspective about the way the world is. It is a way to secure a coherent view, and coherence is so important that we are often unwilling to give up the views we find attractive, despite contradictory evidence.

My point here is that although my primary focus is on what may be called the fine arts, some of the features for which the arts are valued are also exhibited by the sciences. At the risk of oversimplifying the differences between the arts and the sciences, let me say that, in the context of creation, a work of science is a work of art.

3. *Having fixed objectives and pursuing clear-cut methods for achieving them are not always the most rational ways of dealing with the world.* There is a tendency in technologically oriented cultures to conceive of rationality as a method for tightly linking means and ends. To be rational, we tell children (and teachers), that they must first formulate clear-cut objectives for their work, then use these objectives to define means for their achievement, and finally implement and evaluate the effectiveness and efficiency of the means for achieving the desired objectives.

Of course, there is a sense of sweet reason about such a procedure. Yet we often conceptualize and implement this process in mechanical ways: we give students goals for each lesson, we expect teachers to know exactly where they are headed, and we appraise classrooms and the quality of teaching on the basis of their achievement. We try to create a technology of management so that efficiency in learning and teaching is achieved and public accountability is provided. Our narrow conception of rationality is expressed in our incessant search for "what works": It supports the belief that there is, in fact, a single best way, that the main task of researchers is to find it, and that the primary obligation of teachers is to use it. The entire effort to standardize educational outcomes is premised on a conviction that efficient and effective systems can be designed that will take luck out of the educational process.

These beliefs not only affect the conditions of teaching, they also create a climate that affects what and how students learn. Moreover, these views are antithetical to what the arts teach. The arts teach that goals need to be flexible and that surprise counts; that chance, as Aristotle

> Life outside of school is seldom like school assignments—and hardly ever like a multiple-choice test.

wisely remarked, is something that art loves; that being open to the unanticipated opportunities that inevitably emerge in the context of action increases insight; and that purposeful flexibility rather than rigid adherence to prior plans is more likely to yield something of value. No painter, writer, composer, or choreographer can foresee all the twists and turns that his or her work will take. The *work* of art— by which I now mean the *act* of creation—does not follow an unalterable schedule but is a journey that unfolds. The relationship of the maker to the work is not that of lecturer to listener, but a conversation between the worker and the work.

In the context of much of today's schooling, the lessons taught by the arts are much closer to what successful and intelligent corporations do and to what cognitive psychologists are discovering constitute the most sophisticated forms of thinking.[6] These recent psychological discoveries are lessons artists have long understood. What are these lessons?

Solving complex problems requires attention to wholes, not simply to discrete parts;

Most complex problems have no algorithmic solutions;

Nuance counts, and is important;

Purposes and goals must remain flexible in order to exploit opportunities that one cannot foresee.

These newly discovered cognitive virtues are taught in every genuine *work* of art. Yet, ironically, the arts are typically thought of as noncognitive.

What is even more ironic is that, while we say that the function of schooling is to prepare students for life, the problems of life tend not to have the fixed, single correct answers that characterize the problems students encounter in the academic areas of schooling. The problems of life are much more like the problems encountered in the arts. They are problems that seldom have a single correct solution; they are problems that are often subtle, occasionally ambiguous, and sometimes dilemma-like. One would think that schools that wanted to prepare students for life would employ tasks and problems similar to those found outside of schools. This is hardly the case. Life outside of school is seldom like school assignments—and hardly ever like a multiple-choice test.

4. *In addition to their expressive function, the arts perform another function of critical importance.* In all that I have said so far, I have emphasized the contributions that the arts make toward helping students recognize that problems are not restricted to those having single correct answers; that form and content interact; and that purposeful flexibility is a mark of fluid intelligence coping with the vicissitudes of the unpredictable. But I have neglected a contribution that is surely as important. That contribution hinges on a distinction between *expression* and *discovery.* In the arts, students learn that

some kinds of meaning may require the expressive forms that the arts make possible. In this sense, the arts expressively represent; they provide the forms through which insight and feeling can emerge in the public world. Indeed, humans invented the arts to serve expressive functions. For most people who have thought about the arts, this particular function is the one most commonly recognized.

But the arts also make discovery possible. Discovery occurs as students learn through adventures in the arts something of the possibilities of human experience. The journeys they take through the patterned sound we call music, through the visual forms we call painting, and through the metaphorical discourse we call poetry and literature are means through which students can discover their potential to respond. In other words, the arts can help students find their individual capacity to feel and imagine.

While such journeys are experienced through the arts, they can also be secured through the ordinary aspects of daily life when it is approached aesthetically. The world outside of art can become something to explore and relish: through the arts students can learn how to discover not only the possibilities the world offers but also their own possibilities. Expression and discovery are two major contributions the arts make to human development.

> Through the arts students can learn how to discover not only the possibilities the world offers but also their own possibilities.

Just how are such discoveries made? As children learn to manipulate, manage, and monitor the nuances of voice, movement, and visual form, they discover the effects that their own fine-tuning achieves. As form is modulated, so too is feeling. As imagination is given permission to rise, children have the opportunity to enter worlds not tied to the literal, to the concrete, to the practical. Discovery emerges in the appreciation of qualities examined and images pursued. The arts, more than most fields, put a premium on such activities, and those activities can help students discover the special qualities of experience we call aesthetic.

ART AS AN EDUCATIONAL AND DEVELOPMENTAL PRIORITY

Let me close by returning briefly to my initial claim that prevailing conceptions of the arts are based on a massive misunderstanding of their role in human development. This misconception is reflected in the narrow educational priorities of twenty-first-century America. In turn, these priorities are rooted in beliefs that regard mind as fixed rather than developed, that conceive of knowledge as the exclusive property of science, and that consider intelligence as limited to forms of abstract thought dependent on the use of logic. These narrow and misguided conceptions are not ivory tower theories without practical consequences. They influence our educational priorities, shape what we teach, and affect our children's lives. They result in schools that have an antiseptic environment that seldom provides even a nod to our sensuous, poetic, or imaginative sides.

I hope readers realize that my argument here is an optimistic one. What is pessimistic is a fixed view of mind, a conception of knowledge limited to what literal language can convey, and a view of intelligence constrained by the rules of logic. Human intellectual capacity is far wider. The realization of this capacity is surely more likely as we create a richer, more nurturing culture for our students. That culture, as I see it, ought to include significant opportunities for students to experience the arts and to learn to use them to create a life worth living. Indeed, providing a decent place for the arts in our schools may be one of the most important first steps we can take to bring about genuine school reform. Let's hope that, despite the priorities of twenty-first-century America, we have the courage and the wit to take it.

NOTES

1. Bernstein, B. (1971). On the classification and framing of educational knowledge. In M. Young (Ed.), *Knowledge and control* (pp. 47–69). London: Collier, Macmillan.

2. Arnheim, R. (1972). *Visual thinking* (pp.13–14). Berkeley: University of California Press.

3. Eisner, E. W. (1982). *Cognition and curriculum: A basis for deciding what to teach.* New York: Longman.

4. Dewey, J. (1934). *Art as experience* (p. 46). New York: Minton, Balch.

5. Goodman, N. (1978). *Ways of worldmaking.* Indianapolis: Hackett.

6. Resnick, L. (1989). *Toward the thinking curriculum, current cognitive research.* Alexandria, VA: Association for Supervision and Curriculum Development; and Greeno, J. (1989). Perspectives on thinking. *American Psychologist, 44,* 134–141.

What Really Matters in Teaching Children to Read

Richard L. Allington

Richard L. Allington *is professor of education at the University of Tennessee. He is the past president of the National Reading Conference and a member of the board of directors of the International Reading Association. Author of over 100 articles and several books, Dr. Allington currently serves on a number of editorial boards for journals pertaining to literacy, education, and learning disability.*

In every nation there are some children who find learning to read difficult regardless of the nature of the writing system, the assessment plan, the national wealth, or the organization of educational system (Elley, 1992). Even when offered good instruction, some children struggle mightily to become literate. Unfortunately, too many children struggle because they do not have access to sufficient instruction. But just how can sufficient instruction be characterized? In other words, what is it that really matters in designing and delivering instruction to children who find learning to read difficult?

After a century of research on reading instruction and on children who find learning to read difficult, there are only a few things of critical instructional importance that have been identified. Unfortunately, professional debates and discussions often ignore each of these important dimensions of effective instructional environments and interventions. However, it is important to identify and briefly explain what has mattered historically and what matters now in terms of classroom strategies, structures, and environments.

PROFESSIONAL BELIEFS MATTER

Since the study of reading difficulties began around the turn of the twentieth century, three broad factors have been touted regularly as sources of reading difficulties. Each of these factors remains influential in school response to the problem of reading difficulties (Johnston & Allington, 1996).

The Intelligence Factor

First, limited intellectual abilities were viewed as a primary source of the difficulties. But then it was discovered that achievement on purported measures of intelligence and measures of reading achievement did not actually correlate all that well. In fact, terms were invented—hyperlexia and dyslexia—to explain aberrations, those children who read better or less well than was expected. But when educators believed intelligence, or the lack of it, was the source of difficulty, little was offered in the way of instructional interventions because some children were just never going to be readers due to limited intellectual capacity. Some children were "slow learners" and not much could be expected of them. Thus, the "slow it down and make it concrete" instructional plan was widely implemented—virtually ensuring that some children developed only minimal levels of reading proficiency (Allington, 1992).

The "Disadvantage" Factor

However, after noting the less than perfect correlation between measures of intellect and measures of reading, other explanations emerged. Probably the most popular was targeting "disadvantage"—both economic and educational—as a source of the difficulties (McGill-Franzen, 1987). This explanation got a boost from the research showing that many more poor children had difficulty learning to read. Thus, interventions were developed in the hopes of overcoming the disadvantages of poverty. But few of these programs actually seemed to enhance the instruction children received and in some cases the older "slow it down" plan was continued with "disadvantaged" children. The result, therefore, was that many of the "disadvantaged" children failed to develop into readers and writers even after participating in the compensatory education programs (Puma, Jones, Rock, & Fernandez, 1993). Some educators and researchers argued that schools just could not be expected to overcome the negative effects of growing up poor. But the "disadvantage" conceptualization shaped the sorts of instructional programs that were offered.

The Learning Disabilities Factor

A third, and more recently popularized belief about children who find learning to read difficult is that these children suffer a disability (McGill-Franzen, 1987). Usually this disability is characterized in terms of neurological damage or difference that makes perceptual or verbal learning exceedingly difficult, if not impossible. But evidence of a neurological basis for reading difficulties has been difficult to find. If children with such conditions exist they exist in incredibly small numbers, far too few to account for the range of difficulties now observed (Vellutino et al., 1996). Nonetheless, believing in a neurologically based disability meant some children could not be expected to learn to read and so little effective instruction was offered (Allington & McGill-Franzen, 1989). For instance, few individualized educational plans (IEPs) set annual goals for accelerated literacy development (an annual goal of 1.5 years growth per year, for instance) because the disability conceptualization suggested a damaged or limited capacity for learning.

Current Professional Beliefs: Sufficiency of Instruction

Most recently, there has been a growing recognition that reading acquisition is relatively easy for some children and relatively difficult—exceedingly difficult in a few cases—for other children. But only a very few children cannot, seemingly, acquire reading proficiency alongside their peers (Lyons, Pinnell, & DeFord, 1993; Slavin, Madden, Karweit, Dolan, & Wasik, 1993; Vellutino et al., 1996). This might be labeled the sufficiency of instruction conceptualization. Because children vary in the ease with which they acquire literacy and because they arrive at school with varied levels of literacy experience, we should expect that providing a standard instructional program would result in large discrepancies in achievement. Only when the instructional program offers varied levels of instructional intensity can we reasonably expect all children to develop reading proficiency—especially developing that proficiency on a schedule similar to peer development.

However, we must first believe virtually all children can become readers before we even begin to think about how to design instruction to ensure that this happens (Winfield, 1986; Zigmond, 1993). This belief leads us to design programs in which some children have access to larger amounts of higher quality and more intensive instruction.

Beliefs are important because they drive our thinking, our planning, and our actions (Allington, McGill-Franzen, & Schick, 1997). Yet for too long our professional beliefs have literally resulted in educational efforts that produced children who remained largely illiterate. Believing in the inherent educability of all children is a necessary first step in creating schools where all children become readers and writers.

> For too long our professional beliefs have literally resulted in educational efforts that produced children who remain largely illiterate.

CHILDREN NEED TO READ
A LOT TO BECOME READERS

In addition to professional beliefs, it also matters how successful we are at creating instructional environments that foster wide reading by all children, but especially by those children who have found learning to read difficult. Unfortunately, an overwhelmingly consistent finding in the research is that children who find learning to read difficult often participate in educational programs that fail to foster much reading at all. These children do less guided reading with their teachers and less independent, voluntarily reading (Krashen, 2004).

Only occasionally are interventions purposefully designed to alter this situation (Morrow, 1992). More often, instruction for children who find learning to read difficult occupies them with skill games, practice dittos, and drills (Allington, 1983; Allington & McGill-Franzen, 1989). And in some schools children who have difficulty with reading literally have no books in their desks that they can actually read or learn to read from. This occurs even though schools spend substantial additional funds on interventions intended to assist the struggling readers (Guice, Allington, Johnston, Baker, & Michelson, 1996).

The Importance of Instructional Environment

If children are going to engage in substantial amounts of reading, there seem to be at minimum two aspects of the instructional environment left that must be attended to. First, children need access to a large supply of books of appropriate difficulty, books that fit the Goldilocks principle (Fountas & Pinnell, 1996): they are not too hard, not too easy, but just right. This means books that they can read fluently while also understanding the story or information. This is not a new idea. For most of this century fitting children to books has been advocated and teachers have been taught to administer informal reading inventories and, more recently, to gather running records, in an attempt to ensure appropriate book placement. In some schools, unfortunately, there is little evidence that this feature of appropriate instruction is of much concern. For instance, we too often still find classrooms where all children are taught from the same book regardless of how well the book matches their level of literacy development. We find remedial and special education programs that offer little support to either children or classroom teachers in this regard (McGill-Franzen, 1994). Many programs exert little effort to ensure that struggling readers have easy access to a large supply of appropriate books. We find state educational policies that support the purchase of more skill and drill workbooks although classrooms have few, if any, books appropriate for children having difficulty with reading acquisition, and although many school libraries remain underfunded, understaffed, and understocked.

> Children need access to and the freedom to choose books and stories that are interesting and engaging to them to foster independent, voluntary reading.

If we want to foster wider reading there is another important feature of instructional environments that is often overlooked. Children need access to books and stories that are interesting and engaging to them and they need the freedom to choose at least some of the books they read, especially if we are attempting to foster independent, voluntary reading. Again, too few efforts to help children who find learning to read difficult are focused on ensuring a supply of interesting and appropriately difficult books is readily available.

Often we hear talk of the need to motivate reluctant readers but perhaps we should think more about examining the environments we create more carefully rather than characterizing the lack of voluntary reading as a motivational problem located in children. We need to worry more about putting enticing, just-right books in children's hands and less about schemes that bribe children into taking home an uninteresting book that is too difficult.

CHILDREN NEED TO BE TAUGHT

Although there may be some natural readers, most children need good instruction and some need enormous amounts of personalized instruction if they are to become readers. Research on effective instruction suggests that we have not yet found a way to package good teaching. In study after study it is the quality of the teacher, not variation in curriculum materials, which is identified as the critical factor in effective instruction (Bond & Dykstra, 1967; Knapp, 1995; Shanklin, 1990). That is not to say that materials are wholly unimportant, but that investing in teacher development has a better result than investing in curriculum materials. Good teachers and expert teachers produce more readers than other teachers regardless of the curriculum materials used.

Good teachers know their students better and are more precise in targeting instructional needs (Johnston, 1997). Good teachers know more about literacy acquisition and use this expertise in planning instruction. They offer more comprehensive reading instruction with more attention to individual instructional needs (Pressley et al., 1996). These teachers create literacy-rich classrooms and teach strategies using explicit modeling. In other words, these teachers do not simply assign work or attempt to cover some segment of the

> Until we redesign school programs so that children have access to sufficient instruction—of whatever level of intensity and duration is needed—then we will have children who struggle with reading acquisition when compared with their peers.

curriculum material. Instead, these teachers teach actively and teach the useful strategies students need when they need them as opposed to following some predetermined schedule or pacing (Duffy, 1997). These teachers also push children to become more independent and more thoughtful readers.

Good teachers create classrooms where reading and writing activity fill large blocks of time. They develop effective decoding strategies, spelling strategies, and composing and comprehension activities, and they are constantly monitoring children's reading development and intervening when instruction is needed (Goatley, Brock, & Raphael, 1995).

But some children need more intensive instruction than a classroom teacher can provide. Some children will need additional small-group work and some can be expected to need tutorial assistance. Some children will need such help only for the short term, while others will need assistance for the long term. In other words, some children will need extra instruction this Wednesday after school, some will need a tutorial all next week, and some will need the added time that a summer school experience would provide for the remainder of their school career. Unfortunately, all too often we have designed extra-instructional programs in a one-size-fits-all scheme (Walmsley & Allington, 1995), in which everyone will receive three 30-minute small-group sessions every week all year, regardless of their real needs. Almost no one will participate in tutoring because educators have not devised a plan that makes short term tutoring available (even though such efforts are generally more successful than other efforts [Wasik & Slavin, 1993]).

Until we redesign school programs so that children have access to sufficient instruction—of whatever level of intensity and duration is needed—then we will have children who will struggle with reading acquisition when compared with their peers. The key to success is good teachers working within a flexible school framework that allows them to provide the instruction children need.

SCHOOLS WORK BETTER WHEN FAMILIES ARE PARTNERS

Good schools are more important to literacy development than are families (Snow, Barnes, Chandler, Goodman, & Hemphill, 2000), but the most successful schools have fostered and supported family involvement. It is schools that are charged with responsibility for developing reading proficiency, not families. Inviting family involvement, providing families with support in working with their children, and gaining the confidence of the families of children attending the school are all wonderfully important tasks to be undertaken after the school has ensured the adequacy of the school program.

Creating schools where children are neither rewarded nor penalized for their family status must be the first task of educators (Allington & Cunningham, 2001). Once effective school programs are in place—programs that provide children with access to sufficient high-quality instruction—then work on family support and involvement efforts can proceed. Interestingly, once good school programs are in place, family involvement often seems less a problem.

Developing strategies to support families should be the first order of business. For instance, schools might work to ensure all children have an adequate supply of appropriate books to take home in the evening or over the weekend. Extending this support further might involve opening the school library evenings, on weekends, or over the summer as is possible. In some schools this has been accomplished with no added costs by using flexible scheduling of library staff.

Many families simply do not have the discretionary funds to purchase books for a child's bedroom library. A recent study in California reported home supplies of appropriate books varied widely by community with the wealthiest homes reporting nearly 200 age-appropriate books and the less wealthy homes reporting one age-appropriate book available in every other household (Smith, Constantino, & Krashen, 1997). Often the local elementary school has the largest supply of children's books in the vicinity, and yet that supply is often largely unavailable to the parents of children who own no books of their own. To address this problem, schools might develop sponsorships for book give-away programs so that every child receives a number of personal books each year. Schools also might invite parents of preschool age children to use the library themselves.

Families can support school learning in other ways but many will need substantial guidance and support to help effectively. We need to understand that family literacy experiences differ across families, and that family ability to support school instruction also varies (Purcell-Gates, 1995). It often seems that schools would do better to make a greater effort to learn from families than to assume that families need to be taught or told what to do.

So What to Do First?

There are only a very few things that really matter in developing avid and proficient readers. A good beginning is a stocktaking activity that attempts to evaluate reliably just how those things that really matter are addressed in your school. Do children who find learning to read difficult have easy access to appropriate and engaging books and stories? Has the instructional program been designed to offer children access to reading instruction of sufficient quality and intensity to accelerate their literacy development? Is the instruction exemplary and focused on developing independent, engaged readers?

Although there are only a few things that really matter, creating schools that work well for all children is not easy. Changing schools is hard work and it takes time, energy, and expertise. Individuals hold the key in those matters. It is up to you.

References

Allington, R. L. (1983). The reading instruction provided readers of differing abilities. *The Elementary School Journal, 83,* 548–559.

Allington, R. L. (1992). The legacy of "slow it down and make it more concrete." In J. Zutell & S. McCormick (Eds.), *Learner factors/teacher factors: Issues in literacy research and instruction* (pp. 19–30). Chicago: National Reading Conference.

Allington, R. L., & Cunningham, P. M. (2001). *Schools that work: Where all children read and write.* Boston: Allyn & Bacon.

Allington, R. L., & McGill-Franzen, A. (1989). Different programs, indifferent instruction. In A. Gartner & D. Lipsky (Eds.), *Beyond separate education: Quality education for all* (pp. 75–98). Baltimore: Brookes.

Allington, R. L., McGill-Franzen, A., & Schick, R. (1997). How administrators understand learning difficulties: A qualitative analysis. *Remedial and Special Education, 18,* 223–232.

Bond, G. L., & Dysktra, R. (1967). The cooperative research program in first-grade reading instruction. *Reading Research Quarterly, 2,* 5–142.

Duffy, G. G. (1997). Powerful models or powerful teachers? An argument for teacher-as-entrepreneur. In S. Stahl & D. Hayes (Eds.), *Instructional models in reading* (pp. 351–365). Hillsdale, NJ: Erlbaum.

Elley, W. B. (1992). *How in the world do students read? IEA study of reading literacy.* The Hague, Netherlands: International Association for the Evaluation of Educational Achievement.

Fountas, I. C., & Pinnell, G. S. (1996). *Guided reading: Good first teaching for all children.* Portsmouth, NH: Heinemann.

Goatley, V. J., Brock, C. H., & Raphael, T. E. (1995). Diverse learners participating in regular education "Book Clubs." *Reading Research Quarterly, 30,* 352–380.

Guice, S., Allington, R. L., Johnston, P., Baker, K., & Michelson, N. (1996). Access?: Books, children, and literature-based curriculum in schools. *The New Advocate, 9,* 197–207.

Johnston, P. A. (1997). *Knowing literacy.* York, ME: Stenhouse.

Johnston, P. A., & Allington, R. L. (1996). Remediation. In R. Barr, M. Kamil, P. Mosenthal, & P. D. Pearson (Eds.), *Handbook of reading research: Volume II* (pp. 984–1012). White Plains, NY: Longman.

Knapp, M. S. (1995). *Teaching for meaning in high-poverty classrooms.* New York: Teachers College Press.

Krashen, S. (2004). *The power of reading: Insights from the research.* Portsmouth, NH: Heinemann.

Lyons, C. A., Pinnell, G. S., & DeFord, D. E. (1993). *Partners in learning: Teachers and children in Reading Recovery.* New York: Teachers College Press.

McGill-Franzen, A. (1987). Failure to learn to read: Formulating a policy problem. *Reading Research Quarterly, 22,* 475–490.

McGill-Franzen, A. M. (1994). Is there accountability for learning and belief in children's potential? In E. H. Hiebert & B. M. Taylor (Eds.), *Getting reading right from the start: Effective early literacy interventions.* Boston: Allyn & Bacon.

Morrow, L. M. (1992). The impact of a literature-based program on literacy achievement, use of literature, and attitudes of children from minority backgrounds. *Reading Research Quarterly, 27,* 250–275.

Pressley, M., Wharton-McDonald, R., Ranking, J., Mistretta, J., Yokoi, L., & Ettenberger, S. (1996). The nature of outstanding primary grade literacy instruction. In E. McIntyre & M. Pressley (Eds.), *Balanced instruction: Strategies and skills in whole language* (pp. 251–276). Norwood, MA: Christopher-Gordon.

Puma, M. J., Jones, C. C., Rock, D., & Fernandez, R. (1993). *Prospects: The congressionally mandated study of educational growth and opportunity—The interim report* (No. GPO 1993 0-354-886 QL3). Washington, DC: U.S. Department of Education.

Purcell-Gates, V. (1995). *Other people's words: The cycle of low literacy.* Cambridge, MA: Harvard University Press.

Shanklin, N. L. (1990). Improving the comprehension of at-risk readers: An ethnographic study of four Chapter 1 teachers, grades 4–6. *International Journal of Reading, Writing, and Learning Disabilities, 6,* 137–148.

Slavin, R. E., Madden, N. A., Karweit, B. L., Dolan, L. J., & Wasik, B. A. (1993). Success for all: A comprehensive approach to prevention and early intervention. In R. E. Slavin, B. L. Karweit, & B. A. Wasik (Eds.), *Preventing early school failure: Research, policy, & practice* (pp. 175–205). Boston: Allyn & Bacon.

Smith, C., Constantino, R., & Krashen, S. (1997). Differences in print environment: Children in Beverly Hills, Compton and Watts. *Emergency Librarian, 24,* 8–9.

Snow, C., Barnes, W., Chandler, J., Goodman, I. F., & Hemphill, L. (2000). *Unfulfilled expectations: Home and school influences on literacy.* Lincoln, NE: Harvard University Press.

Vellutino, F. R., Sipay, E. R., Small, S. G., Pratt, A., Chen, R., & Denckla, M. B. (1996). Cognitive profiles of difficult-to-remediate and readily remediated poor readers: Early intervention as a vehicle for distinguishing between cognitive and experiential deficits as basic causes of specific reading disability. *Journal of Educational Psychology, 88,* 601–638.

Walmsley, S. A., & Allington, R. L. (1995). Redefining and reforming instructional support programs for at-risk students. In R. L. Allington & S. A. Walmsley (Eds.), *No quick fix: Rethinking literacy programs in America's elementary schools* (pp. 19–41). New York: Teachers College Press; Newark, DE: International Reading Association.

Wasik, B. A., & Slavin, R. E. (1993). Preventing early reading failure with one-to-one tutoring: A review of five programs. *Reading Research Quarterly, 28,* 178–200.

Winfield, L. F. (1986). Teachers' beliefs toward academically at-risk students in inner urban schools. *Urban Review, 18,* 253–268.

Zigmond, N. (1993). Learning disabilities from an educational perspective. In G. R. Lyon, D. B. Gray, J. F. Kavanagh, & N. A. Krasgegor (Eds.), *Better understanding learning disabilities: New views from research and their implications for education and public policies* (pp. 229–250). Baltimore: Brookes.

SECTION 3

Instructing for Intelligence

The general desire to teach for intelligence implies several corollaries worthy of consideration in order to turn this desire into a reality. Spillane maintains that a staff that values intellect is a primary requisite for a school to embark on such instruction. A broad base of factual knowledge, embedded in a rich curriculum, is another necessary ingredient, but *how* that program is presented and dealt with may be even more significant than the content by itself. A teaching staff must provide opportunities for students *to use* the information that matters; and *how it is used,* say many writers, and the behavior or experience it leads to are the essential considerations of pedagogy in a thoughtful school.

The third section of this volume focuses on several major considerations about pedagogical implementation that have emerged over the past two or three decades, as researchers and practitioners have attempted to refine the appropriate teaching methods to deliver an intelligent learning experience. There is no singular approach, it seems, that can guarantee intellectual success. There are, however, powerful tools that have been developed to serve the complex demands of a thoughtful pedagogy. They are described and research about them reviewed in several of the key writings in this section.

Fogarty underlines the role that knowledge about the teaching-learning process and the development of human intellectual potential has played in understanding the dynamics of a learning classroom, citing many of the leading learning theorists of this century: Piaget, Vygotsky, Feuerstein, Gardner, Sternberg, Perkins, and a number of the contributors to this volume. She develops a list of key criteria for classroom success, from maintaining a safe classroom climate, to implementing a balanced approach, to the use of varied assessments. Further, she suggests and describes many of the kinds of strategic applications by which it is possible to realize these key criteria. Bellanca focuses his discussion on teaching practices that research has proven effective. He asks educators to make a conscious choice regarding what teaching for intelligence actually *requires,* and he proposes that extraordinary steps must be taken not only to use traditional content but also to create new content. Teaching for intelligence demands not only respect for the learner's ability to acquire information, but stresses the need for both teachers and students to be competent in *generating knowledge.* Access to experiences that develop such a skill is the *sine qua non* of teaching for intelligence. The readings in this section demonstrate that there is not a singular route to such an objective.

Costa presents an alternative to the strictly strategic approach to becoming "intelligent." For him, teaching is concerned with building classroom experiences that *mediate* a child's continuous learning. Teaching for intelligence is best accomplished by an indirect, facilitating pedagogy akin to Feuerstein's theory of cognitive modifiability and mediated learning experience. According to Costa, building such a dynamic, mediative classroom serves both teacher and student most productively. In intervening between the student or a group of students and the learning environment, the teacher determines the conditions that will engage and promote intellectual growth. In this interaction, the teacher defines, in extensive detail, the learning organization itself. Costa sees leadership of such a collaborative community as a kind of "environmental protection agency." He goes on to articulate what he calls the most important leverage points that must be accomplished by the instructor to make these interventions successful. These include the clarification of goals and outcomes, the establishment of trust, coaching, investing in various forms of leadership, valuing diversity, developing higher process-based curriculum, and focusing on continuous learning. A home for the mind, says Costa, resides in such a classroom environment—one that frees the intellect, develops creative heuristics, and uses pedagogy as an enlivening art.

Interestingly, Strickland approaches classroom instruction in elementary school reading from both strategic and mediative considerations. The problem she attends to is how to differentiate instruction for the variations in student ability that every teacher confronts. The issue of *accessibility* is her key concern. Strickland warns that the best articulated algorithms for learners will not be operable if underlying student capabilities are not developed, and merely "covering the skills," like Sizer's concern for content coverage, is not a sufficient condition for "tapping into the intelligence of every learner." She begins by asking the common instructional questions: how to organize for instruction, what content to teach and how, how to monitor progress, and how to reach low-achieving students. She replies with discussion about flexible groupings and how to plan for them productively; the use of national, and especially local, standards and benchmarks to determine classroom content and plan activities in an integrated way; varying assessments to check student progress in alternative forms of reading performance; and finally, attending to less capable readers with initiatives carried on within the mainstream classroom. Strickland blends solid and traditional techniques in a pedagogy that can grow to be innovative, always keeping in focus the issue of intellectual accessibility. Groups need to be flexible in order to relate to student needs in time; the independence of the reader must always be considered and maintained; appropriate challenges need to be planned for in particular tasks; and consistent monitoring ought to provide data-based decision making for the teacher. Above all, she proposes that teachers initiate new learning gradually, carefully modeling the desired behaviors for key, clear communication. Strickland's teacher is not the fount of all wisdom, but he or she is a master at assessing a student's operable ability and providing for each learner's potential intellectual growth.

This section is concluded with two discussions about how the new pedagogy for intelligence development can become central to current reform in American education. While Cooper and Levine are relatively optimistic, they delineate issues that need to be carefully worked on if successful implementation is to be achieved. They remind practitioners of the need to ensure the basic intelligence paradigm is understood; then, leaders in this approach need to see that the principles of teaching for intelligence are adapted to the realities of classrooms, both for teachers and students. Further, Cooper and Levine say it is important to predict and overcome necessary obstacles, many of which are identifiable from existing research. Finally, they call for expanding the knowledge base of actual teaching thinking research. In that same vein, Levine and Levine present what they believe are key criteria for productive classroom intervention, indicating some promising models that have emerged from ongoing research conducted over the last two decades. These models need to be examined for what they reveal about successful implementation and practice, and their results need to be shared.

Teaching for intelligence is not merely a hoped-for activity in the greater arena of cognitive instruction. This section presents several well-thought out approaches to such pedagogy with rich examples of what each methodology emphasizes. Actual practice suggests these approaches can be interrelated and that further research on promising, current models needs to be pursued. Then, hopefully, the momentum for instructing for intelligence can continue to grow and influence actual school implementations.

Teaching for Intelligence

The Intellectual Life of Schools

Robert R. Spillane

Robert R. Spillane *is Director of the Center for Naval Analyses Corporation's Education Center. He has previously served as Regional Education Officer for Europe and the Newly Independent State of the former Soviet Union in the Office of Overseas Schools, U.S. Department of State. He was New York State Deputy and Superintendent of Boston schools from 1981 to 1985, and in Fairfax, Virginia, from 1985 to 1997. Dr. Spillane, often cited as an exemplary school administrator, developed an effective teacher evaluation program, initiated site-based management and accountability measures, and developed strong support for education in the larger business community.*

Teaching for intelligence sounds like a wonderful thing. Who could be against it? But, as with any great-sounding concept, we need to be careful to define what we mean by it. Intelligence is the ability to understand and manipulate facts and ideas using language and mathematics. The existence of "general intelligence" is one of the most solidly established findings in psychology, as is the belief that intelligence can be assessed (although there is some dispute over the types of "IQ" tests that best measure it). But, contrary to common belief, general intelligence is not fixed, either in individuals or in groups. Worldwide average IQ, for instance, has been rising for several years. Also, there is substantial evidence that educational quality affects IQ levels.

The important question is how one improves the quality of education in a way that increases intelligence. In other words, once we have defined what it *is,* how do we teach for intelligence? There are no "new, improved" ways of doing this. Just as we do not yet have an intelligence pill, we also do not have a newly developed intelligence teaching method. Instead, we need to revisit some of the things that we have known for a long time.

One important element in a school that teaches for intelligence is a staff that values intellect. This means a staff that conveys to students the view that having information and being able to use it to make sense of new information is valuable, and that academic disciplines like math, history, science, and language study are powerful tools for making sense of the world. Staff members who themselves value the life of the mind are invaluable for teaching for intelligence. They must, of course, also be able to convey this value to children, but teachers who are "great with children" but lack intellectual values are unlikely to do a great job teaching for intelligence.

A curriculum that teaches for intelligence must include a great deal of factual knowledge, beginning in the earliest years. This is especially true for students who do not receive background knowledge at home. A broad base of factual knowledge is critical to making sense of new information. If a student does not already know something about a subject, he or she cannot investigate the subject. If a teacher asks a student to comment on or research a topic that the student knows little about, the student will have little idea what questions to ask or what explanations make sense; he or she will be intellectually tied to people who do know—in most cases, teachers. Intelligence means intellectual independence, and only someone who is well informed is capable of such independence.

> Staff members who themselves value the life of the mind are invaluable for teaching for intelligence.

A curriculum that teaches for intelligence must include opportunities to master language and mathematics. This mastery must include drills that help a student to achieve "automaticity," the ability to do many things (such as arithmetic and algebraic computation, spelling, and creation of grammatical sentences) automatically— without conscious thought. Without this automaticity, students will be forever counting on their fingers, struggling with the simplest algebraic equation, looking up spellings, and writing and rewriting the simplest sentences. They will have little time and energy for the complicated mathematical and linguistic expression required for intelligence. Building automaticity is critical and involves some degree of drill and practice.

A curriculum that teaches for intelligence must provide many opportunities for students to use what they have learned in order to investigate, understand, discuss, and comment on significant matters. No student should be asked to investigate or discuss matters about which he or she knows little, or to use math or language beyond the level the student has mastered. However, opportunities for investigation, discussion, and comment should be built into the curriculum as soon as the student has learned enough information and sufficiently mastered language and math to make the exercise authentic. By the end of high school, every student should have achieved sufficient knowledge, mastery, and practice in discussion and expression to, for instance, respond *intelligently* to an article in *The New York Times* on any subject.

A curriculum that teaches for intelligence must prepare students for the inevitable "interdisciplinary" nature of most issues in life. It should do this by helping students develop a strong understanding of the major academic disciplines. The student should understand how, for instance, the natural sciences differ from social science and the humanities disciplines, and how literary study differs from history. Only with this kind of understanding will students be able to evaluate claims and evidence from several disciplines to make judgments about complex issues. In general, "interdisciplinary" instruction should probably come in the early grades (when students cannot be expected to understand what an academic discipline is) and the later grades (after they have achieved that understanding).

Perhaps most of all, teaching for intelligence should be based on respect for students' abilities to acquire information, master math and language, and eventually understand and intelligently comment on complex issues. With this respect, educators can provide the kind of systematic and intellectually serious instruction students need to be intelligent in the real world.

The Intelligence-Friendly Classroom

It Just Makes Sense

Robin Fogarty

Robin Fogarty, a leading proponent of the thoughtful class-room, trains teachers throughout the world in cognitive strategies and cooperative interaction. She operates an education think tank, Robin Fogarty and Associates, and has taught all levels from kindergarten to college, served as an administrator, and consulted with state departments and ministries of education in the United States, Russia, Canada, Australia, New Zealand, and the Netherlands. Dr. Fogarty is the author, coauthor, and editor of numerous publications in professional education.

If we know that intelligence is emotional . . .
    Then it just makes sense to use visceral hooks.
    If we know that intelligence can be nurtured . . .
    Then it just makes sense to create rich environments.
    If we know that intelligence is constructed . . .
    Then it just makes sense to provide tools for the mind.
    If we know that intelligence is developmental . . .
    Then it just makes sense to move from novice to expert.
    If we know that intelligence is experiential . . .

Then it just makes sense to challenge through doing.
If we know that intelligence is expressed in multiple ways . . .
Then it just makes sense to target many dimensions.
If we know that intelligence is modifiable . . .
Then it just makes sense to mediate learning.
If we know that intelligence is elusive . . .
Then it just makes sense to vary the measures we use.

If we know these things and believe what we know to be true, then the intelligence-friendly classroom should be a given. It is as simple and logical as an "if . . . then" syllogism.

DEFINING INTELLIGENCE-FRIENDLY CLASSROOMS

Let's look more closely at the term *intelligence-friendly classroom* and see just what it means. An intelligence-friendly classroom is a classroom in which the teaching and learning process is governed by what is known about developing the intellectual potential of human beings. Literally, intelligence-friendly means friendly to intelligence, which can be understood as both friendly to the growth patterns of human intellect and friendly to the learner in fostering intelligent behavior for use in problem solving, decision making, and creative thinking. Figuratively, the intelligence-friendly classroom serves as a caring companion and mindful guide to the intellect of each and every child in it. Just as a friend in the real world furnishes certain kinds of support that are reliable, time-tested, and tried and true, so intelligence-friendly classrooms provide similar systems of support that foster the ongoing development of human intelligence potential.

In brief, intelligence-friendly classrooms are classrooms that celebrate the joy of the learner's emotional and intellectual world, not through rhetoric and repetition, but through richness and relationships. In this article, we'll take a closer look at these intelligence-friendly classrooms, investigating their theoretical underpinnings briefly and their practical implications in more depth.

THEORETICAL UNDERPINNINGS

Guidelines for the intelligence-friendly classroom are grounded in the works of the leading voices in the field. First, let's quickly examine the various theories of intelligence and explore what each of them implies for the intelligence-friendly classroom.

- Traditional theory of general intelligence. Intelligence is inherited and unchanging.
- Piaget's theory of developmental psychology. Intelligence is developmentally constructed in the mind by the learner, and moves from concrete to abstract stages of understanding.
- Vygotsky's theory of social mediation. Intelligence is a function of activity mediated through material tools, psychological tools, and other human beings.
- Feuerstein's theory of structural cognitive modifiability. Intelligence is a function of experience and can be changed through guided mediation.
- Gardner's theory of multiple intelligences. Intelligence is made up of eight realms of knowing (verbal, visual, mathematical, musical, bodily, interpersonal, intrapersonal, and naturalistic) for solving problems and creating products valued in a culture.
- Sternberg's successful intelligence. Intelligence is triarchic, with analytic, creative, and practical components that need to be balanced.
- Perkins's theory of learnable intelligence. Intelligence is made up of neural, experiential, and reflective components that help us realize the best use of our minds.
- Costa's theory of intelligent behaviors. Intelligence is composed of acquired habits or states of mind that are evidenced in such behaviors as persistence, flexibility, decreased impulsiveness, enjoyment of thinking, and reflectiveness.
- Goleman's theory of emotional intelligence. Intelligence is both cognitive and emotional, with the emotional (self-awareness, self-regulation, motivation, empathy, and social skill) ruling over the cognitive.
- Coles's theory of moral intelligence. Intelligence is composed of cognitive, psychological or emotional, and moral realms.

IMPLICATIONS FOR APPLICATION

The intelligence friendly classroom is an intricate and complex microcosm of nuance and activity that propels the teaching and learning process. The following eight guidelines, derived from the various theories of intelligence, have compelling implications for today's classroom. Each guideline's explanation is followed by a sampling of useful strategies. While some readers may find the suggestions familiar and already part of their current teaching repertoire, others may discover new ideas or, perhaps, novel ways to revisit an old idea with a fresh approach. Whatever the case, these eight guidelines serve as a bridge between theory and practice in the intelligence-friendly classroom.

1. *Set a safe emotional climate.* The intelligence-friendly classroom is a safe and caring place for all learners, regardless of race, color, creed, age, aptitude, or ability, to go about the business of learning. In setting a climate for thinking, risk-taking becomes the norm and learners understand that to learn is to make mistakes as well as to experience successes.

Specific strategies to create a safe emotional climate include establishing classroom rules, promote awareness of verbal and non-verbal teaching behaviors (e.g., wait time), organizing diverse small-group work that feels "safe," tapping into students' emotional and moral intelligences, setting up the room to facilitate student-to-student interactions as well as student-to-teacher interactions, and incorporating learner-centered structures (e.g., multiage groupings) that foster intelligence-friendly learning communities.

2. *Create an enriched learning environment.* An enriched environment requires attention to the physical aspects of the intelligence-friendly classroom. The ideal classroom resembles a children's museum, in which students are implicitly invited to interact with the learning environment. In such a stimulus-rich setting, student-initiated explorations, investigations, and other inquiries are irresistible.

This enriched environment presents science equipment, art supplies, tools and workbenches, toys and building blocks, optical illusion posters, and a captivating variety of developmentally appropriate technological devices. The intelligence-friendly classroom has different mini-environments for quiet reflection, noisy projects, learning centers, and one-on-one tutorials. Sensory input—ranging from print-rich materials, music and recordings, visually appealing bulletin boards, to signs, games, puzzles, and lab setups—provides an intriguing and engaging place for teaching for intelligence.

3. *Teach the mind-tools and skills of life.* Teaching the skills of life involves a broad spectrum of mind and body "tools" that include communication and social skills, the micro-skills of thinking and reflecting, the technological skills needed for the Information Age, mathematical and logical skills used in solving algebraic equations or programming computers, and even the skills needed to learn a craft or to participate in athletics.

More specifically, these skills might include critical thinking skills (e.g., prioritizing, comparing, and judging), creative thinking skills (e.g., inferring, predicting, and generalizing), social skills (e.g., communicating, teambuilding, leading, and resolving conflicts), technological skills (e.g., keyboarding, surfing the Net, and taking virtual field trips), visual skills (e.g., painting, sculpting, and drawing), skills in the performing arts (e.g., dancing, acting, and playing a musical instrument), and athletic skills (e.g., diving, skiing, and swimming).

4. *Develop the skillfulness of the learner.* The developmental path of skill training moves through fairly predictable stages: novice, advanced beginner, competent user, proficient user, and expert. Inherent in this developmental arc is the understanding that skillfulness is achieved through mediation, practice, coaching, and rehearsal.

Skill development often occurs through formal teaching and learning structures, such as direct instruction models that demonstrate the skill for students. Skills also are developed through independent readings and research and through the dialogue, discussion, and articulation of peer coaching, mentoring, and internships. Skill development can even happen in experiences where skills are embedded in application, and in poised moments that encourage peak performances.

5. *Challenge through the experience of doing.* Learning is a function of experience and is shaped by internal processes that actually construct ideas in the mind, as well as by external processes of social interaction. In the intelligence-friendly classroom, a constructivist philosophy of education reigns. Active, experiential learning is the norm as the learner is invited to become an integral part of the teaching and learning process.

Specific strategies that abound in the constructivist classroom include hands-on learning with lots of manipulatives and lab-like situations; small-group, cooperative tasks; the frequent use and unique application of graphic organizers (e.g., concept maps, attribute webs, flowcharts, and Venn diagrams); and authentic experiential curriculum models (e.g., problem-based learning, case studies, project and service learning, performance tasks, and the use of relevant overarching themes).

6. *Target multiple dimensions of intelligence.* The multiple intelligences (MI) approach taps into each learner's unique profile of intelligences. The educational community embraces MI theory because it provides a natural framework for inspired practice. MI approaches to curriculum, instruction, and assessment target a full spectrum of teaching and learning strategies that encompass the many ways of knowing and of expressing what we know. The MI classroom is abuzz with activity as all eight of the intelligences are given fair time in the curriculum, and create authentic, relevant opportunities for development.

This does not mean that every lesson shows evidence of all eight intelligences, but rather that the learning is structured in naturally integrated ways that call upon various intelligences. For example, while creating a school newspaper, students' interview (interpersonal), write (verbal), design (visual), and critique (logical) as natural parts of the process.

7. *Transfer learning through reflection.* The reflective use of learning is the cornerstone of the intelligence-friendly classroom. It drives personal application and transfer of learning. It makes learning personal, purposeful, meaningful, and relevant and gives the brain reason to pay attention, understand, and remember. Reflection is sometimes the missing piece in today's classroom puzzle, as the pacing of the school day often precludes time for reflection. Yet reflection, introspection, and mindfulness must accompany collaborations and discussions because time for reflection is time for internalizing the learning that has occurred.

Specific strategies that enhance reflection include the use of reading-response journals in which the reader writes a personal, immediate response to what has been read; learning logs that record the learner's thoughts, comments, and questions prior to or following a learning experience; lab reports; personal diaries; sketchbooks; writer's notebooks; portfolios; partner dialogues and conversations with a mentor; mediation interventions; and metacognitive strategies of planning, monitoring, and evaluating through self-regulation.

8. *Balance assessment measures.* Human nature demands feedback. Whether that feedback is internally motivated or externally given, all of us who are intent on learning anxiously await critique, judgment, and guidance. In the intelligence-friendly classroom, this critical phase of the learning process is integral to all other interactions. Feedback, analysis, and evaluation are ongoing as well as summative.

Assessment occurs by the traditional means of grades and rankings for required classwork, homework assignments, quizzes, criterion-referenced tests, and standardized tests. To provide the proper balance to the assessment process, both portfolio assessments (e.g., project portfolios, best-work portfolios, electronic portfolios, and videotape analyses) and performance assessments (e.g., speeches, presentations, plays, concerts, athletic performances, and lab experiments) should be utilized.

A FINAL NOTE

In closing, let's circle back for a moment and revisit the title of this article: "The Intelligence-Friendly Classroom: It Just Makes Sense." Think about the intelligence-friendly classroom we've explored, and how it relates to any preconceived notions you might have had as you began to read. Intelligence friendly? What does that mean? What does that look like? Sound like? Did you learn in an intelligence-friendly classroom? Do you teach in one? Would you know one if you saw one?

Of course you would. The intelligence-friendly classroom is no enigma because it makes perfect sense. It draws on the many powers of intelligence of both teacher and learner. It embodies the teaching and learning process in all its glorious colors. It is the science of good, sound pedagogy coupled with the art of uniquely creative minds.

The intelligence-friendly classroom is part of the noble vision of schooling that led many of us into the field. It is the reason that we do what we do. It is about children, and it's about helping those children be as smart as they can be in every way they can be. The intelligence-friendly classroom just makes sense.

Teaching for Intelligence

In Search of Best Practices

James Bellanca

James Bellanca founded SkyLight Professional Development in 1982. As its president, he mentored more than a dozen author-consultants as he led SkyLight in pioneering the use of strategic teaching and comprehensive professional development. Prior to meta-analyses that marked the effectiveness of cooperative learning, graphic organizers, and other cognitive strategies on student achievement, Jim coauthored more than a dozen texts that advocated the application of these tools across the curriculum, with the theme, "not just for the test but for a lifetime of learning." Currently, Bellanca is building on the theories of cognitive psychologist Reuven Feuerstein to develop more effective responses to the learning needs of those low performing students whose academic achievement continues to lag behind those who have greater learning advantages.

Here are two statements from one teacher in the science department of a large, college-directed suburban high school.

When I teach biology, my job is to cover the content. To get all the material required in our curriculum covered, I use two strategies. In class, I lecture or show films to get the material across. In the lab, I work through the lab book with the students. The labs correspond with the text chapters. I use pop quizzes, chapter tests, lab book grades, and a semester final to decide a student's grade for the semester.

* * *

When I teach biology, my job is to interest students in the value of this science. This is much more than giving them information to spit back out on a test or quiz. I have to help them understand how all the information fits together and why it is important. I also have to help them get as excited about biology as I am. In class, I use a variety of methods. First, I teach them how to gather the right information from a variety of sources. These can include some lectures, some films, targeted reading from the text, or online resource materials. I also structure all-class and cooperative-group discussions so that they can relate the specific topics to the "big picture." Finally, I use the lab to engage them in applying the new information. I use the lab book as a start for the students to investigate applications outside the classroom. I use pop quizzes and tests to check what they know about the material. But I also observe and grade how they do lab work, defend their findings, execute outside-of-class projects, contribute to the discussions, and complete the final exam. Unless I actively engage their minds in doing biology, I believe that I have shortchanged their opportunity to understand and to enjoy the subject.

These two views, expressed at different times, reveal changes in beliefs and practices that distinguish this teacher from most of the other biology teachers in the school. This teacher's new practices, developed from a study of Howard Gardner's theory of multiple intelligences, provide concrete examples of "teaching for intelligence."

In this teacher's science department, biology is usually taught as a body of information transferred from the text and each teacher's understanding of the subject directly to the students' heads. At set times, each student is expected to show the teacher how much was absorbed. Test scores document the amount of information recalled on each chapter test. Each day, the teacher enters the room, takes attendance, provides the day's lecture, and answers questions. On some days, the teacher precedes the lecture with a quiz or shows a video to illustrate a key topic. The students are expected to read the chapters, take notes in class, ask questions, follow the lab instructions, complete the workbook pages, and study for the unit tests. If students need assistance they can schedule an appointment with the teacher. The department chairperson explains that these have been accepted practices that have worked well in preparing students for college over the last forty years.

The department chair's claims, supplemented with the school's record of high test scores (its American College Testing Program scores have led the state for the last decade), seem to make the school a strong candidate for the "If it ain't broke, don't fix it" award. However, appearances often belie reality. In the same school we can find students who don't have high grades, strong test scores, or sufficient motivation to achieve. When high-standardized scores are the focus, it is difficult to switch attention to the needs of such students. It is even more difficult to argue how an intelligence-rich model of teaching and learning, which differs from the traditional information-centered model, might benefit the high achievers as well.

The most successful attempts to teach for intelligence replicate the second approach described by the biology teacher. To change one's practices as this teacher did, one must start with some basic assumptions.

The traditional method is not wrong. There are many high-achieving students who thrive with the traditional approach to teaching. However, the traditional method is inadequate for many students who are less achievement driven. If all students are to learn the curriculum, then all need the opportunity to be taught in ways that enrich their learning. This means that the teacher, when faced with less-motivated students, must develop a greater repertoire of methods. Best teaching practices that build on new theories of intelligence—such as Howard Gardner's theory of multiple intelligences, Robert Sternberg's theory of successful intelligence, Daniel Goleman's theory of emotional intelligence, or Reuven Feuerstein's theory of structural cognitive modifiability—provide rich opportunities for teachers who desire to teach for intelligence.

Teaching is a strategic act of engagement. The new theories of intelligence consider the active engagement of students' minds to be a prerequisite to learning. It follows from this concept that teachers and students will benefit when the teacher plans how best to ensure that all students are engaged. Such planning is facilitated when a teacher has a repertoire of proven engagement strategies and the skill to design lessons and units that integrate these strategies with the content so that each student "gets it."

Changing how a teacher teaches takes more than conveying theoretical information. The typical continuing education of teachers looks very much like traditional instruction in junior high and high school classrooms; only the age of the students and the content differ. Theoretical talk dominates. Teachers, as students, hear about learning theories and research results. In some cases, they are given a few descriptions of best practices. If the professor or consultant has any recent classroom experience, the teacher and learners may receive a few practical tips on the side.

Learning to change one's teaching style is as difficult as learning to change one's learning style. Some teachers start the process of change from an abstract, theoretical point of view. They want to study the underlying beliefs, the theory, and the research supporting ideas new to their experience. This approach helps them construct their own framework or "big picture." When they are comfortable with their new beliefs, they begin to test the practical tools that fit. Other teachers must start with a hands-on classroom test of a new method. These teachers will practice the method with their students and evaluate its effects. If the method works well, they look for other similar methods and investigate their theoretical underpinnings. Between these two poles, there are a multitude of individual approaches to initiating change in classroom practice. In all cases, it is essential that the instructor honors the basic learning style of each individual by ensuring that all components of the intelligence-rich models of change are included.

> For teachers to change from using the more traditional, information-centered model of instruction, their experiences in learning how to teach for intelligence need to balance the what, the why, and the how of the new models.

For teachers to change from using the more traditional, information-centered model of instruction, which may have dominated their own learning since perhaps junior high, their experiences in learning how to teach for intelligence need to balance the what, the why, and the how of the new models. The "what" includes descriptions of best practices followed by live or video demonstrations that model how to use these best practices in grade-specific contexts. The "why" includes investigations of the supporting research. The "how" provides mediated role-playing sessions with ample time for problem solving, reflection on application opportunities, collaborative planning for use, a structured assignment to implement the plan, and a collegial assessment of the application results. In this way, the teacher as reflective practitioner can resolve concerns through a low-risk experience that uses what research says about the proper conditions for adult learning transfer.[1]

It is important to note that even the most carefully practiced classroom implementations of approaches new to the teacher/learner are in danger of falling by the wayside. When faced with the contrary, day-to-day classroom pressures that do not take into account the environmental conditions for effective transfer, teachers can abandon the less familiar and risky new practice for the safety and security of their usual approach. Even the teacher most excited about the possibilities of a newly acquired practice needs the right school environment to sustain it. At this point, it is most helpful for the principal, professional developer, or site mentor to step forward and apply research findings on best practice in professional development.

For example, we know that when the teacher/learner has time each week to interact with a peer support team, to share and to plan classroom-specific applications, to reflect on concerns about and problems with those applications, to gather student artifacts and other evidence for assessment, and to make needed adjustments, the targeted changes have an 80 percent chance of becoming regular practice. Without the support team, the chances of successful, long-term implementation can fall below 20 percent.[2] When a school principal encourages the attempts at new approaches and when colleagues respect these endeavors, the chance of long-term implementation increases.[3]

With built-in assessment strategies such as action research, portfolios, implementation checklists, and exhibitions, the focus changes from teacher/learners as acquirers of information to teachers as reflective practitioners who investigate how best practices in theory work for them in the classroom.[4]

When the conditions for change are honored, it is possible for teachers to make dramatic changes in how they teach. As was evident from the statements of the biology teacher quoted at the outset of this article, the changes benefit students as well as the teacher. Case studies of successful changes abound at each grade level. The following example, created by a first-grade teacher and inspired by

Gardner's definition of intelligence as the ability to solve a significant problem or to produce a product, illustrates the productive changes in classroom practice that are possible when those changes are based on the application of a newly understood theory.

SCIENCE CURRICULUM CONTENT: SIMPLE MACHINES

This simple-machines project was based on the theory of multiple intelligences, and integrated required language arts, mathematics, science, and social studies objectives into a single unit. The different intelligences used by the students during the project are identified in parentheses.

Instead of resorting to the text-based approach used in previous years, in which students were shown pictures of a machine with appropriate vocabulary words to memorize, the teacher assigned pairs of students (interpersonal) to create an invented animal that made use of several simple machines (mathematical/logical). After seeing a working example of each machine (e.g., a Lego plane to launch miniature racing cars), the class saw an example, made by the teacher, of a dinosaur that moved (visual/spatial). She pointed out how each simple machine was included and shared a rubric that identified how she would grade each project.

Next, the teacher provided ample supplies and led a whole-class brainstorming session to come up with ideas for the invented animals (interpersonal). Each pair selected its own idea and began the construction process. As the pairs worked, the teacher circulated among them to answer questions and to mediate understandings.

When all the projects were completed, each pair made a formal presentation (verbal/linguistic) to the class. As part of the presentation, the pair was asked to explain why and how they used each of the simple machines, which simple machines were most important in the project, how each partner contributed, and how each felt about the finished product (intrapersonal). The animals were labeled and set out for viewing by the other students and by parents on report card night.

The teacher graded the projects on the multiple dimensions she had outlined in her rubric:

- We used [X number of] machines.
- We helped each other.

- We each talked in the presentation.
- Our animal moved.
- We told which machines were most important.
- Our animal looked like an animal.

This example illustrates how beliefs about learning affect teaching practices. The realization that there is more to teaching than a sharing of information and a testing for recall springs from our ever-expanding understanding that intelligence is modifiable, multiple, and multifaceted. As research provides us with new insights into how human minds work, we are assured that teaching for intelligence is a never-ending challenge, as well as an exhilarating opportunity to help all children become active, engaged, and successful learners. As schools take advantage of the best practices in professional development, the change process ensures more success for teachers who seek to expand their repertoires with the best practices in teaching for intelligence.

NOTES

1. Moye, V. (1997). *Conditions that support transfer for change.* Thousand Oaks, CA: Corwin Press.
2. Joyce, B., & Showers, B. (1985). *Power in staff development.* Arlington, VA: Association for Supervision and Curriculum Development.
3. Bellanca, J. (1996). *Designing professional development for change: A systematic approach.* Thousand Oaks, CA: Corwin Press.
4. Schmuck, R. (1997). *Practical action research for change.* Thousand Oaks, CA: Corwin Press.

Mediative Environments

Creating Conditions for Intellectual Growth

Arthur L. Costa

Arthur L. Costa *is Professor Emeritus of Education at California State University, Sacramento, and codirector of the Institute for Intelligent Behavior in Berkeley, California. He has served as a classroom teacher, a curriculum consultant, an assistant superintendent for instruction, and as Director of Educational Programs for the National Aeronautics and Space Administration. He has made presentations and conducted workshops in all fifty states as well as Mexico, Central America, South America, Canada, Australia, New Zealand, Africa, Europe, Asia, and the Islands of the South Pacific. Active in many professional organizations, Dr. Costa served as the president of the California Association for Supervision and Curriculum Development and was the national president of the Association for Supervision and Curriculum Development from 1988 to 1989.*

Many unconscious factors influence teachers' thinking as they make daily decisions about curriculum and instruction. Their own culture, knowledge of content, their cognitive style, knowledge about their students, and their professional values and beliefs about education influence their judgments about when to teach what to whom. Jack Frymier, however, states:

> In the main, the bureaucratic structure of the workplace is more influential in determining what professionals do than are personal abilities, professional training or previous experience. Therefore, change efforts should focus on the structure of the workplace, not the teachers. (1987, p. 10)

Frymier suggests that less obvious, but vastly more persuasive influences on teacher thought are the norms, culture, and culture of the school setting in which teachers work. Hidden but powerful cues emanate from the school environment. These subtle cues signal the institutional value system that governs the operation of the organization (Saphier & King, 1985).

Recent efforts to bring educational reform will prove futile unless the school environment signals to the staff, the students, and the community that the development of the intellect and cooperative decision making are the school's basic values. While efforts to enhance the staff's instructional competencies, develop curriculum, and revise instructional materials and assessment procedures may be important components in the process of educational re-engineering, it also is crucial that the climate in which parents, teachers, and students make their decisions is aligned with these goals toward the development of intellectual potential. Teachers are more likely to teach for thinking, creativity, and cooperation if they are in an intellectually stimulating, creative, and cooperative environment themselves.

EDUCATIONAL STRESSORS

Classic research by O. J. Harvey (1966) found that teaching is the second most stressful profession. Goodlad (1984), Rosenholtz (1991), Sarason (1993), Fullan (1993), and other authors have identified several potential sources of stress in the profession:

- *Teachers may lack a sense of power and efficacy.* Teachers are often cast at the bottom of an institutional hierarchy, while decisions about curriculum, staff development, assessment, instructional materials, and evaluation—all decisions that affect them directly—are handed down "from above."

- *Teachers feel isolated.* Ours is probably the only profession that performs its most beautiful and creative craft behind closed doors. Contributing to this situation are inflexible schedules and an inadequate amount of time for teachers to reflect and meet, plan, observe, and talk with each other.

- *The art of teaching is often not recognized as such.* The complex, creative, and intelligent act of teaching is often reduced to a rubric, a simplistic formula, or a series of steps and competencies, the uniform performance of which naively connotes excellence and elegance in the art of teaching.

- *Data regarding student achievement is used for political, competitive, evaluative, or coercive purposes.* It neither involves nor instructs school staff members in reflecting on, evaluating, or improving their curriculum and instructional decisions.

- *Educational innovations are often viewed as mere "tinkerings" within the instructional program.* They are so frequent and limited in impact that frustrated teachers sometimes feel "this, too, shall pass." Instead of institutionalizing a significant educational change, deeply entrenched traditional practices and policies in the educational bureaucracy such as assessment, reporting, securing parent understanding and support, teacher evaluation, scheduling, school organization, and discipline procedures are seldom revised to benefit, or benefit from, larger innovations.

The effects of excessive stress on cognition, creativity, and social interaction are well documented (MacLean, 1978). In such barren, intellectually "polluted" school-climate conditions, some teachers understandably grow depressed. Teachers' vivid imaginations, altruism, creativity, and intellectual prowess soon succumb to the humdrum daily routines of unruly students, irrelevant curriculum, impersonal surroundings, and equally disillusioned coworkers. In such an environment, teachers struggle to value the development of students' intellect and imagination.

TOWARD AN ECOLOGY OF THE INTELLECT

The level of teachers' intellectual development has a direct relationship to student behavior and student performance. Higher-level intellectually functioning teachers produce higher-level intellectually functioning students (Sprinthall & Theis-Sprinthall, 1983). Such teachers are identified by their ability to empathize, to symbolize experience, and to act in accordance with a disciplined commitment to human values. These teachers employ a greater range of instructional strategies, elicit more conceptual responses from students, and produce higher-achieving students who are more cooperative and involved in their work. Glickman (1997) concluded that successful teachers are thoughtful teachers that stimulate their students to be thoughtful as well.

To achieve our educational outcome of developing students' intellectual capacities, educational leaders must redefine their role as mediators of the schoolwide and community-wide conditions for continual learning and intellectual development. A mediator is one who deliberately intervenes between the individual or group and the environment with the intention of creating conditions that will engage and promote intellectual growth (Feuerstein, Feuerstein, & Schur, 1997). They design strategies for achieving their vision of a learning organization; they generate data as a means of assessing progress toward that vision; they constantly monitor the intellectual ecology of the school community to determine its contribution to or hindrance of intellectual growth. Their role is analogous to an "Environmental Protection Agency," monitoring and managing the environment to ensure that intellectual growth, creativity, and cooperation are continually sustained and regenerated.

> Educational leaders must redefine their role as mediators by deliberately monitoring and managing the environment. They should ensure that intellectual growth, creativity, and cooperation are continually sustained and regenerated.

Systems analysts believe in "leverage points." These are places within a complex system where a small shift in one condition can produce big changes in the rest of the system. As mediators of the school's "intellectual ecology," the following seven leverage points are interventions intended to enhance continual intellectual growth and sustain the professional zest of the stakeholders in the educational enterprise. While stress cannot be alleviated entirely, perhaps it can be transformed from distress to *eu*stress ("eu" is here taken from the word *euphoria*).

1. Clarifying Goals and Outcomes

Peter Senge (1990) states that leadership in a learning organization starts with the principle of "creative tension." He goes on to describe how creative tension emerges from seeing clearly where we want to be—the vision—and describing truthfully where we are now—our current reality. The gap between the two generates creative tension.

Creative Tension

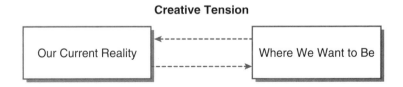

This principle of creative tension has long been recognized by leaders, such as when Martin Luther King, Jr. famously proclaimed, "I have a dream. . . ." King believed that the tension produced through voicing an alternative vision of society would help the nation rise from the depths of prejudice and racism.

This tension, according to Senge (1990), can be resolved by moving the current reality toward the vision. Effective leaders, therefore, stimulate intellectual growth by causing creative organizational tension. Leaders create for themselves—and facilitate their staff's, students,' and the community's—visions of what could be: images of desired states, valued aspirations, outcomes, and scenarios of a better future.

Mission and vision statements, however, are not just exercises. They are employed continually as criteria for making decisions, developing policies, allocating resources, hiring staff, designing curriculum, disciplining, and lesson planning. A school's mission statement is given substance and value when it is systematically assessed. When our values are clear, the decisions we make are much easier. What gives an organization integrity is how the staff members perceive the congruence between its policies, vision, and mission and its daily practices.

2. Building and Maintaining Trust and Collegiality

George Land and Beth Jarman (1998) believe that trust and the ability to work together toward a common vision are what fuel individuals to accomplish amazing results. Trust is a vital element in enhancing cognition. We know that higher level, complex and creative thinking closes down when trust is lacking in the environment or in relationships with others. Teachers are encouraged to inquire, speculate, construct meanings, experiment, self-evaluate, and self-prescribe when the leader manages a trusting environment. Building an atmosphere of trust is the leader's most important task.

Humans, as social beings, mature intellectually when in reciprocal relationships. Collaboratively, individuals generate and discuss ideas, eliciting thinking that surpasses their individual efforts. Together and privately, they express different perspectives, agree and disagree, point out and resolve discrepancies, and weigh alternatives. Because people develop their intellect through this process, collegial interaction is a crucial factor in the intellectual ecology of the school.

The essence of building trust and collegiality is when people work together in order to better understand *how* to work together. People are more likely to engage and grow in higher-level, creative, and experimental thought when they are in a trusting, risk-taking, cooperative climate. Risk taking requires a nonjudgmental atmosphere where information can be shared without fear that it will be used for evaluative purposes.

Baker, Costa, and Shalit (1997) identify eight norms that may serve as standards that are understood, agreed upon, adopted, monitored, and assessed by each participant when working as a facilitating and contributing member of a group. They are the glue that enables school and community groups to engage in productive and satisfying discourse:

Pausing. Taking turns is the ultimate in impulse control (Kotulak, 1997). In a discourse, space is given for each person to talk. Time is allowed before responding to or asking a question. Such silent time allows for more complex thinking, enhances all forms of discourse, and produces better decision making. Pausing is the tool that facilitative group members use to respectfully listen to each other.

Paraphrasing. Covey (1997) suggests we seek to understand before being understood. Paraphrasing lets others know that you are listening, that you understand or are trying to understand, and that you care.

Probing and Clarifying. This is an effective inquiry skill to use when the speaker expresses vocabulary, uses a vague concept, or employs terminology that is not fully understood by the listener. The use of probing and clarifying is intended to help the listener better understand the speaker. In groups, this skill increases the clarity and precision of the group's thinking by clarifying understandings, terminology, and interpretations.

Putting Your Ideas On—and Pulling Them Off—the Table. Groups are most productive when everyone shares their thoughts, dreams, mistakes, assumptions, and opinions. While group members offer ideas, opinions, information, and positions, they attempt to keep their suggestions relevant to the topic at hand. Because there are times when continuing to advocate a position might block the group's functioning, group members also volunteer to withdraw their ideas.

Paying Attention to Self and Others. Meaningful dialogue is facilitated when each group member is sensitive to and conscious of the subtle cues inside themselves and within others in the group. Paying attention to learning styles, modalities, and beliefs when planning for, facilitating, and participating in group meetings enhances group members' understanding of each other as they converse, discuss, deliberate, and make decisions.

Presuming Positive Intentions. People operate on the internal maps of their own reality and, therefore, we assume that they act with positive intentions. This assumption promotes and facilitates meaningful dialogue. Because our language contains overt and covert messages, deeper meanings may be misinterpreted. The subtle (and often not so subtle) ways in which we embed presuppositions in our language can be hurtful or helpful to others. The deliberate use of positive presuppositions assumes and encourages positive actions (Costa & Garmston, 1994).

Providing Data. Groups exercising high levels of communicative competence act on information rather than hearsay, rumor, or speculation. Data serves as an energy source for group action and learning. Seeking, generating, and gathering data from group members, as well as from a variety of other primary and secondary sources, enhances individual and group decision making.

Pursuing a Balance Between Advocacy and Inquiry. Advocating a position as well as inquiring into another's position assists the group's continued learning. Senge, Ross, Smith, Roberts, and Kleiner (1994) suggest that balancing advocacy and inquiry is critical for an organization to perform in order to grow and learn.

Leaders encourage individuals and groups to monitor and assess their own use of these eight norms of collaboration. During meetings and upon their completion, group process observers provide feedback to the group about their performance of the norms. This data is discussed, the effects of the use of norms on group effectiveness are illuminated, and strategies for individual and group improvement are planned (Costa & Kallick, 1995).

3. Coaching

Coaching is one of the most powerful means to overcome the extreme isolation and intellectual depression of teachers. Coaching produces intellectual growth for a variety of reasons:

Coaching enhances instructional thought. The act of teaching is, itself, an intellectual process. Jackson (1990) found that teachers make over 1,300 decisions a day. The behaviors observed in the classroom are artifacts of decisions that teachers make before, during, and after instruction (Shavelson, 1976). The purpose of coaching, therefore, is to enhance the teacher's capacity to plan, monitor, and reflect upon his or her instructional decision making, perceptions, and the intellectual functions. Costa and Garmston (1994) cite that the intent of coaching is to modify teachers' capacities to modify themselves.

People who desire to continually improve their craft seek coaching and profit from being coached. Skillful artists, athletes, musicians, dancers—such as Greg Louganis, Mikhail Baryshnikov, Kristi Yamaguchi, and Jackie Joyner-Kersey—never lose their need for coaching. Likewise in education, to continually perfect their craft, teachers profit from coaching as well.

To work effectively as a member of a team requires coaching. Welding together the individual efforts of team members into a well-organized and efficient unit requires the persistence and stamina of an expert coach. This concerted effort, however, does not just happen. It takes someone—a conductor—who "knows the score" to provide the synergy. It takes time, persistence, practice, and coaching to develop a winning athletic team, a celebrated symphony orchestra, or a successful learning organization.

Few educational innovations achieve their full impact without a coaching component. Joyce and Showers (2002) found that efforts to bring about changes in classroom practice are fruitless unless the teacher is coached in the use of the innovation. Only when the component of coaching was added was the innovation internalized, valued, and transferred to classroom use.

Coaching enhances the intellectual capacities of teachers, which, in turn, produces greater intellectual achievements in

students. The human intellect grows in reciprocity with others. Russian psycholinguist Lev Vygotsky (1980) suggests that intelligence grows in two ways. One is that intelligence develops through our own experience. And the other is that intelligence is shaped through reciprocity with others. Justifying reasons, resolving differences, actively listening to another person's point of view, achieving consensus, and receiving feedback actually increase our intelligence.

Vygotsky's prospective provides a strong theoretical support for coaching as a means of intellectual growth. It is through social interaction that new concepts and intellectual behaviors are formed and grown. And, as was cited earlier, the teacher's level of intellectual development influences the students' level of intellectual development.

4. Investing Leadership in All

> In an intellectual ecology, all the players play all the roles. Leadership is a shared function in the classroom and out.

It was once thought that leadership was invested in a few individuals at the "top" of the organizational hierarchy and that the position of leadership was earned by position, credentials, or the number of academic degrees earned. In an intellectual ecology, however, all the players play all the roles. Leadership is a shared function in meetings, in staff development activities, in action research, in networking between different levels of the organization and, indeed, in classrooms as well (Garmston & Wellman, 1997; Lambert, 1998). Intellectual shifts result when the identities and roles of the participants in the educational process—students, teachers, administrators, and trustees—are redefined. Six major leadership roles include:

Facilitator. Groups conduct meetings for the purpose of shared decision making, planning, and problem solving. These experiences become learning experiences when they involve not only deliberate action but meaning-making through reflection on those actions. Facilitative leaders support data-driven problem solving and solution finding. By establishing such linkages, the data develops deeper importance and becomes a resource rather than a burden to be sidestepped (Costa & Kallick, 1995).

Presenter. Presenters teach groups to develop knowledge, skills, or attitudes that will be applied in the group members' work. Presenting requires clarity about outcomes, interactive teaching strategies, and ways to assess the effectiveness of the learning.

Coach. To coach is to convey a valued colleague from where he or she is to where he or she wants to be. Serving as a coach means mediating—not judging—a colleague's decisions, intellectual functions, and perceptions (Costa & Garmston, 1994).

Consultant. Consultants bring expertise to the relationship and the intention that their expertise be used by the other party. A consultant can be an information specialist who delivers technical knowledge (e.g., purchasing technology), an advocate for content who will influence the group based on his or her broader knowledge (e.g., adopting a curriculum), or an advocate for process (e.g., recommending an open rather than a closed meeting).

Networker. Leaders pay attention to the flow and exchange of energy. Knowing one person's or group's needs and another's talents, information, and resources allows the networker to link people and groups together in mutually supportive relationships for the betterment of the entire group.

Researcher. Meaning develops when individuals and groups generate, interpret, validate, and own the data that results from their decisions and actions. Researching creates situations in which people learn with a higher degree of rigor, and helps support data-driven problem solving.

5. Valuing Diversity

Human beings are made to be different. Diversity is the basis of biological survival. Each of us has a different genetic structure, unique facial features, a distinguishing thumb print, a distinctive signature, a diverse background of knowledge, experience, and culture, and a preferred way of gathering, processing, and expressing information and knowledge. We even have a singular frequency in which we vibrate (Leonard, 2006). Leaders are sensitive to and capitalize on these differences to enhance intellectual growth.

Intellectually effective people seem able to "be at home" in multiple areas of functioning. They move flexibly from one style to another as the situation demands it. They have an uncanny ability to read contextual cues from the situation or the environment as to what is needed. They then draw forth from their vast repertoire those skills and capacities needed to effectively function in any setting.

Organizational life might seem easier if all members of the learning community thought and acted in a similar fashion and remained in their own departments and grade levels. Limitations of time, isolation, and our obsession with the archaic compartmentalization of the disciplines and grades keep school staffs separated; thus, opportunities for teachers' intellectual growth are limited. Leaders realize that humans grow intellectually through resolving differences, achieving consensus, and stretching to accommodate dissonance. They realize there is a greater possibility for making connections, stimulating creativity, and growing the capacity for complex problem solving when such differences are bridged. (In some businesses, this is referred to as "skunkworks"—deliberately bringing together personnel from different departments, positions, and grade levels to make connections and find new and divergent ways to solve problems.)

Interdependent learning communities are built not by obscuring diversity but by valuing the friction those differences bring and resolving those differences in an atmosphere of trust and reciprocity. Therefore, leaders mediate appreciation for this diversity by deliberately bringing together people of different political and religious persuasions, cultures, genders, cognitive styles, belief systems, modality preferences, and intelligences. They structure groups composed of representatives from different schools, diverse departments, community groups, and grade levels to envision, describe learning outcomes, plan curriculum and staff development activities, and allocate resources.

6. Challenging Curriculum Models

Curriculum is like a cemetery. It is etched in stone, visited only on special occasions, filled with dead subjects, aligned in straight rows, and is a monument to the past. Furthermore, we keep putting more in and take nothing out!

Senge (1990) emphasizes that a characteristic of the learning organization is that it challenges existing mental models. The leader, in an atmosphere of trust, challenges existing practices, assumptions, policies, and traditional ways of delivering curriculum. Intellectual growth is found in disequilibrium, not balance. It is out of chaos that order is built, that learning takes place, that new understandings are forged, and that new connections are bridged. Organizations function more consistently with their mission, vision, and goals when they are in creative tension—in productive disequilibrium.

We must finally admit that the process is the content. The core of our curriculum must focus on such processes as thinking, learning to learn, knowledge production, metacognition, transference of knowledge, decision making, creativity, group problem solving, and knowing how to behave when correct answers are not readily apparent. These are the subject matters of instruction. Content, selectively abandoned and judiciously selected because of its potential to contribute to the thinking/learning process, becomes merely the vehicle to carry the processes of learning. The focus is on learning *from* the objectives instead of learning *of* the objectives themselves.

Since these process-oriented goals cannot be assessed using product-oriented assessment techniques, our existing evaluation paradigm must shift as well. Assessment of students' thinking will focus on students becoming more conscious, more reflective, more efficient, more flexible, and more transferable (Costa & Kallick, 1995; Costa & Liebmann, 1997). The leader continually challenges the organization's mental models about what learning is of the most worth as students face an uncertain, technological, and global future (Costa & Garmston, 1998).

7. Learning Continually

Experimentation implies that an atmosphere of choice, risk taking, and inquiry exists. Data are generated without fear that they will be used as a basis for evaluating success or failure. Creativity is more likely to grow in a low-risk atmosphere. Frymier goes on to state:

> The solution is to empower teachers, to help them develop an internalized locus of control. Teachers and principals, supervisors and superintendents, boards of education and state legislators all must appreciate the possibilities of school improvement efforts that marshal the motivations and unleash the talents of those who work directly with children day after day. (1987, p. 10)

For too long, the process of assessment has been external to teachers' goal setting, curriculum, and instructional decision making. School effectiveness, student achievement, and teachers' competence have often all been determined by a narrow range of standardized student achievement test scores in a limited number of content areas: reading, math, and language acquisition. Rank-order test results have been published in newspapers, and awards of excellence have been granted to schools that show the highest gains in scores.

In the process, teachers have become disenfranchised. Educators have had little say about what the tests measure. What these tests do measure is often irrelevant to the curriculum, and the results of testing disclose little about the adequacy of a teachers' curricular and instructional decisions. In many ways, the desire for measurable outcomes has signaled to teachers that they are "incompetent" to assess student achievement. They have, in effect, been told they could not be trusted to collect evidence of students' growth, and that the observations they make daily in the classroom are suspect and of little worth.

The accountability movement caused educators to search for "hard data" by which to assess their efforts. What teachers observed, by inference, therefore, was "soft data." But the "hardest," most objective data available may be collected by an *enlightened* teaching team that systematically and collectively gathers data over time in the real-life, day-to-day interactions and problem solving of the classroom. Conversely, the "softest" and most suspect data may be that which is designed and collected by testing "experts" external to the school setting and ignorant of the school's mission, values, and goals, the community's culture and socioeconomics, and the classroom's mix of learning styles, teaching strategies employed, and the group dynamics in which their tests are administered.

Leaders assist the teaching staff in designing strategies for collecting data and using this assessment data as feedback and a guide to informed and reflective practice. Staff members will need help in learning how to design feedback spirals, including finding multiple ways of gathering such data, establishing criteria for judgment, and in working together to develop common understanding, ascertain the reliability of observations, and report results.

IN SUMMARY

Because learning to think, cooperate, and respect human uniqueness is best learned through imitation and emulation of significant others, leaders strive to model in their own behaviors those same qualities and behaviors that are desired in students and staff.

The development of thinking, individuality, and collegiality as goals of education is not just kid stuff. Education will achieve an intellectual focus when the school becomes an intellectually stimulating environment—a home for the mind for all who dwell there, when all the school's inhabitants realize that freeing human intellectual potential is the goal of education, when staff members strive to get better at it themselves, and when they use their energies to enhance the intelligent behaviors of others. Educational leaders serve as an "Environmental Protection Agency," constantly monitoring the intellectual ecology of the school. Their chief purpose is to ensure that thinking, creativity, and collaboration becomes neither endangered, nor—even worse—extinct.

REFERENCES

Baker, W., Costa, A., & Shalit, S. (1997). The norms of collaboration: Attaining communicative competence. In A. Costa & R. Liebmann (Eds.), *The process centered school: Sustaining a renaissance community.* Thousand Oaks, CA: Corwin Press.

Costa, A., & Garmston, R. (1994). *Cognitive coaching: A foundation for the renaissance school.* Norwood, MA: Christopher Gordon.

Costa, A., & Garmston, R. (1998, Spring). Maturing outcomes. *Encounter: Education for Meaning and Social Justice, 11*(1), 10–18.

Costa, A., & Kallick, B. (1995). *Assessment in the learning organization: Shifting the paradigm.* Alexandria, VA: Association for Supervision and Curriculum Development.

Costa, A., & Liebmann, R. (1997). *Process as content: Envisioning a renaissance curriculum.* Thousand Oaks, CA: Corwin Press.

Covey, S. (1997). *The seven habits of highly effective people.* New York: St. Martin's Press.

Feuerstein, R., Feuerstein, R., & Schur, Y. (1997). Process as content in education particularly for retarded performers. In A. Costa and R. Liebmann (Eds.), *Supporting the spirit of learning when process is content.* Thousand Oaks, CA: Corwin Press.

Frymier, J. (1987, September). Bureaucracy and the neutering of teachers. *Phi Delta Kappan,* p. 10.

Fullan, M. (1993). *Change forces.* New York: Falmer.

Garmston, R., & Wellman, B. (1997). Developing adaptive schools. In A. Costa and R. Liebmann (Eds.), *The process centered school: Sustaining a renaissance community.* Thousand Oaks, CA: Corwin Press.

Glickman, C. (1997). *Supervision of instruction: A developmental approach.* Newton, MA: Allyn & Bacon.

Goodlad, J. I. (1984). *A place called School: Prospects for the future.* New York: McGraw-Hill.

Harvey, O. J. (1966). System structure, flexibility and creativity. In O. J. Harvey (Ed.), *Experience, structure, and adaptability.* New York: Springer.

Jackson, P. (1990). *Life in classrooms.* New York: Teachers College Press.

Joyce, B., & Showers, B. (2002). *Student achievement through staff development.* Baltimore: Association for Supervision & Curriculum Development.

Kotulak, R. (1997). *Inside the brain: Revolutionary discoveries of how the mind works.* Kansas City, MO: Andrews McMeel Publishing.

Lambert, L. (1998). *Building leadership capacity in schools.* Alexandria, VA: Association for Supervision and Curriculum Development.

Land, G., & Jarman, B. (1998). *Break-point and beyond: Mastering the future today.* New York: Leadership 2000.

Leonard, G. (2006). *The silent pulse: A search for the perfect rhythm that exists in each of us.* Layton, UT: Gibbs Smith.

MacLean, P. (1978). A mind of three minds: Educating the Triune brain. In J. E. Chall and M. Mursky (Eds.), *Education and the brain.* Chicago: University of Chicago Press.

Rosenholtz, S. (1991). *Teacher's workplace: The social organization of schools.* New York: Teachers College Press.

Saphier, J., & King, M. (1985, March). Good seeds grow in strong cultures. *Educational Leadership,* pp. 67–74.

Sarason, S. (1993). *The predictable failure of educational reform.* San Francisco: Jossey-Bass.

Senge, P. (1990). *The fifth discipline.* New York: Doubleday.

Senge, P., Ross R., Smith B., Roberts C., & Kleiner A. (1994). *The fifth discipline fieldbook.* New York: Doubleday.

Shavelson, R. (1976). Teacher decision making. *The psychology of teaching methods. 1976 yearbook of the National Society for the Study of Education. Part I.* Chicago: University of Chicago Press.

Sprinthall, R., & Theis-Sprinthall, L. (1983). The teacher as an adult learner: A cognitive developmental view. *Staff development: 82nd yearbook of the National Society for the Study of Education. Part II.* Chicago: University of Chicago Press.

Vygotsky, L. (1980). *Society of mind.* Cambridge, MA: Harvard University Press.

Differentiating Instruction in the Classroom

Tapping Into the Intelligence of Every Learner

Dorothy S. Strickland

Dorothy S. Strickland *is Senior Research Fellow, NIEER, at Rutgers University Graduate School of Education. A former classroom teacher, she is past president of the International Reading Association (IRA). She is active in the National Council of Teachers of English (NCTE) and the National Association for the Education of Young Children. She received IRA's Outstanding Teacher Educator of Reading Award and is the current president of the IRA Reading Hall of Fame. She received the 1994 NCTE Rewey Belle Inglis Award for Outstanding Women in the Teaching of English and the 1998 Outstanding Educator of Language Arts Award.*

Sara glances around her room. She feels lucky to work in a district that is forward looking. She has a nice supply of children's literature, which keeps increasing each year. Her students' writing is everywhere: on the bulletin boards, inside the classroom, and in the corridors just outside. Their work can be read in the library corner and at the publishing table. Like most of the teachers in her school, Sara is gradually changing her instructional practices to reflect new knowledge about learning and teaching. She attempts to contextualize the teaching of skills for reading and writing and to integrate the teaching of all the language arts; she no longer swears by the three reading group format she used routinely for so many years; and she announces with pride that her students now do as much writing in a couple of months as they used to do in an entire year.

By all accounts, Sara and her colleagues are moving with confidence toward more holistic, literature-based instruction. Yet, they share a mixed bag of excitement and uneasiness. There is excitement about the learning that is taking place before their very eyes each day. But there is uneasiness about community concern over attention to the basics. Given the diversity of student abilities and backgrounds in her classroom, even successful teachers like Sara express anxiety over the district's call for uniform high standards. As she prepares for the week ahead, Sara reflects on the issues she continues to find most challenging:

Organizing for instruction. "I know it's important to set high standards for everyone, yet I feel it's even more important to adjust the curriculum to meet individual needs. Too much of my teaching is geared to the whole group. But, it's hard to manage children doing different things at once. Flexible grouping is a real challenge."

"Covering" the skills. "In the past, I taught each skill and checked it off one by one. I suppose that could be called teaching to a uniform standard, but it only worked for some students. Now I try to go beyond merely covering the skills to vary the type and intensity of instruction to children's needs. More children are progressing, but I could sure use some help in making those decisions."

Monitoring progress. "With skill-by-skill teaching, I simply tested periodically to see who was 'getting it' and who was not and moved on to teach the next set of skills. Now, I see the need to continually assess and alter instruction. What I need are some manageable strategies for assessment."

Helping low-achieving students. "I worry about meeting the needs of my low-achieving students. I realize now where I let them down in the past. But I need help with managing materials and time. Also, I need teaching strategies that help these children get what they need within the framework of the regular day.

"In the elementary classroom, at least, treating everyone the same may not mean that everyone is treated fairly. The way I teach now really points up the diversity among my students. It has made differentiating instruction my biggest challenge."

Providing for individual differences is arguably one of the greatest challenges facing language arts teachers today. No doubt this has always been the case, but it has become even more evident as teachers move away from simply *delivering the curriculum* to focus on *making the curriculum accessible* to each and every student. Sara is like many teachers who have embraced some new ideas and experienced some success. She is more reflective about her teaching and more demanding of herself. Teachers like Sara, whether they are new to the profession or seasoned teachers in the midst of change, face new challenges as they attempt to think differently about their role in the classroom and about the reading and writing processes. According to Scharer (1992) and Pace (1992), most teachers find change difficult and anxiety producing. Support from peers and from the profession is important so that teachers know that they are not alone and that the self-questioning they do is in the tradition of reflective teaching.

The issues raised by teachers such as Sara are not the products of failure but the concerns of clear-thinking, reflective practitioners. Moreover, the questions they ask are major issues in language arts instruction today. Educators are attempting to meet public demands for setting high uniform standards for every student in settings where learner variability is inevitable and persistent. They know that setting standards alone does not make learning happen. Learning is highly dependent on effective classroom teaching that offers each child an equal chance to meet those standards. Ironically, this means less standardized teaching and more differentiation of approaches and strategies within a unified framework. This article addresses these issues and offers suggestions from the classrooms of informed and resourceful teachers engaged in the process of change.

> Setting standards alone does not make learning happen. Learning is highly dependent on effective classroom teaching that offers each child an equal chance to meet those standards.

ORGANIZING FOR INSTRUCTION: FLEXIBLE GROUPING

One of the misconceptions that paralleled the advent of "whole language" was the notion that holistically oriented approaches were synonymous with whole-group instruction. Indeed, teachers were continually warned of the dangers of long-term, ability grouping—and rightly so. There is considerable research evidence to support these cautions (Allington, 1983; Hiebert, 1983; Pallas, Entwisle, Alexander, & Stluka, 1994). Resistance to all ability-based instruction in the regular classroom is misguided, however, and often renders lower-achieving students with few opportunities for instruction tailored to their needs. Students who are progressing rapidly may also miss out on opportunities for special projects and the extension of ideas previously introduced to the entire class. Even when teachers attempt to provide frequent individual conferences in reading and writing, there are times when gathering a small group of students who have similar needs is the most effective and efficient way to provide extra support. As Roller so aptly stated: "We must remember that ability grouping and special pull-out programs arose as a solution to the real problem of variability in children's acquisition of literacy. To return to uniform instruction, uniform materials, and uniform expectations is unrealistic. Variability exists" (Roller, 1996, p. 9).

Organizing instruction to account for variability offers students opportunities to work with others whose literacy development is most like theirs as well as those whose skills and abilities differ from theirs. Groups based on instructional needs are continually re-formed according to the results of ongoing evaluation as all children are exposed to a wide variety of heterogeneous grouping for a variety of purposes (Fountas & Pinnell, 1996; Worthy & Hoffman, 1996). Students receive regular, planned opportunities to learn through varied formats, including whole-group, small-group (including pairs), and one-to-one formats, heterogeneous and homogeneous groupings, and direct and indirect instruction. Although variety is emphasized, flexible grouping structures are highly predictable so that students and teachers have a sense of order and continuity.

One possible framework for use in planning for differentiated instruction starts with the assumption that there will be a large block of time designated for language arts each day. While this time is devoted to planned, systematic instruction in reading, writing (including spelling and grammar), and oral language, these skills are addressed throughout the day in all areas of the curriculum. Conversely, topics under study in subject areas such as science and social studies may provide the content through which the language arts are taught during the block of time designated for language arts. I have worked with teachers who had as little as 80 minutes specified for their language arts block and others who had as much as 120 minutes. The suggested format includes a whole-group segment for approximately 30 minutes, a brief planning time of 5 to 10 minutes, and a workshop segment for approximately 60 minutes. Following are some tips for planning.

Start by planning the whole-group activity. Consider each weekly plan as part of a larger unit of work or thematic focus, extending over several weeks' time. During the week under consideration, decide whether to work on a particular story or group of stories, a unit of poetry, or perhaps some informational material linked to the science curriculum. Decide what materials will be used: trade books, core literacy textbooks, content area materials, or collaboratively written charts. Plan lessons using a *whole-part-whole* framework (Strickland, 1998). Start with *whole,* meaningful texts and encourage a variety of types of response. Focus on students' comprehension and construction of meaning. Follow this with explicit attention to specific textual features (the *parts* of written language) and conventions of print. Whole texts provide students with a purposeful basis for looking closely at parts of language. These may include specific phonics elements such as a sound-letter relationship, the use of quotation marks in dialogue, or interesting leads that authors use to grab and hold readers. After highlighting these parts through explicit instruction, reinforce the attention given them by returning to the original text or extending into other *whole* text activities.

Whole-group instruction usually ends with a follow-up assignment for the entire class. It is important that this task be *multilevel,* that is, all students should be able to approach it with a degree of success. Multilevel instruction acknowledges that children come to the classroom with varying backgrounds and abilities. It allows teachers to engage students in similar educational processes with the expectation that there will be variability in individual response. Thus, each child truly has an "equitable opportunity" to move forward toward meeting the curriculum performance standards. Writing assignments such as creating alternative texts (spin-offs based on works students have read and discussed) are examples of multilevel activities. They are a major departure from traditional seatwork activities, which usually are of the clone variety. That is, all children fill in the blanks, copy from the board, or

> Multilevel instruction acknowledges that children come to the classroom with varying backgrounds and abilities.

answer a set of factual questions in which the goal is to have every student produce precisely the same product. Clone assignments keep children busy while the teacher works with small groups. But, because they are geared to the average student, they tend to frustrate struggling learners and offer little or no challenge to those who are progressing rapidly.

Use the planning time to make sure that everyone knows what is expected. Take a few minutes to discuss who, what, where, and when of the workshop activities to follow whole-group instruction. Use name charts, lists, and other devices to help children ascertain who will work in small groups, who has a one-to-one conference with the teacher, whose turn it is to work with a buddy at the computer, which small group may go to the library, and so on. These procedures, as well as classroom routines related to conduct during activity time, need to be introduced gradually during the early part of the year and reinforced as the year proceeds. Each new routine or activity must be explained, demonstrated, and even rehearsed where applicable so that students may work as independently as possible.

Use the workshop for both teacher-assisted and independent activities. One useful way to think about the workshop segment is to envision it in terms of three smaller segments. Each child spends at least one segment to do the follow-up (to whole group) assignment already described. For some students, one segment is spent with the teacher in a small-group, direct instruction format in which the materials and instructional focus are tailored to meet group needs. These students will spend the remaining time at centers, doing research, working on projects, involved in buddy reading, having a one-to-one conference with the teacher, working in a reader response group, or engaging in any of the other various options that may be available. Some students may spend the two remaining segments involved in two or more of these activities. On occasion, three mixed-ability literature response groups might be operating simultaneously, with the teacher circulating among them. Establishing a clear pattern for these activities is extremely important and takes time. Response groups, in particular, need to be introduced in whole-group settings and then modeled by small groups with the remainder of the class observing. In this way, students will experience the process in advance and understand what is expected. My experience indicates that once the patterns are established, these classrooms run smoothly. And, in fact, teachers tell me there are fewer discipline problems because students have opportunities to work in a variety of ways rather than working entirely in whole-group, teacher-directed instruction.

"COVERING" THE SKILLS: ATTENDING TO THE PARTS AS WELL AS THE WHOLE

Providing for individual differences has always been an issue. In the past, however, the primary focus of teachers was given to moving students through a highly linear, skills-based curriculum. The teachers' responsibility was to present the material in a logical and sequential manner. The same scope and sequence was assumed to be suitable for everyone. Adjustments for individual differences focused primarily on the rate at which students moved through a given set of activities and materials. Today's effective teachers are attending to skills within a more purposeful framework. The difference occurs in how, when, and why they teach skills, as well as in the meaning they attach to skills (Dudley-Marling, 1996).

Today's teachers are expected to take greater control over all the decisions involved in the instructional process. They are required to move beyond instruction that merely adjusts to students' rates of learning. At the very least, they must orchestrate a wide array of elements, including student achievement rates, teaching methods, and instructional materials. In order to be effective, they must pay close attention to the performance goals or benchmarks set by the school or district in which they teach. These generally are linked closely to statewide content and performance standards. Au, Carroll, and Scheu stressed the importance of local performance goals: "Because they generally are stated in more specific terms than national, state, and/or district standards, benchmarks help teachers and students understand the expectations at their grade level and work toward them" (Au, Carroll, & Scheu, 2001, p. 293). Teachers are held accountable for the performance goals outlined for their grade level, however, they are frequently given considerable latitude in how they will go about addressing them. Curriculum supervisors have told us that most often they encourage teachers to think of

> Effective teachers attend to skills within a more purposeful framework. The difference occurs in how, when, and why they teach skills, as well as in the meaning they attach to them.

performance goals in an integrated way. Teachers are cautioned against treating them in a linear manner by mindlessly moving through the list, treating each as an isolated objective, checking it off, and moving on to the next. Yatvin (1991) suggested that all teachers have at least an unconscious curriculum that dictates what is noticed that needs to be taught. Ideally, the district's stated curriculum should be the one that teachers draw upon as the basis for capitalizing on teachable moments and for assessing progress.

Determining which skills and strategies will be taught involves (1) teacher familiarity with and attention to school and districtwide standards, (2) student learning opportunities that target the skills and strategies underlying those standards in a systematic and explicit manner within a holistic framework, (3) an abundance of student opportunities for meaningful application of skills and strategies through planned indirect instruction, (4) student accountability for what has been taught, (5) ongoing teacher monitoring of skills used in meaningful and purposeful situations, and (6) multilevel tasks and activities for student application of skills and for monitoring progress.

MONITORING PROGRESS: DOCUMENTATION IS NOT ENOUGH

Monitoring progress is at the heart of a successful program in which instruction is differentiated. Teachers who respect and respond to variability are constantly alert to individual needs and the implications for instruction. They use assessment to focus on students' strengths rather than just their weaknesses (National Center for Fair and Open Testing, 2006). New forms of instruction in the language arts, such as literature response circles and cooperative learning groups, have created a need for new forms of assessment. "Conventional standardized tests, in which students can respond only in a multiple-choice format, cannot adequately assess students' learning of complex forms of reading and writing" (Au et al., 2001, p. 281). Students' progress must be documented on an ongoing basis, but merely documenting progress is not enough. The instructional decisions based on that documentation are what really count. Increasingly, teachers are integrating a system of ongoing, informal classroom assessment into their instructional programs. They have discovered that this type of documentation more truly reveals student needs as opposed to norm-referenced standardized tests, or even teacher-developed paper-and-pencil tests, alone (Calfee & Hiebert, 1988). Viewed in this way, assessment is used to support better teaching and transform schooling rather than reify existing problems and inequalities (Darling-Hammond, 1994).

Students need to know that everything they do in the language arts class is important and that in one way or another, it counts. Self-selected, independent reading and reader response groups sometimes are viewed by students as less important than a test or other types of written work: "After all, we choose the books ourselves" or "We're just talking about what we read." Teachers complain that these activities are difficult to monitor. They want simple but useful management systems for documenting student progress in a variety of areas.

> Teachers who respect and respond to variability are constantly alert to individual needs and their implications for instruction.

By keeping the district's curriculum objectives in mind and offering students many opportunities to participate in activities of the type described under "covering skills," teachers can engage students in holistic, literature-based activities and still chart progress on targeted strategies over time. The information gathered can be analyzed in at least three ways: (1) progress of the individual learner in relationship to him- or herself, (2) progress of the individual learner in terms of the group, and (3) progress of the group as a whole. Each of these ways offers teachers insight into what skills need extra emphasis. Most important, teachers have a sense of where that emphasis should be placed: at the whole-group level, through small, needs-based groups, or through more personalized attention. Following are two examples of systems for monitoring literacy activities that many teachers find difficult to assess.

Monitoring reader response groups. Literature circles offer teachers an opportunity to use oral response to literature as a window into how children are thinking and responding to text (Roser & Martinez, 1995). Strickland worked with several teachers to construct a method for evaluating the reading skills and strategies during such discussions (Strickland, Dillon, Funkhouser, Glick, & Rogers, 1989). Peterson and Eeds (1990) also offered a system for monitoring students' preparation for and participation in literature study groups. A scheme for documenting discussion in these groups, which is based on both efforts, uses a response group assessment form that includes the date, the prompt or focus for the discussion, and the name of the students in the response group. During the discussion, the teacher makes comments next to each child's name regarding the following: (1) preparation for the discussion, (2) the quality of participation, (3) the application of knowledge about literary concepts (e.g., plot, theme, genre, characterization), and (4) the application of knowledge about aspects of reading comprehension (making predictions, getting the main idea, using supporting details, comparing and contrasting, etc.). Teachers may participate in the discussion or merely observe. The strategy has undergone several mutations as teachers attempt to keep the form as simple as possible without sacrificing the content they are after.

Keeping track of independent reading. Reader response journals are a major resource for helping students and teachers keep track of independent reading. Brief one-to-one conferences with children about their self-selected reading also go a long way to giving this kind of activity the stature it deserves as the most important practice for reading development (Anderson, Wilson, & Fielding, 1988; Greaney, 1980). In the past, too often only those children who finished their work early had time for independent reading. Enlightened about its importance, today's teachers are more apt to make independent reading, in and out of school, an integral part of their reading programs. Teachers also are aware that this is an effective way to adjust materials to students' reading levels and interests. Children can, of course, keep their own records of their personal reading. However, the use of personalized conferences transforms record-keeping into a key time for documenting and monitoring progress. A three-ring binder with pages for each child provides a quick and easy method for recording information. Pages can be arranged alphabetically according to each child's last name for easy reference.

Conferences are scheduled for each child every one or two weeks and include the following:

Questions and discussion. Questions that can be asked about any book are useful to get the conversation started; for example, Well, how are you enjoying this book so far? How does this book compare with other books of this type? By this author? At times, the reader response journal itself may become the focus of the discussion.

Oral reading. After a brief discussion the child is asked to read a portion of the book aloud. The selection may be chosen by the teacher or prepared in advance by the student. Some teachers keep an audio-cassette on hand for each child and record the oral reading or the entire conference. Over a year's time, each child has several such conferences recorded to place into a portfolio or to send home to parents as a gift.

Documentation. The teacher engages in a type of diagnostic recordkeeping in which information about the child's reading strategies, reading preferences, and ability to talk confidently about books is noted.

This very simple method of conducting individualized conferences fits easily into the framework for organization outlined. After several conferences, the written documentation may be grouped together and placed in students' portfolios as evidence of the amount, breadth, and overall proficiency of their independent reading.

HELPING LOW-ACHIEVING STUDENTS: TIME, MATERIALS, STRATEGIES

Addressing the needs of struggling readers and writers is one of the most perplexing problems teachers face. Low-achieving students need extra time, materials with which they can feel successful, and strategies that work for them. Attention to these learners within the regular classroom is important for several reasons. Supplementary remedial programs such as Title I and "replacement" programs that substitute for regular in-class instruction have had mixed results over the years (Johnston, Allington, & Afflerback, 1989). Some people argue that such programs cause classroom teachers to over-rely on special help and neglect their responsibility for less able students. Others suggest that where these programs exist, instruction within and outside the classroom often is at odds with each other. Even when such programs are considered successful, most agree that they work best where there is a strong compatible instructional program in the student's regular classroom. The classroom will, no doubt, continue to be the mainstay of students' instructional performance. Therefore, regardless of the supplemental help offered, more attention needs to be given to incorporating the best prevention and intervention procedures into regular classroom instructional practice.

Many of the needs of these students have already been addressed: (1) classroom management that allows for flexible grouping gives low-achieving students more time in small groups and personalized

instructional formats in which their needs can receive specific attention, (2) planned, independent reading activities that encourage
children to select books that match their interests and reading abilities provide the kind of practice they need most, (3) multilevel activities help ensure that students who are struggling will engage in the
same intellectual processes as other students with expectations that
are challenging for them but also realistic, and, of course, (4) consistent monitoring of progress helps to inform instruction so that low-
achieving students receive attention in those areas where they need
help. Two types of activities that have a strong payoff for less able
students are those in which teachers mediate to help make difficult
texts (such as those in the content areas) more readable, and strategies that engage children in a variety of rereading activities.

> **Research suggests that the best readers read widely and often.**

*Making what they "must read" read-
able.* Less able readers need specific
instruction in the use of strategies for com-
prehending texts (Dole, Valencia, Greer, &
Wardrop, 1991; Maria, 1996). Following
are two activities that can help smooth the
way for struggling readers and promote better access to key ideas for
better readers as well.

1. List potentially troublesome vocabulary words and concepts.
Lead students in a discussion of the words and predict what the
selection might be about. Write their predictions on the board and
periodically confirm or disconfirm them during the reading.

2. Read aloud the first paragraph or two after introducing a
selection, as the students follow along. Have several children summarize what they learned or tell one new thing they learned from the
passage you read. Students may volunteer their contributions individually or they may collaborate in pairs or groups and then share
with the class. Continue, asking individual students to read aloud, as
the others follow along. The oral reading should be preceded by
opportunities for everyone to read the passage silently. After the oral
reading make sure to include some of the struggling readers in sum-
marizing or telling something new they learned. When appropriate,
guide students to include some of the new vocabulary in their statements. Their statements should be listed on a chart to form a student-
created summary of the selection. This chart then serves as a reduced
version of the key ideas in the passage. It may be referred to and

reread periodically as a review of the topic, both with the whole group and as a follow-up in small-group, teacher-directed activities with less able readers.

Rereading of familiar texts. Research suggests that the best readers read widely and often (Anderson et al., 1988; Greaney, 1980). Fortunately, the very act of reading helps to build vocabulary and fluency and is the best way to apply developing skills. Unfortunately, research suggests that poor readers actually spend far less time actually engaged in reading than more able readers (Allington, 1983). Rereading opportunities such as choral reading (students read orally together, usually with the teacher as lead reader), echo reading (students "echo" a fluent reader's rendition of a selection, one sentence at a time), read along (students read along silently while listening to a fluent reader read aloud or to a tape recording of the selection), partner reading (two students take turns rereading a selection aloud to one another), and reader's theater (students are assigned roles and reread the selection as a play) are especially helpful. Not only do less able readers and writers need more time involved in direct instruction, they need more time to independently apply what they have learned in situations in which they can experience enough success to self-monitor their own reading and writing behaviors.

CONCLUSION

To be effective, classroom teachers must juggle a myriad of factors simultaneously, and they must do it in a way that creates a positive learning environment for every child they teach. Legislators and administrators who offer policy initiatives calling for uniform standards and high expectations would do well to keep learner variability in mind, not as an excuse for poor performance but as a factor that must be addressed if every child is to succeed. Each day, many teachers demonstrate that this can be done. Many others need help through professional development in order to become more proficient. Recognizing the reality of learner variability and approaching it as a natural part of the instructional process can help students achieve. Rather than something to work around, correct, or complain about, learner variability becomes a factor that teachers and administrators know they have the ability to address. Providing quality instruction and support so that all children have the opportunity to learn is the best way to express belief in the notion that "all children can learn."

Sara reflects:

I have no intention of going backwards to the old ways. I realize that back then I concentrated more on teaching than on learning. It helps to know that the questions I am raising are shared by others. I am striving to make my teaching more skillful and strategic. It is the best hope I can give all my students to help them meet high expectations and standards. Each day I feel that I am growing in my understanding of the teaching/learning process—and my students are achieving. I have made a personal commitment to continue to reflect, rethink, and respond—but never to retreat.

REFERENCES

Allington, R. L. (1983). The reading instruction provided readers of differing reading abilities. *Elementary School Journal, 83*, 548–559.

Anderson, R., Wilson, P. T., & Fielding, L. (1988). Growth in reading and how children spend their time outside of school. *Reading Research Quarterly, 23*, 285–303.

Au, K., Carroll, J., & Scheu, J. (2001). *Balanced literacy instruction: A teacher's resource book.* Norwood, MA: Christopher-Gordon.

Calfee, R., & Hiebert, E. (1988). The teacher's role in using assessment to improve learning. In C. V. Bunderson (Ed.), *Assessment in the service of learning.* Princeton, NJ: Educational Testing Service.

Darling-Hammond, L. (1994). Performance-based assessment and educational equity. *Harvard Educational Review, 64*, 5–30.

Dole, J. A., Valencia, S. W., Greer, E. A., & Wardrop, J. L. (1991). Effects of two types of prereading instruction on the comprehension of narrative and expository text. *Reading Research Quarterly, 26*, 142–158.

Dudley-Marling, C. (1996). Explicit instruction within a whole language framework: Teaching struggling readers and writers. In E. McIntyre and M. Pressley (Eds.), *Balanced instruction: Strategies and skills in whole language.* Norwood, MA: Christopher-Gordon.

Fountas, I. C., & Pinnell, G. S. (1996). *Guided reading.* Portsmouth, NH: Heinemann.

Greaney, V. (1980). Factors related to amount and type of leisure-time reading. *Reading Research Quarterly, 15*, 337–357.

Hiebert, E. H. (1983). An examination of ability grouping for reading instruction. *Reading Research Quarterly, 18*, 231–255.

Johnston, P., Allington, R., & Afflerback, P. (1989). The congruence of classroom and remedial reading instruction. *Elementary School Journal, 85*, 513–528.

Maria, K. (1996). Reading comprehension instruction for disabled readers. In Lillian R. Putnam (Ed.), *How to become a better teacher of reading.* Englewood Cliffs, NJ: Prentice Hall.

National Center for Fair and Open Testing. (2006). Cambridge, MA: www.fairtest.org.

Pace, G. (1992). Stories of teacher-initiated change from traditional to whole language literacy instruction. *Elementary School Journal, 92*, 461–476.

Pallas, A. M., Entwisle, D. R., Alexander, K. L., & Stluka, M. F. (1994). Ability-group effects: Instructional, social, or institutional? *Sociology of Education, 67*, 27–46.

Peterson, R., & Eeds, M. (1999). *Grand conversations.* New York: Scholastic.

Roller, C. M. (1996). *Variability not disability.* Newark, DE: International Reading Association.

Roser, N., & Martinez, M. (Eds.). (1995). *Book talk and beyond: Children and teachers respond to literature.* Newark, DE: International Reading Association.

Scharer, P. L. (1992). Teachers in transition: An exploration of changes in teachers and classrooms during the implementation of literature-based reading instruction. *Research in the Teaching of English, 20*, 408–443.

Strickland, D. S. (1998). What's basic in reading instruction: Finding common ground. *Educational Leadership, 55*, 7–10.

Strickland, D. S., Dillon, R. M., Funkhouser, L., Glick, M., & Rogers, C. (1989). Research currents: Classroom dialogue during literature response groups. *Language Arts, 66*, 193–200.

Worthy, J., & Hoffman, J. V. (1996). Critical questions. *The Reading Teacher, 49*, 656–657.

Yatvin, J. (1991). *Developing a whole language program.* Newark, DE: International Reading Association.

Teaching for Intelligence

Parameters for Change

Eric J. Cooper and Daniel U. Levine

Eric J. Cooper is Executive Director of the National Urban Alliance for Effective Education at Columbia University and cofounder of the Urban Partnership for Literacy with the International Reading Association. He also is Adjunct Professor in the Education Administration Department of Teachers College, Columbia University. He has worked with the College Board as the Associate Director of Program Development and has been an administrative assistant in the Office of Curriculum for Boston Public Schools. He has been a director of a treatment center for emotionally disturbed students, a teacher, a researcher, a counselor, and a Washington Fellow.

Daniel U. Levine is Professor of Education at the University of Nebraska at Omaha. He has worked in urban education for the past forty years. He has served on the boards of the National Urban Alliance for Effective Education and the Phi Delta Kappa Center for Effective Schools. He is the author of several textbooks and numerous articles on educational practice and research.

In the United States, emphasis on education reform for support-ing social change has reached new heights through calls for change in the popular press, educational journals, newsletters, and on the Internet. Yet, significant factors that will stall change reside in how reform is implemented. These factors include the standards for what students know and need to know, how we implement professional development activities, and the ability of reformers to bridge the gap between policy and good implementation (Levine & Cooper, 1991).

In many localities, school system leaders have called for teaching the basics—often forcing districts into implementing a curriculum that divides learning into separate pieces, and teaches skills and knowledge independent of their context (Berryman & Bailey, 1992). Yet, recent analyses cited in the popular press suggest the importance of teaching advanced thinking in the context of meaningful subject matter and in conjunction with a new reality of the workplace. This indicates, for example, that there should be no difference in the high school courses taken between a future engineer and an auto-trade journeyman (Barth, 1997). All students will have to be taught advanced thinking.

How localities deal with the implementation of change and the change process often decides the ability of a school system and community to remain competitive in the global economy and remain a viable place to live (White, 1997). It is our contention that there are some general conclusions that are particularly pertinent for projects to improve students' performance in thinking and other higher-order skills. The general conclusions can be summarized as follows:

- Successful innovations to improve instruction in thinking and other higher-order skills will generally have to be relatively large and complex.
- If educators select a thinking-skills approach that utilizes specific teaching materials in order to enhance manageability for teachers or for other reasons, care should be taken to allow, encourage, and assist participating teachers in adapting the materials to the realities of their classrooms.
- Whether or not the selected thinking-skills approach utilizes specific sets of teaching materials, project administrators should attempt to identify core components that require fidelity in implementation, and they should work with teachers to ensure that these components are stressed and implemented well.

- Because thinking-skills approaches require large, complex, and difficult changes in the behaviors and attitudes of teachers and students, even more stress than usual should be placed on ensuring that innovations are manageable and capable of being implemented by teachers, and that prerequisites and antecedents of successful implementation are firmly in place. These should include attention to considerations such as planning time, class size, change overload, amount of paperwork, adaptability in participating classrooms, compatibility with other demands, capacity for inspiring commitment, and large-scale staff development.
- Predictable obstacles that should be addressed in advance include school realities that stress classroom order and passive learning, students' preferences for lower-order skills, student and teacher compromises that trade obedience for undemanding instruction, low-level learning scripts for low achievers, and teacher preferences for easy-to-teach lessons.
- Projects to improve students' thinking are likely to be greatly hampered when student assessment focuses on low-level skills.
- Successful implementation of approaches for improving thinking skills requires concerted stress on revising organizational and institutional arrangements and structures.
- Initiation of effective projects for improving thinking skills is an imposing challenge not to be undertaken lightly (Levine & Cooper, 1991, p. 388).[1]

A second overriding issue frequently addressed in research and analysis on the change process involves the extent to which initiative and decision making should emphasize "top-down" mandates or "bottom-up" participation. Top-down approaches tend to emphasize fidelity to a mandate. Bottom-up participation emphasizes adaptation, placing greater stress on widespread participation in determining the nature and details of implementation. Recent movements have signaled an acceptance of the possibilities for faithful implementation of core components in a predetermined approach to innovation. Likewise, current research and analysis seem to be moving toward more stress on the importance and value of appropriate top-down initiative. During the 1970s and 1980s, many researchers and academic observers emphasized the need for teacher participation in initiating and guiding innovation. During the 1990s, however, some research has shifted toward a more balanced conclusion.

Probably the best example of the recent recognition of the role of top-down leadership in bringing about successful change has been provided in longitudinal studies conducted by Miles (1983) and his colleagues. Miles summarized much of this research in an article in which he outlined the forces leading to the "institutionalization" of innovation as follows:

> ... high administrative commitment tends to lead to both administrative pressure on users to implement the innovation, along with administrative support, which often shows up in the form of assistance to users. Both the pressure and the assistance tend to lead to increased user effort. . . . the harder people worked at an innovation, the more committed they grew; that commitment was also fueled by increasing technical mastery of the innovation.
>
> Commitment and mastery both lead toward increasing stabilization of use . . . [which is] aided if administrators decide to mandate the innovation, which also naturally increases the percentage of use . . . [that in turn encourages institutionalization]. (Miles, 1983, p. 18)

Emphasizing top-down action in bringing about change is not necessarily the same, of course, as de-emphasizing bottom-up participation. For one thing, the conclusions just quoted were concerned with institutionalization, not just initial mastery and implementation. Certainly Miles and his colleagues would not ignore or play down the importance of teacher participation and commitment in designing and implementing innovation. In addition, their conclusions continue to emphasize the importance of "teacher-administrator harmony" and of both "teacher mastery/commitment and administrative action" (Miles, 1983, p. 19). Nevertheless, their data and conclusions do provide an important balance to the work of some others who have minimized the necessity for and possibilities of strong top-down mandates and action in carrying out innovation successfully.

Hall and Hord (1987) and Crandall, Eiseman, and Louis (1986) have also reviewed research related to the top-down/bottom-up issue, reaching conclusions similar to those of Miles and his colleagues. Elaborating on some of the important considerations involved in devising and implementing innovations, Hall and Hord stressed that "mandates and decrees" are helpful in providing clear indications of priority. Crandall, Eiseman, and Louis concluded that a strategy based on mandates by strong leaders "appears to require five elements: absence of debilitating conflict; an effective, debugged innovation; continuity of leadership; frequent reminders that successful and faithful implementation is important; and adequate resources and support" (Crandall et al., 1986, pp. 40–41).

IMPLICATIONS FROM RESEARCH

The legacy of research from the 1980s is the conclusion that teachers must change their teaching practices in the direction of concentrating more time and effort on concept development, cognitive development, reasoning, thinking, higher-order comprehension skills, and advanced subject matter (Harris & Cooper, 1985). A strong base of research linking cognitive development to prior knowledge in learning emerged in the late 1970s (Langer, 1982). Those studies concluded that, particularly when reading is the learning mode, students with much prior knowledge and experience relevant to a subject have less difficulty learning new material, and retain more than students with inadequate or incomplete prior knowledge and experience. Students need the benefit of teachers who know how to access prior knowledge that the students might not be aware of, which might help them with the material to be learned (Cooper & Sherk, 1989).

> Students need the benefit of teachers who know how to access prior knowledge that the students themselves might not be aware of.

Finding ways to help students relate what they already know to what is to be learned is often called preteaching or preparation. Research has suggested that teachers accomplish this in several ways. One way is by encouraging students to make predictions before a reading and/or learning task (Cooper & Sherk, 1989). Predicting—based on the students' prior knowledge of the topic of a reading selection and on what students think the reading selection will be about—helps students to become aware of their knowledge base. It also helps them to focus closely upon how the text informs the reader (Cooper & Sherk, 1989).

Another transportable practice is to allow students to examine the structure of textual material before detailed reading takes place. For example, when students determine that they are going to read a narrative selection, they can then review their knowledge of the narrative structure (i.e., a narrative has a setting, characters, a beginning, and is often structured in patterns of time/sequence and problem/ solution). If the selection is an expository one, students can be alerted to look for signals that indicate a particular relationship of ideas (organizational patterns such as cause-effect, comparison-contrast, problem-solution, or chronology and sequence). Teachers are in the best position to point out such distinctions to their students and to determine how best to utilize the text for problem solving and decision making (Cooper & Sherk, 1989).

In considering the ideas introduced in this brief article, readers should keep in mind that innovations to improve instruction, changes in thinking, and other higher-order skills (e.g., reflective, critical, and creative analysis in the translation and application of knowledge) generally have to be relatively large and complex. Even given the urgent response needed to address the deepening gulfs between American haves and have-nots, we cannot expect significant change to happen school by school or teacher by teacher. Many students are school dependent for learning advanced skills, yet teachers have not had the support to be prepared to offer effective instruction to enhance higher-order skills (e.g., MacGinitie & MacGinitie, 1986). The knowledge base for teaching thinking is still relatively undeveloped in terms of classroom practices (Marzano et al., 1988). Emphasizing higher-order skills also constitutes a major change in many or most classrooms and schools (Goodlad, 2004; Perkins, 1995), and many students will need close guidance and assistance (i.e., mediation) from highly skilled teachers (Marzano et al., 1988).

The general complexity and large magnitude of change involved in innovative projects to improve instruction in thinking was underlined in an analysis of teaching thinking skills prepared by Nickerson, Perkins, and Smith (1985). Although the authors note that thinking-skills approaches vary considerably with respect to considerations such as the amount of class time devoted to instruction, the specific skills addressed, and the amount of special training for teachers, these approaches emphasize similar general conclusions. Teachers of thinking need to be facilitators of knowledge; students must explore and discover knowledge rather than passively absorb it; many teachers resist approaches that do not yet offer a clear and definite technology; assessment of thinking skills is still relatively primitive; and that significant time-on-task opportunity has to be available to students. Furthermore, implementation of any thinking-skills programs should ensure that tasks are intrinsically interesting to students, that objectives and exercises are "calibrated" to "students' current level of knowledge and abilities," that reasons for student success or failure are explicitly addressed, that considerable feedback is provided to students, and that practice is provided in "a variety of problem contexts" (Nickerson et al., 1985, pp. 342–343)—no small job for any classroom teacher. If we are to recognize the importance of teaching advanced thinking in preparing students to go to institutions of higher education, successfully compete in the workplace of the twenty-first century, and become lifelong learners, we will have to recognize that sustained and cohesive professional development is necessary to reach our goals. Nothing less than total commitment by all stakeholders in school communities, state departments of education, and the federal government to this end is needed.

NOTE

1. Levine, D. U., & Cooper, E. J. (1991). The change process and its implications in teaching thinking. In L. Idol and B. Jones (Eds.), *Educational values and cognitive instruction: Implications for reform* (p. 381). Hillsdale, NJ: Lawrence Erlbaum Associates. Reprinted with permission.

REFERENCES

Barth, P. (1997, November 26). Want to keep American jobs and avert class division? Try high school trip (A little physics goes a long way, too). *Education Week,* pp. 30–33.

Berryman, S. E., & Bailey, T. R. (1992). *The double helix of education and the economy.* New York: Teachers College Press.

Cooper, E. J., & Sherk, J. (1989). Addressing urban school reform: Issues and alliances. *Journal of Negro Education, 58*(3), 315–331.

Crandall, D. P., Eiseman, J. W., & Louis, K. S. (1986). Strategic planning issues that bear on the success of school improvement efforts. *Educational Administration Quarterly, 22*(3), 21–53.

Goodlad, J. I. (2004). *A place called school.* New York: McGraw-Hill.

Hall, G. E., & Hord, S. M. (1987). *Change in schools.* Albany: State University of New York Press.

Harris, T. L., & Cooper, E. J. (1985). *Reading, thinking, and concept development.* New York: The College Board.

Langer, J. A. (1982). Facilitating text processing: The elaboration of prior knowledge. In J. A. Langer and M. Smith-Burke (Eds.), *Reader meets author/Bridging the gap.* Newark, DE: International Reading Association.

Levine, D. U., & Cooper, E. J. (1991). The change process and its implications in teaching thinking. In L. Idol and B. Jones (Eds.), *Educational values and cognitive instruction: Implications for reform.* Hillsdale, NJ: Lawrence Erlbaum Associates.

MacGinitie, W. H., & MacGinitie, R. K. (1986). Teaching students not to read. In S. DeCastell, A. Luke, and K. Egan (Eds.), *Literacy, society, and schooling.* Cambridge, England: Cambridge University Press.

Marzano, R. J., Brandt, R. S., Hughes, C. S., Jones, B. F., Presseisen, B. Z., Rankin, S. C., and Suhor, C. (1988). *Dimensions of thinking. A framework for curriculum and instruction.* Alexandria, VA: Association for Supervision and Curriculum Development.

Miles, M. B. (1983). Unraveling the mysteries of institutionalization. *Educational Leadership, 41*(2), 14–19.

Nickerson, R. S., Perkins, D. N., & Smith, E. E. (1985). *The teaching of thinking.* Hillsdale, NJ: Lawrence Erlbaum Associates.

Perkins, D. (1995). *Outsmarting IQ—The emerging science of learnable intelligence.* New York: Simon and Schuster.

White, K. A. (1997, November 26). Jobs will follow better schools, Miami-Dade leaders say. *Education Week,* p. 7.

Considerations in Introducing Instructional Interventions

Daniel U. Levine and Rayna F. Levine

Daniel U. Levine *is Professor of Education at the University of Nebraska at Omaha. He has worked in urban education for the past forty years. He has served on the boards of the National Urban Alliance for Effective Education and the Phi Delta Kappa Center for Effective Schools. He is the author of several textbooks and numerous articles on educational practice and research.*

Rayna F. Levine *is a retired principal of William Volker Applied Learning Magnet School, a nationally recognized Blue Ribbon school in Kansas City, Missouri. She has worked in urban education and public schools for more than twenty years as a teacher, a coordinator of instruction, a principal, and in central administration as Director of Elementary Schools. She has coauthored a text and several articles.*

M any recent analyses have clarified issues involving the successful implementation of approaches for bringing about significant improvement in the functioning of public schools. For example, Fullan and Miles (1992) examined the dangers inherent in introducing a large set of fragmented interventions. McKenzie

(1995) provided useful material for analyzing and improving the effectiveness of site-based management teams in schools. Researchers participating in the Consortium for Policy Research in Education (1996) have identified central considerations in building capacity for school reform.

Our goal in this article is to contribute to this area of analysis by focusing on issues dealing with selection and implementation of instructional interventions that have a fighting chance to bring about substantial improvement in students' academic performance. We will consider aspects of selection implementation that involve

- neglect of critical prerequisites for successful implementation,
- selection of interventions low in "doability,"
- potential for mischievous misimplementation,
- lack of attention to predictable pitfalls, and
- downplaying of schoolwide and sociological perspectives.

NEGLECT OF CRITICAL PREREQUISITES

Researchers have identified a number of prerequisites for success when implementing major instructional interventions. Using varied terminology but usually focusing on similar basic concepts, they have identified requirements such as the following (Bullard & Taylor, 1994; Levine & Cooper, 1990; Levine & Lezotte, 1990; Stringfield, Milsap, Scott, & Herman, 1996):

- Massive staff development, conducted primarily at participating school sites.
- Availability of one or more full- or largely full-time instructional specialists who provide classroom-level technical assistance to teachers.
- Regular monitoring to assess the workability and success of instructional arrangements at each stage of the implementation process.

We will not repeat the arguments and evidence that supports the importance of these or other prerequisites for meaningful instructional reform. Instead, we will briefly review some of the reasons why critical prerequisites are too often ignored when planners design and proceed to implement ambitious change efforts.

Failure to recognize a prerequisite in the first place. Decision makers frequently seem unaware of the existence of a given prerequisite. Many reform plans, for example, assume that already overloaded principals somehow can find the time and possess the knowledge to help their teachers master difficult new instructional techniques and strategies. Similarly, reform plans too often assume that traditional staff development approaches involving occasional large-session workshops or short-term, superficial training for a few teacher leaders will result in sustained, meaningful change throughout a participating school.

Relatively high costs of prerequisites. Reform plans that include necessary prerequisites such as full-time instructional specialists in each school or ongoing, site-based staff development for entire faculties generally require considerable additional expenditures. In many cases, concentrating resources to fund these prerequisites to the extent necessary would limit reform efforts to only a few schools at a time. This approach risks allegations of favoritism or discrimination from constituents at other schools and thereby limits political support for the plan. It is easier to ignore expensive prerequisites and proceed "full speed ahead," particularly since decision makers receive accolades, publicity, and relief from criticism or state scrutiny when initiating large-scale plans that seek to reform entire systems. Failure will not be evident until a few years later, when administrators have already begun to implement other new, similarly underfunded "reforms."

> In our experience, it is astounding how quickly some administrators cave in to pressures for unplanned reform.

A "do something, do anything" mentality. Tendencies to proceed with interventions that ignore the prerequisites for successful change are exacerbated by perceptions that educational problems are too severe to allow for inaction or delay in bringing about systemwide improvement. Strong pressures from community groups, the school board, or high-level business executives cause administrators to believe they are being urged to "do something, do anything." In our experience, it is astounding how quickly some administrators cave in to such pressures. Does a fully formed plan exist? Does that plan provide adequate resources and arrangements for staff development? Does it place unreasonably burdensome time demands and recordkeeping tasks on already overloaded teachers? No matter—again, going through the motions may satisfy critics at least temporarily, until the next reform effort replaces the current failed one a few years down the road.

LOW DOABILITY INTERVENTIONS

Some interventions devised to improve students' performance are inherently more difficult to implement than others. This truism frequently receives little or no explicit attention when deciding on an intervention, or developing plans to implement it. For example, although the possible payoff from individualized, continuous-progress instruction potentially is greater than that from traditional mixtures of whole class and small group instruction, problems in implementing continuous-progress arrangements are so pervasive that they are seldom addressed successfully in practice.

Similarly, although the potential benefits of heterogeneous grouping include improved performance among low-achieving students as well as important gains with respect to desegregation and school climate, productive heterogeneous grouping is extremely difficult to implement in most schools. This is true because it typically requires relatively small classes, well-trained and highly motivated teachers, and the introduction of a range of new instructional strategies. Only in the past decade have advocates of heterogeneous grouping devoted meaningful attention to school and classroom level challenges in delivering heterogeneous instruction effectively, and begun to identify practical strategies to address these challenges (Wheelock, 1993).

Given the predictable problems encountered in implementing widely advocated reforms such as individualized instruction and heterogeneous grouping—not to mention performance assessments and portfolio-based accountability approaches, inclusion of students with disabilities in regular classes, interdisciplinary curricula emphasizing critical thinking, multiage grouping, and [insert your own favorite contemporary instructional reform approach], it would be prudent for decision makers to study research on the implementation requirements and demonstrated effectiveness of their proposed interventions. Perhaps they should use a "doability" index such as the following to summarize the results of their review:

1. Almost never works; hardly ever will

2. Works occasionally when very well implemented by an outstanding faculty

3. Works occasionally when very well implemented by a capable faculty

4. Usually works when very well implemented by an outstanding faculty

5. Usually works when very well implemented by a capable faculty

6. Almost always works given competent implementation by a mostly capable faculty (probably a null category).

Enhancing implementability. Some innovative approaches are basically nonimplementable in most situations because they are complex to the point that they are counterproductive. Even though such approaches may incorporate excellent ideas that could improve student achievement, teachers cannot effectively implement highly complex approaches hour after hour, day after day, week after week. In some cases, educators can draw usefully on such approaches by radically simplifying them so they can actually be used in the typical classroom. Examples of potentially useful, but overly complex approaches include: implementation of certain elaborate and highly prescribed models for teaching students in accordance with their distinctive learning styles; comprehensive use of cooperative learning arrangements; and planning and delivering all lessons in a specified sequence of steps.

Teachers in some districts have substantially improved instruction by drawing on approaches such as those listed above while explicitly simplifying their implementation. For example, educators in Johnson City, New York, have implemented mastery learning effectively, in part because they followed a relatively simple rule that corrective instruction for initial nonmasters must be delivered in a mode different from the original lesson (Levine, 1985). By way of contrast, teachers in many other districts have stumbled trying to continually utilize a variety of learning modes that presumably address each student's learning style. As this example shows, simpler is often better when simplification makes a promising approach more implementable in real schools and classrooms.

Interventions High in Potential for Mischief

Proposals for major institutional reform should also be assessed according to their "Potential for Mischief Quotient" (PFMQ).

Assessing proposed reforms in this way recognizes that some are much more susceptible to misimplementation. For example, mastery learning, when well implemented, may produce impressive gains in higher-order skills, but too many mastery learning implementations have involved superficial efforts to ensure that students acquire easily taught low-level skills (Levine, 1985).

Another good example is apparent when one visits schools implementing so-called "whole language" approaches that stress the use of literature to teach reading. Frequently lacking comprehensive, ongoing training in how to help poor readers—and working virtually unsupervised and unmonitored—some teachers using this approach do little more than distribute materials and "let the children read." It is tempting for teachers to take this easy way out because their students appear to be functioning in accordance with expectations as they motor through lots of books. Other instructional and organizational approaches that are particularly high in PFMQ include

- *Block scheduling in secondary schools.* This reform's effectiveness depends to some extent on whether teachers know how to meaningfully plan and deliver appropriate instructional activities using the expanded time. Students must also learn independently in extended blocks of time. In many schools, block scheduling is implemented without assessing or attending to problems involved in helping students who are unprepared or unmotivated to function meaningfully on their own or in small groups (Smith & McNelis, 1999).
- *Self-esteem improvement efforts that give little or no attention to learning strategies and skills.* One reason why these approaches have high PFMQ is because they implicitly encourage users to disregard and postpone the hard work involved in actually bringing about achievement gains that might serve as a stable and potent basis for enhanced self-esteem. In turn, the failure of such approaches to improve achievement enables detractors to more credibly go to an opposite extreme and ignore the importance of efforts to bolster students' self-esteem.

In this section, we have cited several superficially attractive ideas that sound as if they offer considerable potential for improving the quality of education. One of them—mastery learning—even has extensive research regarding its effectiveness when well implemented. Susceptible as they are to mischievous misinterpretation and misimplementation, they easily become faddish approaches likely to drop out of sight when the pendulum swings back toward their equally attractive-sounding opposites.

Approaches high in PFMQ share several characteristics. First, implementing them effectively requires more time, commitment, training, resources, and a great deal of hard work. At the same time, they lend themselves to a kind of quick and dirty implementation that appears to conform to the underlying model. Thus, busy teachers can discharge their responsibilities by implementing surface features while ignoring more challenging aspects. With mastery learning, for example, teachers may welcome the chance to teach and reteach small mechanical skills if doing so relieves (or is allowed to relieve) them of responsibility for developing students' mastery of higher-order skills.

> The improvement efforts that are most susceptible to misimplementation easily become faddish approaches.

Second, approaches that are high in PFMQ generally require significant additional resources to implement effectively, while their susceptibility to surface implementation allows planners to gloss over the fact that needed resources have not been secured. In schools with a substantial proportion of students who do not function well independently, for example, both whole language and block scheduling require relatively low ratios of staff-to-students so that faculty can provide appropriate individual help. In both cases, it is easy for administrators to point to activities and arrangements that theoretically indicate the approach is being implemented even though its fundamental presuppositions are violated in practice.

It is probably no accident that approaches high in PFMQ frequently have been promulgated under the banner of buzzwords or phrases popular during the time period they are most widely implemented—mastery learning in the 1980s and whole language in the early 1990s were yesterday's fads fated to be replaced by today's and then tomorrow's fads. Hype in professional journals and newsletters of their promised benefits provided cover for administrators concerned more with responding to political pressures and the desire to be seen as "doing something" than with recognizing the predictable probabilities that these reforms will be mischievously misimplemented.

We would like to be able to discuss approaches that are very low in PFMQ, but when we limit our consideration to reforms substantial enough to have long-range impact on student performance, we cannot think of any. The best we can do is to identify several that are relatively low in PFMQ. Among approaches we have encountered that can be placed in this category are:

- *The Higher Order Thinking Skills (HOTS) approach developed by Stanley Pogrow (1992, 1996) and his colleagues.* Because HOTS can be implemented by one carefully selected and specially trained teacher or a small cadre of teachers and paraprofessionals, and because it provides participating instructors with detailed and concrete curricular and instructional materials to help them get started, it has produced positive outcomes in a majority of implementations. Even though HOTS involves "pulling" low achievers out of regular classrooms for supplementary instruction, it differs from most other compensatory education pullout arrangements (which usually are very high in PFMQ) in that it stresses active, engaged learning of meaningful material rather than low-level, remedial instruction emphasizing mechanical skills.
- *Assessment using the Degrees of Reading Power (DRP) test.* Unlike other machine-scored tests designed to assess students' reading comprehension, the DRP was constructed to help teachers select materials that are appropriate for independent reading and for instruction aimed at improving the functional comprehension of a particular student or group of students. Since teachers are not given a set of scores indicating performance on subskills (e.g., identifying main idea), they are less likely to be diverted (or allowed to divert themselves) into introducing a long list of subskills that are of questionable value in improving reading comprehension (Sherk, n.d.).

LACK OF ATTENTION TO PREDICTABLE PITFALLS

We have noted that instructional and organizational reforms designed to improve student performance frequently fail in part because they neglect critical prerequisites for successful implementation, involve interventions that are highly complex, and/or inherently possess high potential for misimplementation. Besides attending to these general issues that should be considered in assessing any proposal for a sizable reform effort, planners also should recognize that particular interventions introduce their own unique pitfalls. For example:

- Some interventions require that unusually large amounts of assistance be provided to teachers. Expecting already over-loaded building administrators to provide such help meaningfully on a day-to-day basis is a recipe for failure. The recent movement toward inclusion of exceptional education students into regular classrooms exemplifies this pitfall because it frequently assumes that teachers know how, have adequate time, and are able to differentiate instruction appropriately for a very diverse group of students who differ greatly in previous achievement. Failure to address this predictable pitfall all but guarantees that participating teachers will either try to ignore inclusion students as much as possible or will spend inordinate amounts of time and energy attending to their special needs to the detriment of other students.
- Mastery learning, as noted above, is particularly susceptible to mindless instruction, emphasizing the testing and reteaching of lower-order skills, and whole language approaches may easily morph into a version of laissez-faire nonteaching.
- Problems encountered in the operation of computer laboratories also tend to be highly predictable. Chief among these are tendencies to assign classes to a lab for only one or two periods per week—too little for meaningful learning but sufficient to squeeze in every class in the school. In elementary schools, educators frequently fail to coordinate instruction in the lab with regular classroom learning, especially where computer time is also teacher planning time. Too often the software available is little more than electronic worksheets. Students have little control over computer-generated activities, and the small skill drills merely duplicate similar assignments in the classroom.

Such problems are highly predictable because they emerge directly from "natural" tendencies in the operation of schools. For example, the tendency to process all classes through the lab arises in part because it is easier to give every class equal time than to devise and defend flexible schedules that provide more time for some students than others as part of a larger school improvement plan. Since the problems are predictable, proactive administrators could take action early in the planning process to ensure that computer labs will be used productively to enhance student performance.

Somewhat comparable problems arise in the implementation of after school programs often established to help low achievers, or provide expanded learning opportunities for students. If "natural" forces in program development and operation run their course, the problems encountered are likely to include:

- selection of teachers proceeds according to seniority, political influence, certification, or other criteria unrelated to suitability and motivation for working in the program,
- class sizes may be larger than can be accommodated for, given available resources, and
- planned activities constitute an uncoordinated hodgepodge that will likely have little or no discernible impact on student achievement.

Identifying and taking early action to avoid or solve predictable problems in implementing given innovations may be even more important than selecting interventions with relatively low potential for misimplementation. Even those that are relatively low in PFMQ frequently will not be successful unless likely problems are proactively identified and attended to, whereas even the most difficult and complex interventions sometimes are successful if their problematic aspects, such as massive staff development requirements, are adequately addressed. Over the years we have encountered a few schools that successfully implemented high PFMQ approaches, such as individualized instruction, mastery learning, and computer laboratories, usually because their leaders were able to work through problems that resulted in ineffective implementation at other locations. Any approach can be successful somewhere if enough is done to anticipate and overcome the predictable difficulties that will arise when attempts are made to implement it. Our problem is not with the isolated sites where innovations are successfully implemented; instead,

> Identifying predictable problems and taking early action to avoid or solve them may be more important than selecting interventions with relatively low potential for misimplementation.

our concern is the need to make school reform a reality across districts that are not now adequately serving all students.

DOWNPLAYING OF SCHOOLWIDE AND SOCIOLOGICAL PERSPECTIVES

Still another reason why instructional innovations are frequently ineffective is because they ignore sociological perspectives involving impact on the school as a whole. Instead, interventions are generally assessed only in terms of psychological perspectives focused on individual students.

Inclusion policies provide instructive examples of innovations that have been assessed mostly on a psychological basis. In our experience, evaluators have most often examined the effects on inclusion students placed in regular classrooms, but seldom have they provided meaningful data regarding classroom- or school-level outcomes. Slower pacing of instruction, increased frustration among teachers and administrators, lack of appropriate staffing, diversion of funds from other interventions and services, and similar potentially negative effects frequently are unexamined in determining whether inclusion programs in a given school or district are successful or unsuccessful.

Similarly, grade retention practices have been evaluated almost entirely in terms of effects on retained students, even though their major purpose and potential benefits frequently are schoolwide: to demonstrate to all students—not just those retained—that lack of effort and/or failure to meet specified standards will have serious consequences. Although information regarding unusually effective schools indicates that in at least some cases rigorous promotions policies have played an important part in effectuating high expectations (Levine & Lezotte, 1990), we know little about how these policies were developed and implemented. To what extent do rigorous policies result in an initial spurt in retentions but then, if properly implemented, decline to relatively low levels? How can a faculty work cooperatively to implement a productive policy? These questions seldom have been investigated; all but a handful of the hundreds of studies dealing with retention have restricted their analyses to effects on students who have been retained.

CONCLUSION

Our major purpose in writing this article has been to delineate some of the questions that decision makers should consider in selecting among and proceeding with proposals for substantially improving the effectiveness of instruction in public schools. Among the most important of these questions are

- What are the critical prerequisites for successful implementation of a given intervention?
- How difficult is the intervention to implement, and what can be done to make it less complex so that it is implementable?
- How susceptible is the intervention to misimplementation?
- What pitfalls in implementation are most likely to be encountered, and what can be done to avoid them?

Ignoring or otherwise neglecting these and related questions and issues is likely to result in what some observers have referred to as "illusory" or "phantom" implementation or even, in more extreme cases, "reforms" that are delusional and hallucinatory (Levine & Lezotte, 1990). Whether such interventions should be characterized as illusory or instead as delusional, they seldom, if ever, will result in meaningful improvements in schools, classrooms, or student performance.

REFERENCES

Bullard, P., & Taylor, B. O. (1994). *Keepers of the dream.* Chicago: Excelsior.

Consortium for Policy Research in Education. (1996). *Public policy and school reform.* Philadelphia: University of Pennsylvania Graduate School of Education.

Fullan, M., & Miles, M. M. (1992). Getting reform right. *Phi Delta Kappan, 73*(10), 745–752.

Levine, D. U. (Ed.). (1985). *Improving student achievement through mastery learning programs.* San Francisco: Jossey-Bass.

Levine, D. U., & Cooper, E. J. (1990). The change process and its implications in teaching thinking. In L. Idol & B. F. Jones (Eds.), *Education values and cognitive instruction.* Hillside, NJ: Erlbaum.

Levine, D. U., & Lezotte, L. W. (1990). *Unusually effective schools.* Bloomington, IN: Phi Delta Kappa Center for Effective Schools.

McKenzie, J. (1995). The site-based decision-making guide for practitioners, at Internet site http://fnopress.com/classics.html.

Pogrow, S. (1992). What to do about chapter 1. *Phi Delta Kappan, 73*(8), 624–630.

Pogrow, S. (1996). Reforming the wannabe reformers. *Phi Delta Kappan, 77*(10), 656–663.

Sherk, J. K. (n.d.). *DRP materials matching: Adjusting the system.* Kansas City, MO: University of Missouri at Kansas City.

Smith, D. L., & McNelis, M. J. (1999). *Status report on alternative scheduling in Tennessee high schools.* Center for Research in Educational Policy: University of Memphis.

Stringfield, S., Milsap, M. A., Scott, E., & Herman, R. (1996, April). *The three year effects of promising programs on the academic achievement of students placed at risk.* Paper presented at the annual meeting of the American Educational Research Association, New York.

Wheelock, A. (1993). *Crossing the tracks.* New York: New Press.

SECTION 4

Special Concerns of Teaching for Intelligence

While teaching for intelligence is an educational position hard to disagree with, there is a realization in this period of reform that many groups of learners may not easily succeed in achieving the hoped-for objectives. Special concerns need to be examined relative to teaching the underserved, as well as the most fragile constituencies in schools, such as students in poverty, the learning challenged, the very young, and the unmotivated. Can past experiences of working with talented and gifted students shed any light on how to present accelerated learning to the most needy? These are topics, drawn from both research and practical studies, addressed in the fourth section of this volume.

The world of poverty-stricken and restless students of the drug-infested south Bronx is poignantly drawn by Kozol's sharp pen. It is a world devoid of intelligence, it seems; one weighed down by rotten luck, accumulated difficulties, and near hopelessness. Yet, Kozol returns regularly to this New York neighborhood, and with him comes the rare chance that something fundamental might change, that a real education might offer different possibilities to a child caught in this foul environment. According to Kozol, it is an investment many ought to be making and encouraging others to support.

Ginsburg challenges current educators to both devise exciting and stimulating instruction and create developmentally appropriate educational activity for preschool students. Working in the area of mathematics education, his research has refuted the myth that poor, minority children have short attention spans and limited intellectual ability. When interested and motivated, these youngsters showed they can develop elegant strategies in mathematics operations. They were as curious and persistent as any preschoolers, and they particularly enjoyed social learning interactions developed by sensitive, caring teachers. Ginsburg presents an alternative scenario to Kozol's bleak, depressed neighborhood.

VanTassel-Baska seeks a program that can address the needs of most talented or gifted students and, at the same time, provide for multiple outcomes in cognitive, affective, aesthetic, and social areas. For the advanced learner, she suggests, the youngster's precocity (especially in domain-specific contexts) must be honored. Teachers must also encourage the breadth of their higher-order thinking skills and their ability to make interdisciplinary connections and discover systemic relationships. Much collaboration is still required between Schools of Education and Colleges of Liberal Arts and Sciences to further consider the research being done in this complex field. Unfortunately, as VanTassel-Baska points out, only a few ventures have really been pursued to the point where they have yielded reliable, informative data.

An exception to the paucity of research on teaching for intelligence and actually delivering a promising program is the work of Renzulli, who presents his schoolwide enrichment model in this section. Originally an advocate of special education for the gifted and talented, Renzulli now proposes "challenging and enjoyable high-end learning" across a full range of student populations, at different levels, and with varied demographics. Renzulli is practical; he considers how teachers must be supported while learning gradual change, and he is ever diligent about how to use the precious time teachers have available for productive ends. What is most interesting about his relatively complex model is its unique way of dealing with the demands of the regular curriculum while simultaneously addressing the need to inspire and to be creative in providing for students' cognitive enrichment. Renzulli would modify use of the ubiquitous textbook so that time would be freed for the student to be challenged by an exciting, self-selected project in an area about which he or she is curious and motivated. The research findings on implementing Renzulli's model, at various sites across the country, make his contribution to this volume a rich resource in teaching for intelligence and for implementing real innovations in the classroom.

Finally, this section and this volume concludes with Comer's moving study of the climate and conditions needed to create an environment in which children—even the poorest and most neglected—can learn to think intelligently. His personal story adds a touching view of nurturing and inspiration. His doubts about the false reliance on IQ scores makes one wonder how we determine what real quality is and how respect for learning actually develops. Comer stresses the importance of the *community* of knowing, of developing "no-fault" support for the learner in a child-centered school. He reports on numerous schools that have successfully implemented his Yale Child Study Center Model of schooling, emphasizing consensus and collaboration. Like his friend Feuerstein, Comer makes the world think differently about children. Given opportunity, guidance by caring teachers, and encouragement to learn to manage their own environment, every child from Alabama to the south Bronx can learn and achieve at the highest level possible. Teaching for intelligence is the key to a whole new world of being. Every child deserves a chance to experience it.

Working With Kids Like Mario

Jonathan Kozol

Jonathan Kozol moved in 1964 from Harvard Square to a poor black neighborhood of Boston and became a fourth-grade teacher in the Boston public schools. He has devoted the subsequent three decades of his life to issues of education and social justice in America. He is the author of numerous books, including the award-winning Death at an Early Age, Homeless Families in America, Amazing Grace, *and* Savage Inequalities. *His book,* The Shame of the Nation: The Restoration of Apartheid Schooling in America *addresses the racial resegregation and deterioration of public schools in the United States.*

I've been working with kids like Mario one way or the other for most of my life. Started out back in 1964, thirty-four years ago, in the segregated public schools in Boston, and I have spent most of the decades since working with black and Hispanic kids, much of the past five years with children in New York, off and on in the south Bronx. In all, I have made about 200 visits up to the south Bronx to talk to children, mothers, fathers, teachers, and preachers who face challenges I couldn't have even dreamed of thirty years ago. I usually go up by the train. While you are here in New York you can take the same trip if you'd like. Number 6 train. Get on in front of Bloomingdale's, 57th Street and Lexington Avenue. One of the richest neighborhoods in the entire Western world. Get off fifteen minutes later on Brook Avenue in the south Bronx. Poorest section of the poorest congressional district in America. Also one of the physically sickest neighborhoods that I've visited in my entire life.

When I was writing *Amazing Grace,* doctors at the hospital told me nearly one-fourth of all the young women who came into the hospital to have a baby tested positive for HIV. Imagine what that means. You visit kindergarten. I love to start the day visiting kindergarten when I'm up there because it is cheerful. It should be cheerful. If you know the numbers, you can't engage in phony boosterism, and you can't be artificially optimistic. That's not good theology. You know the numbers, and you look at these little babies in front of you, and you are thinking to yourself, 1, 2, 3, 4, every fourth child may lose his or her mother to an early death and many will follow their mothers to the grave.

Challenging Preschool Education

Meeting the Intellectual Needs of All Children[1]

Herbert P. Ginsburg

Herbert P. Ginsburg is the Jacob H. Schiff Professor of Psychology and Education at Teachers College, Columbia University. For the past thirty years, he has conducted research on cognitive development, particularly the development of children's mathematical thinking, both within the United States and in various countries around the world. He has used the knowledge gained from research to develop several kinds of educational applications, including mathematics textbooks and video workshops designed to enhance teachers' understandings of children's learning of mathematics. He is now studying preschoolers' mathematical thinking.

This article is about *challenging* preschool education—"challenging" in two senses. First, we need to question current conceptions of preschool education. These conceptions tend to underestimate children and result in programs that fail to stimulate young children as much as they want and need to be stimulated in order to enjoy preschool and prepare for school (which in turn also needs to be made more exciting, stimulating, and enjoyable than it is now!). Second, we need to make preschool education more challenging than it is now for all children. We need to devise exciting, simulating, and, at the same time, developmentally appropriate preschool programs. In this article, I describe research showing that all preschoolers are capable of interesting mathematical thinking, want to engage in it, and enjoy doing so. This research suggests ways to create a mathematics education that is both "developmentally appropriate" for preschoolers and more stimulating and enjoyable than what they now receive.

WHAT SHOULD PRESCHOOL EDUCATION INVOLVE?

Across the United States, and indeed around the world, an increasingly large number of families—both two-parent and one-parent families—require child care because of work. In New York City, for example, there are hundreds of private daycare centers and nursery schools, and the New York City Agency for Child Development (ACD) serves some 50,000 preschool children, most of them poor African American and Latino children, in various daycare and Head Start settings. New York State has introduced an initiative to mandate universal preschool education. All four- and five-year-olds in New York State now have the right (although not necessarily the opportunity) to attend a preschool. The public schools in many states are opening preschools and, in some cases, kindergartens for the first time.

As these demographic trends intensify, there is a great deal of ferment in early childhood education. Everyone of course agrees that we must provide preschoolers with safe care and we must enhance their physical, social, and emotional development. But many now recognize that these goals, although essential, are not sufficient. Many early childhood educators and parents are grappling with the fundamental question of how we can improve *education* for the children in daycare and preschool, particularly four- and five-year-olds.

- States like Texas have undertaken the task of rethinking what preschool education ought to cover. This has led to the development of Texas' Prekindergarten Curriculum Guidelines.

- The National Science Foundation and the U.S. Office of Education have funded new initiatives to develop mathematics and science curricula for preschool and kindergarten children.
- Programs like *Sesame Street, Blue's Clues,* and *Reading Rainbow* are planning to expand the intellectual content of their preschool offerings.
- Large textbook publishers are considering whether to produce preschool materials and what form they should take.

This article aims to contribute to the discussion of the nature, goals, and content of preschool education. I argue that we need to *educate* preschoolers in at least two ways: we must promote their current intellectual development, and we must prepare them for schooling so that they can succeed in their academic work.

Further, we have a special responsibility to provide poor children and disadvantaged minority children with effective early education. Because they lack the advantages and resources available to middle-class children, because they are at risk of school failure and at risk of attending failing schools, and because they are likely to be short-changed when it comes to receiving a decent elementary school education, they need all the early preparation they can get.

Unfortunately, we have not done very well by these children. We generally provide very little financial support to early childhood programs. Daycare providers and preschool teachers receive little training, are poorly paid, and often must make do with minimal facilities and equipment. This is yet one more example of this country's shameful neglect of its children.

Further, the educational community has developed little in the way of interesting educational activities for preschoolers. Often, daycare providers perceive no alternative but to seat the children in front of the television or to impose on them dreadful workbooks for the purpose of teaching reading, writing, and arithmetic.

> Aside from a few exclusive nursery schools, education receives low priority in most daycare and preschool settings.

Sad to say, it is a fact that aside from a few exclusive nursery schools, education receives low priority in most daycare and preschool settings. In most cases, adults do little to foster development of the mind beyond helping children to count and to recognize common shapes, and beyond reading books to children and teaching them to make the letters. These of course can be worthwhile activities, but as we shall see, they do not come close to responding to preschool children's cognitive needs.

Why this lack of attention to preschool *education*? One reason, I think, is that we have lacked both a clear understanding of young children's cognitive development and a coherent vision of the very nature and goals of early childhood education. The National Association for the Education of Young Children (Bredekamp & Copple, 1997) correctly advises us to avoid rote drill in the preschool—also not a very good idea as the mainstay of education at the older grades, too!—and, instead, to present young children with developmentally appropriate learning activities.

But many preschool educators are unclear about the notion of developmentally appropriate practice. Should young children be limited to relatively simple and concrete forms of learning as is often the case in many preschool facilities? Is it developmentally appropriate for four-year-olds to learn some mathematics and reading? What kinds of activities will get them ready for school? What role should adults play in guiding the learning and development of preschool children? Until we have theory and evidence that help us answer questions about the nature of preschoolers' minds and about the ways in which they can be helped to learn, it will be very hard to develop appropriate preschool programs.

Psychological research conducted over the past twenty or thirty years can help illuminate some of these issues. Psychologists have made important discoveries about preschoolers' minds, about the deep questions preschoolers implicitly ask, and about the ways in which preschoolers attempt to construct an understanding of the world. As a result of this research, psychologists are now in a position to suggest a focus and goals for preschool education, and can offer new insights into both "developmentally appropriate" learning and teaching for preschoolers and into the tangled issue of school readiness. In this article, I focus on research dealing with preschoolers' mathematical thinking because it offers a fascinating view of preschoolers' minds and their intellectual motivation and suggests some important lessons for preschool education. To convey the essence of this work, I describe in detail a few examples. Keep in mind, however, that

> It is a myth that young children have a short attention span for intellectual activities.

these examples are entirely representative of preschoolers generally; they are not odd or unusual cases.

A CLINICAL INTERVIEW WITH ABDUL

Here is an interview with Abdul: newly four, a recent immigrant from Africa, and a member of a low-income family. At the time I saw him, he was attending a local daycare center that did not devote much effort to mathematics education beyond simple counting. I asked him and other children in the center if they would like to have a turn "playing some games" with me. In "clinical interviews" like these, I give the child activities to engage in, games to play, materials to work with, and continually ask the child to describe how he or she is thinking and solving the various problems. The interview lasts anywhere from twenty to forty minutes. I end the interview sooner than that if the child does not like it. But that seldom is the case. Most children thoroughly enjoy these activities and often do not want to leave. After all, young children seldom receive so much individual attention from an adult who is interested in their thinking.

Abdul was no exception. He thoroughly enjoyed the various activities, stayed in the interview for some thirty to forty minutes, and in the end practically had to be dragged away so that other children could participate. It is a myth that young children have a short attention span for intellectual activities. If interested, four- and five-year-olds—and even some three-year-olds—can work at least thirty to forty minutes on challenging tasks. This is a general phenomenon: under the right conditions—and the right conditions usually are not the conditions of standard testing—young children are capable of an attention span much longer than that normally attributed to them.

I placed on the table five red checkers and asked Abdul to count them.

Interviewer (I): How many red ones are there?

Abdul counted very carefully, touching each checker as he counted it, and concluded very firmly that there were five altogether.

Abdul (A):   Five!

I: Very good. Now let's make believe that you have five red apples.

A: [interrupts, eagerly exclaiming] I'll do it, I'll do it.

Abdul was extremely excited about all of the tasks and often wanted to get involved in a very active way, touching objects, moving them. He basically tried to take over the interviewer's role, so that it was necessary to calm him down a bit.

I: No, it's my turn. You have five red apples here, and you go to the store and you get some more. *[I placed three more red checkers on the table, separate from the first group of five. Referring to the new group of three, I asked:]* How many apples are here?

Abdul held up three fingers.

I: How many is that?

A: Three.

I: How many do you have altogether now?

Abdul carefully moved all of the checkers into one group containing two rows of four checkers each, like this:

He touched each checker, pair by pair, and counted it out loud. As he counted the fifth, he looked up to check my expression and in doing so skipped the sixth, so that he concluded that there were seven altogether.

Consider what has happened so far. First of all, Abdul showed a high degree of motivation in these apparently simple and perhaps dull counting tasks. Abdul's vivid interest in mathematical questions was evident; his excitement was palpable. The same cannot be said of many children in school. Abdul's behavior indicates that mathematical tasks can be "motivationally appropriate" for four-year-olds. A corollary is that it would be developmentally inappropriate to prevent young children from engaging in activities like these.

Most of us have been so turned off by many years of deadly schooling in mathematics—what the philosopher Arlo Guthrie calls "the boring method of education"[2]—that we forget how intrinsically fascinating basic mathematical questions are. From the little child's point of view, profound mysteries and puzzles are involved in such questions as, If I count these things this way—ball, pen, paper—and I get "three," what happens if I count them in another way—paper, pen, ball? I called the paper "three" the first time, but then I called the ball "three." How can they both be "three"? And what does "three" mean anyway? I call the ball "ball" and I also call it "three." Does "three" refer to the ball only or to the paper, pen, and ball? And if so, is this the same "three" that can also be used to describe a unicorn, Alexander the Great, and a popsicle? In the child's mind, these are questions worth careful thought, and they deliver pleasurable engagement.

Second, Abdul's work also shows that he possessed an "everyday" concept (Vygotsky, 1996) of addition as combining things (later he showed that he saw subtraction as taking things away). After all, combining (getting more) and taking away (or losing) are fundamental emotional events in children's lives. Is it not essential that they learn about these things, even if their parents are unaware of their doing so?

Abdul had *ideas* about addition and subtraction as well as techniques for calculation. He knew that adding involves combining sets, and he used counting to accomplish the result. At the outset, his idea of addition was sound, and so was his strategy. In fact, his strategy—placing objects in pairs—was elegant in the way it arranged objects in a manner highly convenient for counting. But although the spirit is willing, the flesh can be weak: he failed to execute the strategy, skipping an object when he looked up at me. The resulting wrong answer, it is clear, does not provide an accurate measure of either his basic idea or his strategy for calculation. To understand children, we usually need to get beyond standard testing: we need to observe, to question in flexible ways, and to interpret sensibly, as is possible in the clinical interview.

I saw that Abdul was wrong simply because he skipped an object. Instead of telling him that he was wrong or giving him the right answer, I asked him to try again.

I: OK, Abdul, do it again, more carefully.

At this point I thought that Abdul was about to go down a dangerous path. He undid the two by four arrangement of checkers and instead placed them in a circle. I was concerned with his strategy because a circle is a decidedly inelegant arrangement of objects for the purpose of counting. Unless he was able to remember where he started, he might not know where to stop counting. But Abdul proved my pessimism unwarranted. He counted all of the checkers once and only once, stopping at the right place and getting the correct answer—eight. This might be taken to show that what is the most rational approach for an adult may not necessarily be the most effective method for a child. Adults, be humble: let children try it their (apparently inferior) way.

I: OK. Now Big Bird comes and takes away some apples. How many are left?

Abdul noted that two were taken away, counted those remaining, and correctly reported that six were left.

I: Now Big Bird brings *back* the two apples. How many are there now?

Abdul sighed deeply and began to count again the set of eight apples. Of course, knowing that if two apples were taken away from but then returned to a set (of any size), the adult would not have to count but would immediately *know* that the set must have what it started with, which in this case was eight. Once again Abdul counted accurately his not particularly well-arranged collection and concluded, as if it were a completely new result, that the number was eight.

In this episode, Abdul demonstrated some reasoning difficulties characteristic of young children. He failed to understand the inverse relation between addition and subtraction. He did not see that if you start with eight, take away two, and then return two, eight checkers *must* remain. It is a logical necessity; you do not need to calculate to get the answer—you just need to *think*. But young children generally have difficulties with "reversibility" problems of this sort (Piaget, 1965).

We have seen that despite evident limitations, Abdul, like most other four-year-olds from all social classes and ethnic groups, has some knowledge and skill in counting, addition, and subtraction, as well as considerable interest in these topics. How does the child develop notions like these? The child lives in an environment replete with quantitative events and relations. "My brother has more cookies than I do," a clear inequality, or, "The daddy bear gets the largest bed, the mommy bear the middle bed, and the baby bear the smallest," a simple and morally appropriate functional relation. In coping with these situations, the child, aided by tools provided by the culture—chiefly, a system for counting—*must* develop mathematical ideas. As Vygotsky put it, ". . . children's learning begins long before they enter school. . . . children begin to study arithmetic in school, but long beforehand they have had some experience with quantity—they have had to deal with operations of division, addition, subtraction, and the determination of size. Consequently, children have their own preschool arithmetic, which only myopic psychologists could ignore" (Vygotsky, 2006, p. 84). Vygotsky was right about the preschool arithmetic but wrong about who ignores it. Not only psychologists, but parents and teachers are also often unaware of the child's labors and mostly do not provide help.

This example of preschool children's intellectual competence and curiosity is significant and should not be ignored. As Montessori put it, "Ah, before . . . dense and willful disregard of the life which is growing within these children, we should hide our heads in shame and cover our guilty faces with our hands!" (Montessori, 1988).

But I have shown you only one example. You may well ask, How general are phenomena like these? We have conducted research showing that this one little boy is not at all atypical. An everyday mathematics—a system of knowledge not imposed by adult instruction, but at least partly constructed by the child—is extremely widespread. Our research has shown that before entering school, children all over the world—schooled children and unschooled children, children from literate societies and children from illiterate societies, poor children and affluent children—develop concepts like these (Ginsburg, Choi, Lopez, Netley, & Chi, 1997). Indeed, our research, as well as investigations by many others (Ginsburg, Klein, & Starkey, 1998), shows that key aspects of early everyday mathematics, like Abdul's concrete addition and subtraction, may well be universal.

WHAT DOES PLAY TELL US ABOUT CHILDREN'S MATHEMATICAL THINKING?

In attempting to understand young children's competence, we cannot rely on only one method. We must approach the issue from many directions. Clinical interviews show how children respond to adult questions. But what is the nature of children's *spontaneous* mathematical thinking? Do they think about addition and subtraction in their everyday lives? Are mathematical issues meaningful to their ordinary activities? What does "free play" reveal about their mathematical competence?

> The young child lives in an environment replete with quantitative events and relations. In coping with these situations, the child *must* develop mathematical ideas.

To find out, I have spent considerable time in daycare centers in New York City. My students and I have made observations in the classrooms, we have conducted workshops and interviews with the parents, and we have played with the children, most of whom are from low-income African American and Latino families. We have, as in the case of Abdul, conducted interviews with these same children. In the course of making observations in the classrooms, we noticed that in their everyday play, children seem to be dealing with "mathematical questions" in one way or another.

To investigate the issue carefully, we have been making videotapes of children's everyday activities and examining the mathematics inherent in them. Our technique is simple: after the children have become familiar with us and our equipment, we videotape individual children for a 15-minute period during free play. The target child, fitted with a cordless microphone, is taped during whatever he or she does and wherever the activity takes place (except the bathroom) during the free play period, which in most cases is scheduled for the early morning. We have taped some 90 children in this way (including, for purposes of comparison, low-, middle- and upper-income children).

Here is an example involving Steven's counting.

"Let me see," Steven said as he carefully poured the small beads in his hand onto the table. "Oh, man—I got one hundred." Then he started counting the beads on the table. He picked out the beads one by one, and counted, "One, two, three. . . ." When Steven reached the tenth bead, Barbara joined in, saying, "Ten, eleven, twelve. . . ." However, Barbara was not actually counting the beads although she *said* the number words in sequence. They continued counting, reaching "Twenty-five, twenty-six. . . ." Steven dropped the twenty-sixth bead, but ignored it and continued counting, picking out the next and saying "twenty-seven." Barbara kept pace, and they continued. Steven dropped the thirtieth bead. He paused for a second and said, "Wait! I made a mistake."

Notice that when he poured the beads on the table, Steven postulated a specific number of beads. Instead of saying "many" or "lots of," like many young children, he said "one hundred." He knew that a large number, whether or not it is exact, attaches to a rather large collection of beads. In this he was reasonably accurate; he did not say ten or twenty, which in fact would have been far from the mark. So Steven began by offering a plausible estimate of a large collection.

His subsequent behavior suggests that he wanted to determine whether his estimate was correct: did he really have one hundred beads? He employed counting to answer the question. Not only did he have skill in counting, he clearly knew that counting tells how many. As he counted the beads, Steven made several mistakes because the beads were difficult to grab.

> Interestingly, Steven's classmates did not ask what he was doing or why he wanted to count the beads. His counting turned into a spontaneous social activity.

Once or twice, he uttered a number word without picking up a bead; when he dropped the bead in his hand, he continued counting without replacing it. At first, he did not seem to care much about his mistakes. But when he dropped the thirtieth bead, he stopped counting. He seemed concerned at this point that his counting was not correct.

Steven poured the beads in his hands on the table and started to count them again. "One, two, three. . . ." When he counted "three," Barbara picked out one bead, showed it to him, and said, "I have one." But Steven ignored her and continued to count. When he counted "five," Barbara joined him. When he counted "ten," Barbara again showed her beads to Steven, "I got, look. . . ." But Steven again ignored her and continued counting. Barbara kept pace with him, uttering the same number words. When he counted "twelve," Barbara shouted meaningless words in his ear, as if she wanted to destroy his concentration. Steven ignored her again, and kept counting, "Nineteen, twenty [at twenty, he put out two beads], twenty-one. . . ." When Steven counted up to forty-seven (almost entirely correctly), a girl asked him, "What do you count?" Again, he ignored her and kept on counting. After "forty-nine," Steven paused. As Barbara said "fifty," Steven followed her, "—ty, fifty-one, fifty-two. . . ."

Steven's decision to count the beads all over again seemed to indicate that he was now really serious about the counting; he wanted his counting to be done right. He ignored Barbara's distractions and concentrated his attention on counting, which may have provided a sense of mastery. Interestingly, Barbara, who earlier interrupted his counting by shouting meaningless words in his ear, rescued him from being stuck at forty-nine. Her help allowed his counting to continue.

When they counted "fifty-two," Ruthie came to the table, picked out one bead, and joined their counting, "fifty-two, fifty-three . . ." Madonna also came to the table, tried to find a place, picked out one bead, and joined the counting, "fifty-six, fifty-seven . . ." The girls' counting sometimes violated the one-to-one correspondence rule; they sometimes selected several beads at once or sometimes did not select a single bead. After seventy-nine, Steven again paused. As the girls said, "eighty," Steven continued the counting, "eighty, eighty-one . . ." When they counted "eighty-five," the girls competed with one another to grab more beads. The plastic container was turned over, and the beads in the container dropped on the table and the floor and rolled in every direction. The girls grabbed the beads, trying to get more than one another. Through this entire disturbance Steven kept on counting, "eighty-six, eighty-seven . . . ninety-four."

Steven's counting turned into a social activity. Ruthie and Madonna came to the table in turn and spontaneously joined Steven's counting. Interestingly, they did not ask what he was doing or why he wanted to count the beads. They did not appear to enumerate the beads, although they correctly said the number words in sequence. Rather, they seemed to enjoy the repetitive behaviors of picking out the beads and saying the number words in a certain tune and rhythm. Steven did not care about them or what they were doing; he did not exchange a single word with them. But Steven used the help they gave him. He paused after seventy-nine, and as they said "eighty," he too said it and continued counting. For a while, the girls enjoyed picking out beads and saying the number words with Steven, but they soon became interested in having more beads than one another. Their fight over the beads led to chaos. Through this distraction, Steven's persistence in counting was surprising. He made several mistakes, but this time did not correct them. He seemed to be determined to reach one hundred no matter what.

After he picked out the ninety-fourth bead, he found no more beads on the table. He bent over and picked out a bead from those on the floor, and continued counting, "ninety-five, ninety-six, and ninety-seven . . ." (inaudible after ninety-seven). After Madonna shouted "one hundred!" raising her arm, Steven, Barbara, and Ruthie joined in, saying "one hundred!" right after her. Then Steven concluded, "We all got one hundred."

Clearly, Steven wanted to reach one hundred. Interestingly, even though the girls did not know that Steven had one hundred in mind as the end point of his counting, they all stopped counting once they reached one hundred and gave a cheer. It was a special number for all of them, worth celebration.

Steven's example is instructive in several ways. He set for himself a goal at the outset, namely to count to one hundred. Why this goal? Big numbers are challenging for little children—even though most state curriculum guidelines do not recommend counting this high and even though many early childhood educators do not believe children, especially poor children, can do it. A very popular children's book, *How Much Is a Million?* (Schwartz, 1985), explores such issues as how long would it take if you wanted to count from one to one million. How long? The answer given is twenty-three days. Perhaps Steven too wanted to know what a large number of objects actually look like, which is a question fascinating even to jaded (or mathematically challenged) adults. Further, Steven knew what counting is for and used it with skill. He generally worked with great care, sometimes but not always repeating his count when he made a mistake. He was generally accurate but, more importantly, exerted effort and, despite major distractions, stayed focused on achieving his goal. Notice, too, that other children found his work fascinating, occasionally helped out, and joined the counting party. Intellectual work is a social event for young children; indeed, social interaction seems to stimulate intellectual activity.

> Intellectual work is a social event for young children; indeed, social interaction seems to stimulate intellectual activity.

Is Steven typical? Mathematical activity appears to be a fairly frequent occurrence in the low-income children we studied, comprising slightly less than half of children's play (about 45%). In this group, the most frequently occurring mathematical activity was concerned with *patterns and shapes* (e.g., pattern and shape detection, prediction, or creation— 36%); and then *dynamics* (e.g., exploration of processes of change or transformation—22%); *relations* (e.g., magnitude evaluation or comparison—18%); *classification* (e.g., sorting, grouping, or categorization—13%); and *enumeration* (e.g., quantification or numerical judgment—11%). Interestingly enough, we found "enumeration"—the topic most frequently investigated in psychological research—relatively rarely occurring in children's play. Instead, these preschool children engaged heavily in pattern analysis and geometric thinking in their free play (Ginsburg, Inoue, & Seo, 1999).

DESIGNING PRESCHOOL EDUCATION

We have seen that both interviews and naturalistic observation reveal that preschoolers, including poor children, can and do engage in significant mathematical activities. Now, the question is how these psychological insights can guide attempts to provide preschoolers with a productive education. The research offers several lessons.

One is that we should raise our expectations concerning what preschoolers can do. At present, the expectations are low. The Agency for Child Development aims at teaching children "relatively easy skills and concepts."[3] Most American kindergarten texts expose children to numbers no higher than thirty-one, the largest number of days that can appear on the calendar.[4] Even Big Bird and the Count could stand to gain from some higher education.

As you have seen, children are ready for more than the typical curriculum offers. Count to thirty-one? That's adult's play, not child's play. Of course, our research is not the only evidence. We know that young children can get deeply engaged in work with computers (Shade, 1997), often putting their parents' efforts to shame (Papert, 1996). You might say that children have voted with their mice for a higher level of developmentally appropriate activity. We know that at Reggio Emilia, children can engage in meaningful projects in which the intensity of the intellectual effort surpasses the ten- or twenty-minute attention span normally attributed to four-year-olds (Raines, 1997). So the first goal should be to give preschoolers exciting things to do.

Some might object that a curriculum of this type may be harmful. It might hurry children, put too much pressure on them, arouse anxiety, or distort their emotional development. Of course any approach executed badly—from Bank Street to Montessori—can produce negative effects. But these need not occur. Implemented with sensitivity and skill, a challenging preschool curriculum should be a good deal of fun for preschoolers. It satisfies their intellectual needs. They enjoy learning, are eager to learn, and have not yet been taught that they are not capable of learning. Indeed, failing to provide preschoolers with challenging experiences is harmful: it deadens their curiosity and teaches them at an early age that schooling does not respond to their needs. A challenging curriculum is particularly important for poor, disadvantaged children. They need to excel in academic work as early as possible because of the disadvantages they will face in school, and their early success may convince adults that there is no excuse for failing to educate these children.

Second, a developmentally appropriate curriculum—that is, interesting and challenging activities for young children—should respond, at least in part, to children's everyday interests, to their "personal curriculum." The research shows that in their free play preschool children implicitly "pose" important questions, like what combination of colors produces another.

> A developmentally appropriate curriculum should respond to children's everyday interests—their "personal curriculum."

Of course, they do not ask these questions explicitly. Rather, their behavior suggests that they are interested in and struggling with a variety of intellectual problems. One approach to determining the content of the curriculum, then, is to attempt to discover preschoolers' implicit questions and then to develop activities that can help preschoolers explore these issues and learn something about them. Think of the origins of "curriculum" as the teacher's attempt to help individual children explore, make explicit, formalize, and learn about issues in which they already have an interest. Later, this attempt can be made with many children; then, it is "curriculum" in the formal sense.

Third, understanding children's minds helps us think more deeply about goals for preschool education.[5] Our research suggests two major goals for preschool education. First, it should help children engage in activities enabling them to elaborate on their everyday knowledge. This everyday knowledge deals with interesting questions, and it is the child's own personal and valued possession. A second goal should be to help children understand the relations between their everyday knowledge and the ways in which the culture has come to systematize and formalize it. This type of personal knowledge is only a beginning: children need to learn how the questions they ask can be approached in a more organized, mature, and public fashion.

Fourth, how should we go about "teaching" this kind of curriculum? It is obvious that traditional, direct instruction is inappropriate for preschoolers. We certainly don't want them to engage in dull and disembodied workbook activities. But it also is clear that by itself free play is insufficient. We have seen that in daycare center settings preschoolers can go only so far in their spontaneous investigations, as valuable as these can be. At some point, children require adult assistance to formalize and generalize ideas, to become conscious of them, and to communicate them to others.

What form of adult assistance should be used with preschoolers? It should certainly be sensitive to preschoolers' distinctive psychology—to their concerns, their state of mind, their motivations, and to their modes of constructing the world. Beyond that, it is hard to say what form it should take. Experimentation is required, ideally in the kind of laboratory school John Dewey founded many years ago.

In brief, my argument is that the preschool curriculum should:

- involve high expectations,
- draw on children's everyday interests,
- aim toward the integration of everyday and formal knowledge, and
- involve some form of adult assistance, not free play alone.

CONCLUSION

Children's informal mathematical knowledge takes many forms and is more complex and interesting than usually expected. Whether or not they are somewhat behind or ahead of their more advantaged peers, poor children are capable of engaging in exciting, challenging learning—learning that our research shows is developmentally appropriate. We need to meet preschoolers' intellectual needs by providing them with stimulating intellectual activities, based at least in part on their demonstrated interests, which seem to go far beyond what current state curricula and the early childhood education community seem to recognize as appropriate for preschoolers. We should accept the challenge of challenging early childhood educators to create challenging education for our young children.

NOTES

1. The research described in this paper was supported by a generous grant from the Spencer Foundation, Grant Number 199800041.

2. Listen to his hilarious spoof of education in the song "Inch by Inch" on the disk *Precious Friend,* with Pete Seeger, Warner Brothers 3644, 1982.

3. "The Agency for Child Development discourages programs from attempting to develop . . . skills within the narrow academic confines of having children orally recite 'their numbers and A, B, C' and having them complete paper-and-pencil worksheets. Instead, programs should sequentially develop these skills by using many varied and integrated activities and methods. Each day children should actively participate in a complementary variety of 'hands-on' activities which include: block scheduling, language development, arts, crafts, outdoor play, woodworking, music, manipulative toys, socio-dramatic play, field trips, cooking, sand and water play, and science exploration. The program gives children opportunities to acquire relatively easy skills and concepts and master them before being introduced to more advanced skills" (Agency for Child Development 1996, 1).

4. The official State of Texas guidelines for textbooks require teaching kindergartners the "use of numbers to describe how many objects are in a set (through 20)" (State of Texas, 1997, Ch. 1, pp. 1–2). To be fair, this is a minimum goal, but as is well known, many teachers will teach to it, making it the final goal.

5. This is of course an old idea. According to the father of child study, "All now agree that the mind can learn only what is related to other things learned before, and that we must start from the knowledge that the children really have and develop this as germs . . ." (Hall, 1981, p. 154). Or as Dewey put it many years ago: "[Knowing] how the mind works in the construction of number, [the teacher] is prepared to help the child to think number. . . ." (McLellan & Dewey, 1907, p. 22). And of course we also want to help the preschool child to "think science" and "think reading" and think many other things. Doing this requires, as (Dewey, 2001) proposed, that we determine how the child's ". . . experience already contains within itself elements—facts and truths—of just the same sort as those entering into formulated study; and, what is of more importance, of how it contains within itself the attitudes, the motives, and the interests which have operated in developing and organizing the subject-matter to the plane which it now occupies. From the side of the studies, it is question of interpreting them as outgrowths of forces operating in the child's life, and of discovering the steps that intervene between the child's present experience and their richer maturity" (Dewey, 2001).

REFERENCES

Agency for Child Development. (1996). *Program assessment instrument.* New York: Author.

Bredekamp, S., & Copple, C. (Eds.). (1997). *Developmentally appropriate practice in early childhood programs* (Revised ed.). Washington, DC: National Association for the Education of Young Children.

Dewey, J. (2001). The child and the curriculum. In *The School and Society & The Child and the Curriculum.* Mineola, NY: Dover Publications.

Ginsburg, H. P., Choi, Y. E, Lopez, L. S., Netley, R., & Chi, C. Y. (1997). Happy birthday to you: Early mathematical thinking of Asian, South American, and U.S. children. In T. Nunes & P. Bryant (Eds.), *Learning and teaching mathematics: An international perspective* (pp. 163–207). East Sussex, England: Erlbaum (UK) Taylor and Francis.

Ginsburg, H. P., Inoue, N., & Seo, K. H. (1999). Preschoolers doing mathematics: Observations of everyday activities. In J. Copley (Ed.), *Mathematics in the early years.* Reston, VA: National Council of Teachers of Mathematics.

Ginsburg, H. P., Klein, A., & Starkey, P. (1998). The development of children's mathematical thinking: Connecting research with practice. In I. Sigel & A. Renninger (Eds.), *Handbook of child psychology: 5th ed., Vol. 4, Child psychology and practice* (pp. 401–476). New York: John Wiley and Sons.

Hall, G. S. (1891). The contents of children's minds on entering school. *Pedagogical Seminary, 1,* 139–173.

McLellan, J. A., & Dewey, J. (1907). *The psychology of number and its applications to methods of teaching arithmetic.* New York: D. Appleton.

Montessori, M. (1988). *The Montessori method* (Reissue ed.). New York: Schocken Books.

Papert, S. (1996). *The connected family: Bridging the digital generation gap.* Atlanta, GA: Longstreet Press.

Piaget, J. (1965). *The child's conception of number* (C. Gattegno & F. M. Hodgson, Trans.). New York: W.W. Norton and Co., Inc.

Raines, S. C. (1997). Developmental appropriateness: Curriculum revisited and challenged. In J. P. Isenberg & M. R. Jalongo (Eds.), *Major trends and issues in early childhood education: Challenges, controversies, and insights* (pp. 75–89). New York: Teachers College Press.

Schwartz, D. M. (1985). *How much is a million?* New York: Lothrop, Lee, and Shepard Books.

Shade, D. D. (1997). The role of computer technology in early childhood education. In J. P. Isenberg and M. R. Jalongo (Eds.), *Major trends and issues in early childhood education: Challenges, controversies, and insights* (pp. 90–103). New York: Teachers College Press.

State of Texas. (1997). *Texas essential knowledge and skills for mathematics.* Austin, TX: Author.

Vygotsky, L. S. (1996). *Thought and language* (A. Kozulin, Trans.). Cambridge, MA: The MIT Press.

Vygotsky, L. S. (2006). *Mind in society: The development of higher psychological processes* (New ed.). Cambridge, MA: Harvard University Press.

Infusing Higher Order Thinking Into Science and Language Arts

Joyce VanTassel-Baska

Joyce VanTassel-Baska is the Jody and Layton Smith Professor of Education and Director for the Center for Gifted Education at the College of William and Mary. Her research focuses on studies in curriculum and instructional interventions with gifted students and work on variables associated with the development of talent, especially for disadvantaged learners. She is the past president of CEC-TAG and is on the board of directors for the National Association for Gifted Children (NAGC). She is the author of twenty books and more than 345 articles, scholarly reports and book chapters. She was selected as a Fulbright Scholar to New Zealand in 2000.

How do we address the needs of our best learners in schools? This central question can be answered in several ways, all of which relate to the teaching of higher order thinking. Through the use of inquiry models that promote both convergent and divergent thinking, high-ability students may be best served.

VanTassel-Baska (1993a) examined research support for curriculum promoting higher order thinking:

Studies of thinking have strongly contributed to understanding curriculum directions for the gifted. Expert-novice comparisons in various fields (Berliner, 1985; Sommers, 1982) have yielded differences favoring experts in metacognitive acts like planning and revising. A collection of research on expertise has revealed that the successful utilization of these skills may be content-specific. Rabinowitz and Glaser (1985) found that expert performance entailed a large knowledge base of domain-specific patterns, rapid recognition of situations in which these patterns apply, and the use of forward reasoning based on pattern manipulation to reach solutions.

Further support for such domain-specific research comes out of studies that use general content-independent cognitive strategies and that find no clear benefits outside the specific domains in which they are taught (Pressley, Snyder, & Carigha-Bull, 1987). Thus, research on transfer suggests that "thinking at its most effective [level] depends on specific context-bound skills and units of knowledge that have little application to other domains." (Perkins & Saloman, 1989, p. 119)

Teaching thinking skills to the gifted, then, or any learner, requires an integrated approach, with attention to several variables simultaneously. Curriculum for the gifted must always be concerned about multiple outcomes in the cognitive, affective, aesthetic, and social areas. Such curriculum can be deliberately designed in an integrated fashion to address all of these dimensions through an approach that recognizes the importance of three interrelated aspects:

1. Advanced content that honors the child's level of precocity in domain-specific areas,

2. Higher level thinking and problem-solving processes that honor the gifted child's ability to explore topics in greater depth resulting in substantive products, and

3. The use of interdisciplinary concepts, problems, and issues that honor the child's ability to make connections within and across domains of knowledge (VanTassel-Baska, 1992).

For the past eight years, with the support of special grants from the United States Department of Education, we at the Center for Gifted Education have been involved in the process of designing, field testing, and revising curriculum for gifted learners based on this conceptual model. Key aspects of curriculum development have included collaboration with experts in the content domains of science and language arts in the development process; review of existing curriculum materials based on validated criteria for what constitutes: an appropriate curriculum generally, an exemplary curriculum in the subject areas, and an appropriate curriculum for gifted learners; the development of teacher training workshops on core strategies integrated into the units; and conducting three phases of research: on student learning gains, teacher implementation issues, and school change as a result of using the College of William and Mary curriculum units.

> Teaching thinking skills to the gifted learner, and to all learners, requires an integrated approach, with attention to several variables simultaneously.

THE PROCESS OF CURRICULUM INFUSION

Several key features were part of the curriculum development process that appeared to make a difference with respect to the infusion of higher order thinking into the curriculum, the degree of acceptance in schools, and key aspects of classroom implementation (VanTassel-Baska, 1993b; VanTassel-Baska, Gallagher, Bailey, & Sher, 1993). These features included the following:

The importance of frameworks. Each of the curriculum projects has developed a set of goals and underlying objectives that provided the anchor point for curriculum development, implementation, and assessment. These frameworks, developed on the Integrated Curriculum Model (ICM) cited in earlier work (VanTassel-Baska, 1992, 1994, 1995), served as a coherent structure for all phases of the work.

The curriculum, instruction, and assessment (CIA) relationship. The interplay of curriculum, instruction, and assessment is a critical understanding in the curriculum design enterprise. It becomes even more critical as teachers implement a new curriculum that they understand how these three pieces fit together to enhance learning.

The collaborative nature of the development work. Our work was only possible because of the efforts of individuals with varying expertise and perspectives. For instance, the inclusion of a molecular biologist as a major player in developing science curriculum cannot be underestimated with respect to the integrity of the effort. Similar expertise was enlisted in English and the language arts.

The alignment of national, state, and local standards. Part of the task in these projects is to show how one can serve high-end learners and address state and local concerns for curriculum mastery. Given that both projects were modeled on the National Standards work, the alignment tasks were very straightforward.

The linkage to other exemplary materials. We have also worked to link our materials to other exemplary materials found through an extensive evaluation process (Johnson, Boyce, & VanTassel-Baska, 1995). In science, we have aligned our work with several materials developed at Lawrence Hall of Science, including Great Explorations in Math and Science (GEMS), Full Option Science System (FOSS), and Insights. In language arts, we have established a relationship with the Junior Great Books Program, modeling our literature selections and questions after its approach.

Training on materials. Based on our preliminary work with these projects, we decided to develop a training model that was grounded in enhancing chances for strong implementation. Therefore, our training efforts modeled those employed by many National Science Foundation (NSF) projects, using materials as the basis for teaching strategies necessary for classroom use. Such an approach proved to be a critical component of our efforts. We have now conducted training in over thirty states and have implementation sites in twenty-two of them as a result. National training was also conducted at the College of William and Mary over a three-year period.

THE RESEARCH AGENDA

The research agenda for the project emerged out of the need to move beyond pilot efforts in teacher developer classrooms. Toward that end we began to look more closely at questions of impact. The overall model for how the curriculum development effort links to research may be found in Figure 4.1. Currently, the Center faculty, staff, and graduate students are engaged in a series of studies that are examining aspects of the implementation of the curriculum and its underlying pedagogy in schools. These studies may be clustered around the following categories:

Curriculum Effectiveness Studies

We are engaged in a series of curriculum effectiveness studies that are examining the curriculum impact by unit, by developmental level (primary, intermediate, and middle school), by classrooms over time (implementation of three or more units), and by teachers over time (three-year implementations). Moreover, the Center is also conducting replications of basic student impact studies at new sites (VanTassel-Baska, Hughes, Johnson, Boyce, & Hall, 1997).

Classroom Implementation Studies

We also are interested in understanding how the curriculum works on a day-to-day basis at the classroom level. Thus, we are exploring teacher behaviors, use of specific strategies and embedded assessments (non-usable material, modifications, and extensions), and classroom interaction processes.

Special Population Studies

We also wish to understand the impact of the curriculum on special populations of students, especially disadvantaged and minority students. Two questions of interest are (1) how effective is the curriculum with disadvantaged and minority students? and (2) are the effects differential or comparable to those found with more advantaged populations? Comparisons of student outcome effects with other special populations are of interest as well. One dissertation study, for example, is focusing on the teaching of persuasive writing through the use of the Paul model with gifted, learning disabled, and average students (Hughes, in preparation).

Classroom and School Studies of Change

Finally, we have an interest in studying how the curriculum impacts school change and reform. Consequently, we are studying teacher use of the units over three years and more to determine collective impacts on school and district use over time (VanTassel-Baska, Avery, Little, & Hughes, under review). We are specifically

Figure 4.1   Model of Curriculum Development Process

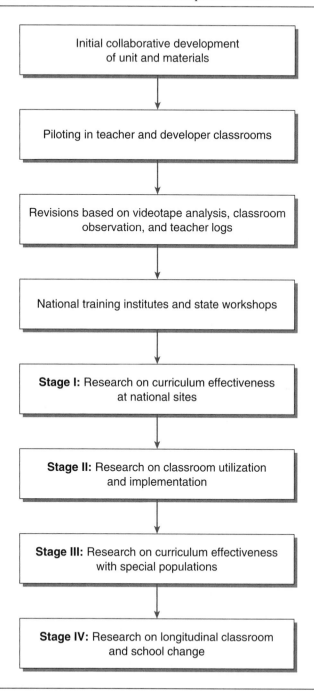

interested in how institutionalized the curriculum becomes in selected districts as judged by its presence in district policies, its classroom utility, and perceptions of it among relevant stakeholders, such as parents, students, and teachers.

NATURE OF PRELIMINARY FINDINGS

In the area of science we have found significant but modest gains for experimental groups on a pre- and postmeasure of integrated science process skills (Fowler, 1990). Content analysis of student responses across 45 classrooms reveals students do not demonstrate gains in skills such as planning data collection, planning to control variables, interpreting data, and drawing conclusions. All of these skill areas require higher order thinking. Individual students, however, are showing strong improvement even in these areas.

The following example represents a preassessment for science learning in Grade 3. The prompt is the question "Are earthworms attracted to light?" The protocol is a 22-point scale judging initial layout, examination of data, and evaluation of results.

Student A pretest response:

First, I would put some earthworms in a container. There would be lights and some dirt. I would put several different earthworms in it. If more earthworms liked the light, then that would be right. If more didn't like the light, then that would be right. I would try this with about seven groups and decide if they liked light.

The student in this pretest response reveals much about what he knows and doesn't know about the scientific design process. First, he demonstrates a narrative orientation to the prompt rather than a scientific one. He has an idea of "procedures" and is able to demonstrate a rudimentary manipulation of materials. He also has a sense about the setting of criterion levels for judging the results of experiments.

After 25 hours of instruction in a specially designed problem-based science curriculum unit, Student A's post-test response to the prompt "Are bees attracted to diet cola?" is as follows:

Materials: Diet cola, 3 large containers, 3 small containers, 6 bees

Hypothesis: If you give bees diet cola then they will be attracted to it

1. Gather 6 bees, diet cola, 3 large containers, 3 small containers.

2. Put 2 bees in each large container.

3. Pour 5 ml of diet cola in each small container.

4. Set the small container of diet cola in each large container that has bees in it.

5. Watch and observe to see if the bees are attracted to the diet cola.

6. You should record if the bees like diet cola on a chart like below.

Bee	If they are attracted to diet cola
1	
2	
3	
4	
5	
6	

In this posttest response, the same student is able to perform many more scientific research tasks well. He can delineate materials, provide clear and specific procedures, formulate a hypothesis, understand the need for a data table, demonstrate precision with respect to the experiment, and demonstrate an understanding of repeated trials. His protocol score has risen from a 5 to a 14.

Has this student learned from the curriculum? Yes, in several interrelated science processes, but he still does not evince a deep understanding of the role of interpretation of results linked to the original problem, nor clear ways to judge the results of the experiment.

Why is there such limited growth overall? Three hypotheses that are being explored include (1) that the curriculum may not be faithfully implemented, (2) that teachers teach what they know and therefore may not be focusing on the higher level science skills, and (3) that an integrated curriculum model may inhibit strong growth in any given area (VanTassel-Baska, Bass, Ries, Poland, & Avery, 1998).

Teacher's qualitative responses were overwhelmingly positive in respect to using the problem-based units of study, noting that students found the units highly motivating and interesting—a perspective shared by teachers as well. Evidence of significant learning based on problem-based learning (PBL), however, is yet to be documented (Boyce, VanTassel-Baska, Burruss, Sher, & Johnson, 1997).

In the area of language arts, we have found significant and impressive gains in literature, persuasive writing, and linguistic competency for experimental classes using the curriculum (VanTassel-Baska, Johnson, Hughes, & Boyce, 1996).

An example of a performance-based assessment task and the analysis of learning that has occurred in the area of language arts may also be examined. The prompt is "Should the poem 'Autobiographia Literaria' be required reading for students in your grade level?" The protocol focuses on the development of claim, data, warrant, and conclusion and has a 20-point scale.

The preassessment response for a student in Grade 5 follows:

> In my opinion this poem has a good message because kids can relate to it. The first reason I say this is he writes about a child and his feelings, which can relate to children. Second this poem shows how much you can change in a lifetime, which teaches children. Finally this will help child who is feeling different know that he is not alone.

In a preliminary content analysis of this piece, we can note that the student's language fluency is low and relatively awkward; the fundamental structure of persuasive writing is modeled with an introduction, three reasons, but no conclusion; and the student exhibits sensitivity to literature as he discerns the theme of loneliness that changes once the narrator has been exposed to poetry.

Let us now examine the post assessment after thirty hours of instruction in a College of William and Mary language arts curriculum unit. The prompt reads, "Should the poem 'Where the Rainbow Ends' be required reading for students in your grade level?" The same student's individual response reads:

I really liked this poem "Where the Rainbow Ends" by Richard Rive. I think other kids my age would agree with me. I'm concerned about racism mainly because I'm Jewish and I know about the Holocaust. I totally agree with this poem. It's true that getting along together will be a part tune to learn.

Most kids, no matter what their parents say, will play with whoever they like. I never ask my friends their religion, I just play with them. If these kids read this poem it will enforce positive beliefs that hopefully they will pass on to their children as well.

Because he uses the metaphor of music to explain a difficult idea, it makes it easier for kids to understand. The line "There is no white music and no black music" makes the idea that there is no difference between white and black people very clear.

It's important for fifth graders to read a poem by a black poet and then see that it is no different than one written by a white poet. This shows us that there is no white and black poetry—just poetry.

This is an excellent poem for a fifth grade class. We should read words by writers from all different ethnic groups, the metaphor makes his point clear to everyone, and since most kids don't discriminate Mr. Rive's poem makes you feel you are right to think that way.

The student demonstrates competency in several areas of the prompt. His language fluency is very strong, and he has cast a well-articulated response. The persuasive structure of his argument is also very strong in both the basic areas and the elaborative structure. He shows unusually heightened sensitivity to literature, apparent from his reference to the poem's central metaphor and his ability to articulate its relationship to the social realm. He also is sensitive to multicultural literature and its value. Moreover, he displays a recognition of the insidiousness of racism and its negative impact on society.

Has this student learned from the curriculum? Yes, we would argue, he has grown in several dimensions. He exhibits ideational fluency and elaboration (creativity), writing skills essential to high-level development (i.e., thesis, argument, and a conclusion), enhanced literary analysis and interpretation skills, and a social understanding of similarities and differences among people. His protocol score moved from a 10 to a 20.

Individual content analyses reveal different patterns of growth, however. Overall findings led to follow-up implementation studies and new questions. Why, for example, is there less growth in literature analysis and interpretation than in writing for the majority of learners? Several hypotheses emerged around this question. One is that the curriculum units have a stronger emphasis on teaching the persuasive writing model directly than they do in teaching literary analysis. A second hypothesis is that the assessment of literary analysis and interpretation may not be taught to students as a self assessment rubric, as is the case for writing. A third hypothesis to be entertained focuses on the possibility of uneven implementation of the units, with more emphasis placed on persuasive writing.

In schools, we have found extensive evidence of the institutionalization of the curriculum with many constituent groups voicing strong support for its impact. Teachers remarked that the units helped students look for the big picture instead of just memorizing a lot of isolated information, while promoting teacher learning as well. Several administrators noted that teachers have learned to draw back and act as coaches, letting kids hit or miss the mark. Regarding the language arts curriculum, teachers noted that after students have been exposed to more than one unit, they began to see improvements in habits of mind, writing and self-reflection skills, and in their overall ability to work cooperatively in groups.

> Students agreed that the gifted materials keep their minds working. One perceptive young man observed: "We get smarter as the units get harder."

Parents cited the benefits of the units' carryover into the home. One parent noted: "When my child hears a speaker, he starts to critique what is being said and how things are interrelated." Another parent related: "This notion of having three arguments has now permeated our life. We wanted to go bowling and my son kept saying 'elaborate.'" Students agreed that the gifted materials keep their minds working, and one perceptive young man observed: "We get smarter as the units get harder."

IMPLICATIONS FOR PRACTICE

The benefit of using sound, well-designed curriculum is a clear implication in all of our studies. Until the field is ready to critique existing materials and seek uniform high quality, student learning will not be positively impacted. Variability in instructional technique also appears to be critical, particularly the use of inquiry—a central focus of all curriculum units in both science and language arts. The use of assessment as a direct vehicle for learning is also strongly recommended. It must be habitual, and rubrics need to be taught to students with well-defined criteria for guiding judgment. Monitoring implementation in the school context is also essential to curriculum success. Moreover, the role of the principal and how staff development needs are addressed greatly influence positive effects.

In addition, there is a need for equal emphasis on the dynamics of curriculum, instruction, and assessment in the teaching and learning enterprise. Balanced emphasis on these dynamics may be the most vital force to yield the positive change in education desperately sought by so many.

Key variables in the curriculum development cycle need to include equal attention to each part of the cycle. For curriculum, appropriate goals and outcomes are essential to begin the process, followed by activities that address those outcomes in a substantive manner. The curriculum must also be exemplary for the subject matter under study, representing the new national standards projects in all subject areas. It also should be designed according to high ability needs to ensure the level of challenge necessary for all students' success.

Appropriate instructional emphasis requires the use of multiple types of strategies that simultaneously reflect classroom management of various groups, flexible use of differentiated materials, and the manipulation of core strategies. An emphasis on inquiry must be present to ensure the mental engagement of the learner. A balance also needs to be struck between direct instruction and facilitation. The encouragement and use of higher-level questions toward a focus or goal is likewise a critical component of instruction for gifted learners. Furthermore, effective use of individual, small group, and large group activities forms a basic part of effective teaching.

Assessment has to be viewed as integral to the teaching process, yielding important diagnostic information used to promote learning. Assessment should be frequent and ongoing, and include both performance-based and standardized measures. Most important as a teaching tool is the use of specific criteria for judgment of performance. Through these teachers can instill standards of excellence toward which students may aim.

While the curriculum, instruction, and assessment dynamic is important, it is also critical that school administrators see their role as instructional leaders, ensuring that a learning dynamic is taking place in an appropriate way. Thus, monitoring classroom implementation is essential to the integrity of the process. The role of the principal as a visible instructional leader in classrooms puts the emphasis on student growth, where it belongs. In such a system, emergent staff development needs can be discerned through judging day-to-day practice. Teacher leaders can also act as catalysts in this process, engaging in peer coaching and other means to promote positive change.

Finally, it is important to specify what we mean by positive change for any learner, and what our understanding of the gifted contributes to this often used but vague term. There are three essential components to judging positive change in a school context: enhanced learning for students, a climate of excellence, and learning-centered students, parents, and teachers. Until student learning is at the center of judgments made about any reform, it is a meaningless exercise in the techniques of schooling. In respect to a climate of excellence, a school must provide visible symbols that learning matters. Lastly, learning-oriented stakeholders in the educational process are a necessary part of positive change. Teachers, parents, and students must collectively accept that the process of learning over a lifetime is a core value to be nurtured and internalized.

> To create a climate of excellence, a school must provide visible symbols that learning matters.

Can appropriate curriculum become a reality in schools? The answer is a tentative "yes." We have 55 school districts in our national network of schools, using both the science and language arts units, and 100 districts using one or more units. Reports and ongoing work with these districts indicate a reawakening of concern for coherence and quality in curriculum. Real learning for our best students has become a reality.

REFERENCES

Berliner, D. (1985). *Presidential address to the American Educational Research Association.* San Francisco, CA.

Boyce, L. N., VanTassel-Baska, J., Burruss, J. D., Sher, B. T., & Johnson, D. T. (1997). A problem-based curriculum: Parallel learning opportunities for students and teachers. *Journal for the Education of the Gifted, 20,* 363–379.

Fowler, M. (1990). The diet cola test. *Science Scope, 13*(4), 32–34.

Hughes, C. (2000). *A comparative study of teaching critical thinking through persuasive writing to average, gifted and students with learning disabilities.* Doctoral dissertation, Indiana University in Pennsylvania.

Johnson, D. T., Boyce, L. N., & VanTassel-Baska, J. (1995). Science curriculum review: Evaluating materials for high-ability learners. *Gifted Child Quarterly, 39*, 36–43.

Perkins, D., & Saloman, G. (1989). Are cognitive research skills context bound? *Educational Researcher, 18*(1), 16–25.

Pressley, M., Snyder, B., & Carigha-Bull, T. (1987). How can good strategy use be taught to children? Evaluation of six alternative approaches. In S. M. Corner & J. D. Hagman (Eds.), *Transfer of learning* (pp. 81–120). New York: Academic.

Rabinowitz, M., & Glaser, R. (1985). Cognitive structure and process on highly competent performance. In E. D. Horowitz & M. O'Brien (Eds.), *The gifted and talented: Developmental perspectives* (pp. 75–98). Washington, DC: American Psychological Association.

Sommers, N. (1982). Revision strategies of student writers and experienced writers. *College Composition and Communications, 31*, 378–387.

VanTassel-Baska, J. (1992). *Planning effective curriculum for gifted learners.* Denver, CO: Love Publishing.

VanTassel-Baska, J. (1993a). Theory and research on curriculum development for the gifted. In K. A. Heller, F. J. Minks, & A. H. Passow (Eds.), *International handbook of research and development of giftedness and talent* (pp. 365–386). New York: Pergamon Press.

VanTassel-Baska, J. (1993b). The National Curriculum Development Projects for high ability learners: Key issues and findings. In N. Colangelo, S. G. Assouline, & D. L. Ambroson (Eds.), *Talent development* (Vol. 2, pp. 19–38). Dayton, OH: Ohio Psychology Press.

VanTassel-Baska, J. (1994). *Comprehensive curriculum for gifted learners* (2nd ed.). Boston: Allyn & Bacon.

VanTassel-Baska, J. (1995). The development of talent through curriculum. *Roeper Review, 18*, 98–102.

VanTassel-Baska, J., Avery, L. D., Little, C. A., & Hughes, C. E. (2000). An evaluation of the implementation of curriculum innovation: The impact of the William and Mary units on schools. *Journal for the Education of the Gifted, 23*(2), 244–270.

VanTassel-Baska, J., Bass, G., Ries, R., Poland, D., & Avery, L. (1998). A national pilot study of science curriculum effectiveness for high ability students. *Gifted Child Quarterly, 42*, 200–211.

VanTassel-Baska, J., Gallagher, S. A., Bailey, J. M., & Sher, B. T. (1993). Scientific experimentation. *Gifted Child Today, 16*(5), 42–46.

VanTassel-Baska, J., Hughes, C. E., Johnson, D. T., Boyce, L. N., & Hall, D. R. (1997, April). Language arts curriculum effectiveness study: Results of a curriculum developed for high ability students. Presentation given at the annual meeting of the American Educational Education Association, Chicago, IL.

VanTassel-Baska, J., Johnson, D. T., Hughes, C. E., & Boyce, L. N. (1996). A study of language arts curriculum effectiveness with gifted learners. *Journal for the Education of the Gifted, 19*, 461–480.

A Practical Approach for Developing the Gifts and Talents of All Students

Joseph S. Renzulli

Joseph S. Renzulli *is Professor of Gifted Education and Talent Development at the Neag Center, University of Connecticut, where he also serves as Director of the National Research Center on the Gifted and Talented. He has served on numerous editorial boards in the field of gifted education and has served as a senior research associate for the White House Task Force on Education for the Gifted and Talented.*

If there is one thing upon which most leaders of educational reform agree, it is that remedial models for school improvement have failed. Attempts to boost achievement test scores from "the bottom" through highly prescriptive mastery learning models have frustrated low-achieving students and dragged down the performance of average and high-achieving youngsters. An alternative to what one student called the "drill-and-kill" approach is an enrichment-based model that uses "high-end learning" strategies and accelerated content to improve the performance of all students.

The advent of instructional technology and easy access to the Internet have now put the resources necessary for high-end learning within easy reach of all teachers. After describing the enrichment model upon which this chapter is based, I will describe an online enrichment program that one teacher said was the equivalent of

". . . having a dozen teaching assistants in my classroom every day, all day!"

The Schoolwide Enrichment Model (SEM) is a detailed blueprint for total school improvement that is flexible enough to allow each school to develop its own unique program based on local resources, student populations, school leadership dynamics, and faculty strengths and creativity. Although this research-supported model is based on highly successful practices that have their origins in special programs for gifted and talented students, its major goal is to promote both challenging and enjoyable high-end learning across the full range of school types, levels, and demographic differences. It is not intended to replace or minimize existing services to high-achieving students. Rather, its purpose is to integrate these services into "a rising tide lifts all ships" approach to school improvement, and to expand the role of enrichment specialists by having these persons infuse specific practices for high-end learning into the total school program. The Schoolwide Enrichment Model provides educators with the means to:

- Develop the talent potentials of young people by systematically assessing their strengths, providing enrichment opportunities, resources, and services to develop their strengths, and using a flexible approach to curricular differentiation and the use of school time.
- Improve the academic performance of all students in all areas of the regular curriculum and to blend standard curriculum activities with meaningful enrichment learning.
- Promote the continuous, reflective, growth-oriented professional development of school personnel to such an extent that many faculty members emerge as leaders in curriculum and staff development, program planning, etc.
- Create a learning community that honors ethnic, gender, and cultural diversity and that promotes mutual respect, democratic principles, and the preservation of the earth's resources.

A Case in Point

Two afternoons a week, twelve-year-old Kelvin goes to an enrichment cluster at the Noah Webster School in Hartford, Connecticut. When he was selected for the program, Kelvin said, "It feels good, but I was amazed. I was about to faint! I was super, super surprised." The reason for Kelvin's amazement is that he never considered himself to be a good student, at least not in the traditional way we usually view students. And the program was not exactly the place where you found kids like Kelvin, who lives in subsidized housing and whose family manages to survive on a monthly welfare check and food stamps.

But the program in which Kelvin is enrolled looks at talent development in a different way. Based on a plan called the Schoolwide Enrichment Model, the program seeks to identify a broad range of talent potentials in all students through the use of a strength assessment guide called the Total Talent Portfolio. This guide helps to focus attention on student interests and learning style preferences as well as strengths in traditional subjects. These strengths serve as building blocks for advanced achievement. Kelvin's strongest academic area is mathematics, and through a process called curriculum compacting, he is now being provided with mathematics material that is two grade levels above the level of math being covered in his classroom.

Kelvin, who once described himself as a "mental dropout," now finds school a much more inviting place. He is hoping to enter the research he is doing on airplane wing design in his enrichment cluster into a state science fair competition. He is also thinking about a career in engineering, and the enrichment specialist at his school has helped him apply for a special summer program at the University of Connecticut that is designed to recruit and assist minorities into mathematical- and engineering-related professions. "School," says Kelvin, "is a place where you have must-dos and can-dos. I work harder on my must-dos so I can spend more time working on my can-dos."

THE SECRET LABORATORY OF SCHOOL IMPROVEMENT

Kelvin represents one example of the ways in which numerous students are being given opportunities to develop talent potentials that too many schools have ignored for too many years. The type of program in which Kelvin is enrolled is not a radical departure from present school structures, but it is based on assumptions about learners and learning that are different from those that have guided public education for many years. We must consider new ways of solving problems, methods other than using the levels of consciousness that created these problems if there is to be any hope of turning around a public education system that is slowly but surely deteriorating into a massive warehouse of underachievement, unfulfilled expectations, and broken dreams. The factory model of schooling that gave rise to the clear and present danger facing our schools cannot be used to overcome the very problems that this model of schooling has created. And yet, as we examine reform initiatives, it is difficult to find plans and policies that are qualitatively different from the old top-down patterns of school organization or the traditional linear and sequential models of learning that have dominated almost the entire curriculum used in our schools. Transcending these previous levels of consciousness will not be an easy task. If there is any single, unifying characteristic of present-day schools, that characteristic is surely a resistance, if not an immunity, to change. The ponderous rhetoric about school improvement and the endless lists of noble goals need to be tempered with a gentle and evolutionary approach to change that school personnel can live and grow with rather than be threatened by. If traditional methods of schooling have failed to bring about substantial changes, we must look at different models that have shown promise of achieving the types of school improvement we so desperately have sought.

This article describes a plan that has demonstrated its effectiveness in bringing about significant changes in schooling. The plan, entitled the Schoolwide Enrichment Model (SEM), is a systematic set of specific strategies for increasing student effort, enjoyment, and performance and for integrating a broad range of advanced-level learning experiences and higher-order thinking skills into any curricular area, course of study, or pattern of school organization. The general approach of the SEM is one of infusing more effective practices into existing school structures rather than layering on additional things for schools to do. This research-supported plan is designed for general education, but it is based on a large number of instructional methods and curricular practices that had their origins in special programs for high-ability students.

> Special programs have been the true laboratories of our nation's schools, because they present ideal opportunities for testing new ideas and experimenting with potential solutions to long-standing educational problems.

In many respects, special programs of almost any type have been the true laboratories of our nation's schools because they have presented ideal opportunities for testing new ideas and experimenting with potential solutions to long-standing educational problems. Programs for high potential students have been an especially fertile place for experimentation because such programs usually are not encumbered by prescribed curriculum guides or traditional methods of instruction. It was within the context of these programs that the thinking skills movement first took hold in American education and the pioneering work of notable theorists such as Benjamin Bloom, Howard Gardner, and Robert Sternberg first gained the attention of the education community. Other developments that had their origins in special programs are currently being examined for general practice. These developments include a focus on concept rather than skill learning, the use of interdisciplinary curriculum and theme-based studies, student portfolios, performance assessment, cross-grade grouping, alternative scheduling patterns, and perhaps most important, opportunities for students to exchange traditional roles as lesson-learners and doers-of-exercises for more challenging and demanding roles that require hands-on learning, firsthand investigations and the *application* of knowledge and thinking skills to complex problems.

Research opportunities in a variety of special programs allowed researchers at the Neag Center for Gifted Education and Talent Development at the University of Connecticut to develop instructional procedures and programming alternatives that emphasize the need to (1) provide a broad range of advanced level enrichment experiences for *all* students, and to (2) use the many and varied ways that students respond to these experiences as stepping-stones for relevant follow-up on the parts of individuals or small groups. This approach is not viewed as a new way to identify who is or is not "gifted." Rather, the process simply identifies how subsequent *opportunities, resources,* and *encouragement* can be provided to support continuous escalations of student involvement in both required and self-selected activities. This approach to the development of high levels of multiple potentials in young people is purposefully designed to sidestep the traditional practice of labeling some students "gifted" (and, by implication, relegating all others to the category of "not gifted"). The term *gifted* is used in our educational lexicon only as an adjective, and even then, it is used in a developmental perspective. Thus, for example, we speak and write about *the development of gifted behaviors* in specific areas of learning and human expression rather than gifted-ness as a state of being. This orientation has allowed many students opportunities to develop high levels of creative and productive accomplishments that otherwise would have been denied through traditional special program models.

Practices that have been a mainstay of many special programs for "the gifted" are being absorbed into general education by reform models designed to upgrade the performance of all students. This integration of gifted program know-how is viewed as a favorable development for two reasons. First, the adoption of many special program practices is indicative of the viability and usefulness of both the know-how of special programs and the role enrichment specialists can and should play in total school improvement. It is no secret that compensatory education in the United States has largely been a failure. An overemphasis on remedial and mastery models has lowered the challenge level faced by the very population that programs such as Chapter I attempt to serve. Second, *all* students should have opportunities to develop higher-order thinking skills and to pursue more rigorous content and firsthand, investigative activities than those typically found in today's "dumbed-down" textbooks. The ways in which students respond to enriched learning experiences should be used as a rationale for providing all students with advanced-level follow-up opportunities. This approach reflects a democratic ideal that accommodates the full range of individual differences in the entire student population, and it opens the door to programming models that develop the talent potentials of many at-risk students who traditionally have been excluded from anything but the most basic types of curricular experiences. But in order to operationalize this ideal, we need to "get serious" about the things we have learned during the past several years about both programming models and human potential.

The application of gifted program know-how into general education is supported by a wide variety of research on human abilities (Bloom, 1985; Gardner, 1993; Renzulli, 1998; Sternberg, 1984). This research clearly and unequivocally provides a justification for much broader conceptions of talent development. These conceptions argue against the restrictive student selection practices that guided identification procedures in the past. Laypersons and professionals at all levels have begun to question the efficacy of programs that rely on narrow definitions, IQ scores, and other cognitive ability measures as the primary method for identifying which students can benefit from differentiated services. Traditional identification procedures have restricted services to small numbers of high-scoring students and excluded large numbers of at-risk students whose potentials are manifested in other ways that will be described in a later section that describes an SEM component called the Total Talent Portfolio. Special services should be viewed as opportunities to develop "gifted behaviors" rather than merely finding and certifying them. In this regard, we should judiciously avoid saying that a young person is either "gifted" or "not gifted." It is difficult to gain support for talent development when we use statements such as "Elaine is a gifted third grader" as a rationale. These kinds of statements offend many people and raise the accusations of elitism that have plagued special programs. But note the difference in orientation when we focus on the behavioral characteristics that brought this student to our attention in the first place: "Elaine is a third grader who reads at the adult level and who has a fascination for biographies about women of scientific accomplishment." And note the logical and justifiable services provided for Elaine:

1. Under the guidance of her classroom teacher, Elaine was allowed to substitute more challenging books in her interest area in place of the third-grade reader. The schoolwide enrichment-teaching specialist helped the classroom teacher locate these books, and they were purchased with funds from the enrichment program budget.

2. Elaine was allowed to leave the school two afternoons a month (usually on early dismissal days) to meet with a mentor who is a local journalist specializing in gender issues. The schoolwide enrichment-teaching specialist arranged transportation with the help of the school's parent volunteer group.

3. During time made available through curriculum compacting in her strength areas (i.e., reading, language arts, and spelling), the schoolwide enrichment teaching specialist helped Elaine prepare a questionnaire and interview schedule to be used with local women scientists and women science faculty members at a nearby university.

Could even the staunchest anti-gifted proponent argue against the logic or the appropriateness of these services? When programs focus on developing the behavioral potential of individuals or small groups who share a common interest, it is no longer necessary to organize groups merely because they all happen to be "gifted third graders."

THE SCHOOLWIDE ENRICHMENT MODEL

The programming model that the researchers at the Neag Center for Gifted Education and Talent Development have advocated since the early 1970s has always argued for a behavioral definition of giftedness and a greater emphasis on applying gifted program know-how to larger segments of the school population. The model is currently being used in hundreds of school districts across the country, including major urban areas such as New York City, Detroit, St. Paul, San Antonio, and Fort Worth. The present reform initiatives in general education have created a more receptive atmosphere for more flexible approaches that challenge all students and, accordingly, we have organized the Schoolwide Enrichment Model so that it blends into school improvement activities currently taking place throughout the country. Space does not permit a detailed description of the full model; however, the following sections describe the school structures upon which the model is targeted and the three service-delivery components. A graphic representation of the model is presented in Figure 4.2.

School Structures

1. *The Regular Curriculum.* The regular curriculum consists of everything that is a part of the predetermined goals, schedules, learning outcomes, and delivery systems of the school. The regular curriculum might be traditional, innovative, or in the process of transition, but its predominant feature is that authoritative forces (i.e., policy makers, school councils, textbook adoption committees, state regulators) have determined that the regular curriculum should be the "centerpiece" of student learning. Application of the SEM influences the regular curriculum in three ways. First, the challenge level of required material is differentiated through processes such as curriculum compacting, textbook content modification procedures, and group jumping strategies. Second, the systematic content intensification procedures used to replace eliminated content with selected, in-depth learning experiences increase the challenge level by introducing the broad underlying principles of a discipline. Third, the types of enrichment recommended in the Enrichment Triad Model (described below) are integrated selectively into the regular curriculum activities. Although the Neag Center researchers' goal in the

Figure 4.2   The Schoolwide Enrichment Model: Relationship Between Two Types of Components of the Model and School Structure

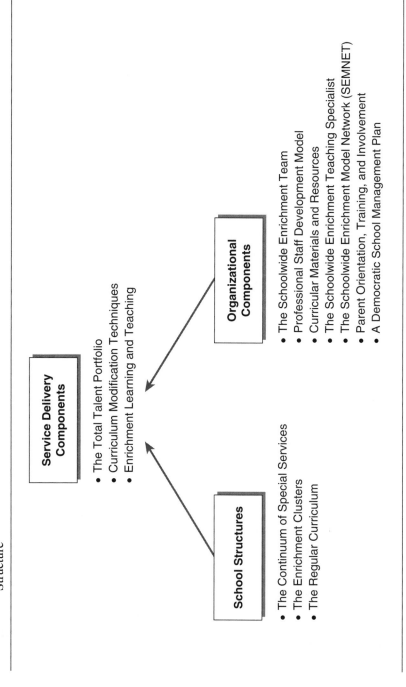

Service Delivery Components

- The Total Talent Portfolio
- Curriculum Modification Techniques
- Enrichment Learning and Teaching

Organizational Components

- The Schoolwide Enrichment Team
- Professional Staff Development Model
- Curricular Materials and Resources
- The Schoolwide Enrichment Teaching Specialist
- The Schoolwide Enrichment Model Network (SEMNET)
- Parent Orientation, Training, and Involvement
- A Democratic School Management Plan

School Structures

- The Continuum of Special Services
- The Enrichment Clusters
- The Regular Curriculum

SEM is to influence rather than replace the regular curriculum, the application of certain SEM components and the related staff development activities have resulted in substantial changes in both the content and the instructional processes of the entire regular curriculum.

2. *The Enrichment Clusters.* Enrichment clusters are nongraded groups of students who share common interests and who come together during specially designated time blocks to pursue these interests. Like extracurricular activities and programs such as 4-H and Junior Achievement, the main rationale for participation in one or more clusters is that *students and teachers want to be there.* All teachers (including music, art, physical education, etc.) are involved in teaching the clusters, and teacher involvement in any particular cluster is based on the same type of interest assessment used for students. Community resource persons should also be invited to organize enrichment clusters. The model for learning used with enrichment clusters is based on an inductive approach to the pursuit of real-world problems rather than traditional, didactic modes of teaching. This approach, entitled enrichment learning and teaching, is purposefully designed to create a learning environment that places a premium on the development of higher-order thinking skills and the authentic application of these skills in creative and productive situations. The theory underlying this approach is based on the work of constructivist theorists such as Jean Piaget, Jerome Bruner, and John Dewey and the general application of constructivist theory to classroom practice. Enrichment clusters are excellent vehicles for promoting cooperativeness within the context of real-world problem solving, and they also provide superlative opportunities for promoting self-concept. A major assumption underlying the use of enrichment clusters is that *every child is special if we create conditions in which that child can be a specialist within a specialty group.*

Enrichment clusters are organized around major disciplines, interdisciplinary themes, or cross-disciplinary topics (e.g., an electronic music group or a theatrical or television production group that includes actors, writers, technical specialists, costume designers, etc.). The clusters are modeled after the ways in which knowledge utilization, thinking skills, and interpersonal relations take place in the real world. Thus, all work is directed toward the production of a product or service. There are no lesson plans or unit plans. Rather, direction is provided by the following six key questions:

1. What do people with an interest in this area do?
2. What products do they create and/or what services do they provide?
3. What methods do they use to carry out their work?
4. What resources and materials are needed to produce high-quality products and services?
5. How, and with whom, do they communicate the results of their work?
6. What steps need to be taken to have an impact on intended audiences?

The enrichment clusters are not intended to be the total program for talent development in a school, but they are major vehicles for stimulating interests and developing talent potentials across the entire school population. They are also vehicles for staff development in that they provide teachers an opportunity to participate in enrichment teaching and subsequently to analyze and compare this type of teaching with traditional methods of instruction. In this regard, the model promotes a spillover effect by encouraging teachers to become better talent scouts and talent developers, and to apply enrichment techniques to regular classroom situations. Enrichment clusters are used by some schools on a one-half day per week basis and in other schools they meet daily. At the Webster Elementary School in St. Paul, Minnesota, for example, a broad array of interdisciplinary clusters is offered daily. At the Southeast School in Mansfield, Connecticut, enrichment clusters are offered two afternoons a month, and they are taught jointly by teachers, administrators, and parent volunteers. One of the most popular clusters is called Flight School and was organized by the superintendent of schools, who is a licensed pilot.

3. *The Continuum of Special Services.* A broad range of special services is the third school structure targeted by the model. A diagram representing these services is presented in Figure 4.3. Although the enrichment clusters and the SEM-based modifications of the regular curriculum provide a broad range of services to meet individual needs, a program for total talent development still requires supplementary services that challenge young people who are capable of

working at the highest levels of their special interest areas. These services, which ordinarily cannot be provided in enrichment clusters or the regular curriculum, typically include individual or small-group counseling, direct assistance in facilitating advanced-level work, arranging for mentorships with faculty members or community persons, and making other types of connections between students, their families, and out-of-school persons, resources, and agencies. For example, the schoolwide enrichment coordinator in the LaPorte, Indiana, School Corporation developed a Parent-Teacher Enrichment Guide for the city and surrounding area that includes information about a wide variety of enrichment opportunities for parents and teachers.

> The Schoolwide Enrichment Model encourages teachers to become better talent scouts and talent developers.

Direct assistance also involves setting up and promoting student, faculty, and parental involvement in special programs such as Future Problem Solving, Odyssey of the Mind, the Model United Nations Program, and state and national essay, mathematics, and history contests. Another type of direct assistance consists of arranging out-of-school involvement for individual students in summer programs, on-campus courses, special schools, theatrical groups, scientific expeditions, and apprenticeships at places where advanced-level learning opportunities are available. Provision of these services is one of the responsibilities of the schoolwide enrichment-teaching specialist or an enrichment team of teachers and parents who work together to provide options for advanced learning. A schoolwide enrichment teaching specialist in Barrington, Rhode Island, estimates she spends two days a week in a resource capacity to the faculties of two schools, and three days a week providing direct services to students.

Service Delivery Components

1. *The Total Talent Portfolio.* The case study of Elaine presented earlier is an example of the ways in which the Schoolwide Enrichment Model targets specific learning characteristics that can serve as a basis for talent development. Our approach to targeting learning characteristics uses both traditional and performance-based assessments to compile information about three dimensions of the learner—their abilities, interests, and learning styles. This information, which focuses on strengths rather than deficits, is compiled in

Figure 4.3   The Continuum of Services for Total Talent Development

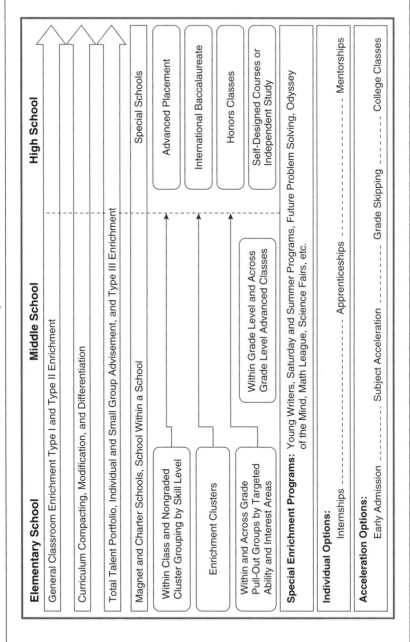

a folder called the Total Talent Portfolio (see Figure 4.4) and is used to make decisions about talent development opportunities in regular classes, enrichment clusters, and in the continuum of special services. Two questions summarize the intent of the Total Talent Portfolio: "What are the very best things we know and can record about a student's best work?" and "What are the best ways we can utilize this information to nurture the student's talent?" This expanded approach to identifying talent potentials is essential if we are to make genuine efforts to include more underrepresented students in a plan for *total* talent development. This approach is also consistent with the more flexible conception of *developing gifts* and talents that has been a cornerstone of our work and our concerns for promoting more equity in special programs.

2. *Curriculum Modification Techniques.* SEM's second service-delivery component is a series of curriculum modification techniques designed to (1) adjust levels of required learning so all students are challenged, (2) increase the number of in-depth learning experiences, and (3) introduce various types of enrichment into regular curricular experiences. The procedures used to carry out curriculum modification are curriculum compacting, textbook analysis and the surgical removal of repetitious material from textbooks, and developing a planned approach for introducing greater depth into regular curricular material.

Curriculum compacting (Reis & Renzulli, 1992) is a systematic procedure for modifying or streamlining the regular curriculum in order to eliminate repetition of previously mastered material, upgrading the challenge level of the regular curriculum, and providing time for appropriate enrichment and/or acceleration activities. This process includes (1) defining the goals and outcomes of a particular unit or segment of instruction, (2) determining and documenting which students have already mastered most or all of a specified set of learning outcomes or who are capable of mastering them in less time than their peers, and (3) providing replacement activities for material already mastered through the use of instructional options that enable a more challenging and productive use of the student's time. These options include content acceleration, individual or group research projects, peer teaching, and involvement in nonclassroom activities discussed in the section on the continuum of services. A key feature of these options is that students have some freedom to make decisions about the topic and the methods through which the topic will be pursued. Curriculum compacting might best be thought of as *organized common sense,* because it simply recommends the natural pattern that teachers ordinarily follow when individualizing instruction. Compacting also might be thought of as the "mirror image" of remedial procedures that have always been used in diagnostic/prescriptive models of teaching.

The second procedure for making adjustments in regular curricular material is the examination of textbooks to determine parts that can be economized through textbook analysis and the "surgical" removal of repetitious drill and practice material. The textbook is the curriculum in the overwhelming majority of today's classrooms; despite all of the rhetoric about school and curriculum reform, this situation is not likely to change in the near future. Until such time that high-quality textbooks are universally available, it is essential to deal with the curriculum situation as it currently exists. Although curriculum compacting is one procedure that can be used to get an unchallenging curriculum "off the backs" of students who are in need of curriculum modifications, the procedure is a form of "damage control." Therefore, we need to take a more proactive stance to overcome the well-documented low levels of American textbooks.

The procedures for carrying out the textbook analysis and surgical removal process are based on the argument that "less is better" when it comes to content selection, and it is necessary to make wise decisions when determining which material will be covered in greater depth. The first step in the process might best be described as "textbook triage." Each unit of instruction is examined by grade-level teams to determine which material is needless repetition of previously covered skills and concepts. When repetition is eliminated, teachers then decide which material is necessary for review and which material is important enough to cover in either a survey or an in-depth manner. What teachers teach is at the very heart of professional competency. The textbook analysis and surgical removal process offers teachers an opportunity to come together as a group of professionals around specific tasks within and across grade levels and subject areas to perform these important operations.

> What teachers teach is at the very heart of professional competency.

Adding more in-depth learning experiences is the third curriculum modification procedure. This approach is based on the work of

Figure 4.4 The Dimensions of the Total Talent Portfolio

Abilities	Interests	Style Preferences			
Maximum Performance Indicators	Interest Areas	Instructional Styles Preferences	Learning Environment Preferences	Thinking Styles Preferences	Expression Style Preferences
Tests • Standardized • Teacher-Made Course Grades Teacher Ratings Product Evaluation • Written • Oral • Visual • Musical • Constructed (Note differences between assigned and self-selected products) Level Participation in Learning Activities Degree of Interaction with Others	Fine Arts Crafts Literary Historical Mathematical/Logical Physical Sciences Life Sciences Political/Judicial Athletic/Recreation Marketing/Business Drama/Dance Musical Performance Musical Composition Managerial/Business Photography Film/Video Computers Other (Specify)	Recitation & Drill Peer Tutoring Lecture Lecture/Discussion Discussion Guided Independent Study* Learning/Interest Center Simulation, Role Playing Dramatization, Guided Fantasy Learning Games Replicative Reports or Projects* Investigative Reports or Projects* Unguided Independent Study* Internship* Apprenticeship* *With or without a mentor	Inter/Intra-Personal • Self-Oriented • Peer-Oriented • Adult-Oriented • Combined Physical • Sound • Heat • Light • Design • Mobility • Time of Day • Food Intake • Seating	Analytic (School Smart) Synthetic/Creative (Creative, Inventive) Practical/Contextual (Street Smart) Legislative Executive Judicial	Written Oral Manipulative Discussion Display Dramatization Artistic Graphic Commercial Service
	Ref: Renzulli 1997	Ref: Renzulli & Smith, 1978	Ref: Amabile & Gryskiewicz, 1989; Dunn, Dunn, & Price, 1984; Gardner, 1993	Ref: Sternberg, 1984, 1988; Sternberg & Lubart, 1992	Ref: Kettle, Renzulli, & Rizza, 1998; Renzulli & Reis, 1985

Phenix (1986), who recommends that a focus on representative concepts and ideas is the best way to capture the essence of a topic or area of study. Representative ideas or concepts consist of themes, patterns, main features, sequences, organizing principles and structures, and the logic that defines an area of study. Representative ideas and concepts can also be used as the bases for interdisciplinary or multidisciplinary studies.

While the use of representative concepts allows teachers to capture the essence of an area of study, it also allows them to introduce economy into content selection. The vast amount of material within any given discipline prevents unlimited coverage of content; therefore, material must be selected so that it is both representative and maximally transferable. Excellent resources are available to assist in this process. Books such as the *Dictionary of the History of Ideas* (Weiner, 1973) contain essays that cover every major discipline, and the emphasis of the essays is on interdisciplinary and cross-cultural relationships. The essays are cross-referenced to direct the reader to other articles containing similar ideas in other domains. Additional resources can be found in books such as *The Syntopicon: An Index to the Great Ideas* (Adler, 1990), which lists concepts, ideas, and themes around which curriculum can be developed.

In-depth teaching is also concerned with the level of advancement or complexity of the material. First and foremost, the material must take into consideration the age, maturity, previous study, and background experiences of students. Beyond these considerations, three principles of content selection are recommended. First, curricular material should be selected so that it escalates along the hierarchy of knowledge dimensions: facts, conventions, trends and sequences, classifications and categories, criteria, principles and generalizations, and theories and structures. Second, movement toward the highest level, theories, and structures should involve continuous recycling to lower levels so that facts, trends, sequences, etc., can be understood in relation to a more integrated whole rather than as isolated bits of irrelevant information. Third, the cluster of diverse procedures surrounding the acquisition of knowledge, that dimension of learning commonly referred to as "process" or thinking skills, should itself be viewed as a form of content. These more enduring skills form the cognitive structures and problem-solving strategies that have the greatest transfer value.

A final characteristic of in-depth learning is a focus on methodology. This focus is designed to promote an understanding of, and appreciation for, the *application* of methods to the kinds of problems that form the essence of various fields of knowledge. The goal of this emphasis on methodology is to cast the young person in the role of a firsthand inquirer rather than a mere learner of lessons, even if this role is carried out at a more junior level than that of the adult professional. This role encourages young learners to engage in the kinds of thinking, feeling, and doing that characterizes the work of the practicing professional because it creates the confrontations with knowledge necessary for active, rather than passive, learning.

3. *Enrichment Learning and Teaching.* The third service delivery component of the SEM is enrichment learning and teaching. Enrichment learning and teaching is based on the ideas of a small but influential number of philosophers, theorists, and researchers.[1] The work of these theorists, coupled with the Neag Center's research and program development activities, has given rise to the concept we call enrichment learning and teaching. The best way to define this concept is in terms of the following four principles:

1. Each learner is unique and, therefore, all learning experiences must be examined in ways that take into account the abilities, interests, and learning styles of the individual.

2. Learning is more effective when students enjoy what they are doing and, therefore, learning experiences should be constructed and assessed with as much concern for enjoyment as for other goals.

3. Learning is more meaningful and enjoyable when content (i.e., knowledge) and process (i.e., thinking skills, methods of inquiry) are learned within the context of a real and present problem and, therefore, attention should be given to opportunities to personalize student choice in problem selection, the relevance of the problem for individual students at the time the problem is being addressed, and authentic strategies for addressing the problem.

4. Some formal instruction may be used in enrichment learning and teaching, but a major goal of this approach to learning is to enhance knowledge and thinking skill acquisition that is gained through formal instruction with applications of knowledge and skills that result from students' own construction of meaning.

The ultimate goal of learning that is guided by these principles is to replace dependent and passive learning with independent and engaged learning. Although all but the most conservative educators will agree with these principles, much controversy exists about how these principles or similar ones might be applied in everyday school situations. A danger also exists that these principles might be viewed as yet another idealized list of glittering generalities that cannot be manifested easily in schools that are entrenched in the deductive model of learning. Developing a school program based on these principles is not an easy task. Over the years, however, the researchers at the Neag Center for Gifted Education and Talent Development have achieved a fair amount of success by gaining faculty, administrative, and parental consensus on a small number of easy-to-understand concepts and related services and by providing resources and training related to each concept and service delivery procedure. Numerous research studies (summarized in Renzulli & Reis, 1994) and field tests in schools with widely varying demographics have been conducted. These studies and field tests have provided opportunities for the development of large amounts of practical know-how that are readily available for schools that would like to implement the SEM.

THE ENRICHMENT TRIAD MODEL

In order for enrichment learning and teaching to be systematically applied to the learning process, it must be organized in a way that makes sense to teachers and students. An organizational pattern called the Enrichment Triad Model (Renzulli, 1977) is used for this purpose. The three types of enrichment in the model are depicted in Figure 4.5. Before discussing the role and function of each type of enrichment, it is necessary to discuss three considerations that relate to the model in general.

Learning in a Natural Way

The Enrichment Triad Model is based on the ways in which people learn in a natural environment rather than the artificially structured environment that characterizes most classrooms. Just as scientists "look to nature" when they attempt to solve particular types of problems, the process of learning is examined as it unfolds in the nonschool world. This process is elegant in its simplicity. External stimulation, internal curiosity, necessity, or combinations of these three starting points cause people to develop an interest in a

Figure 4.5   The Enrichment Triad Model

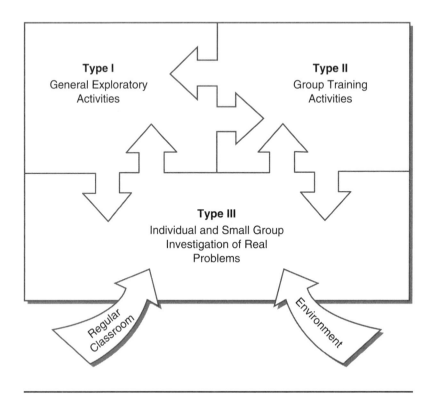

topic, problem, or area of study. Humans are, by nature, curious, problem-solving beings, but in order for them to act upon a problem or interest with some degree of commitment and enthusiasm, the interest must be a sincere one and one in which they see a personal reason for taking action. Once the problem or interest is personalized, a need is created to gather information, resources, and strategies for acting upon the problem.

Problem solving in nature almost always results in a product or service that has a functional, artistic, or humanitarian value. The learning that takes place in real-problem situations is *collateral learning* that results from attacking the problem in order to produce a product or service. It was precisely this kind of natural problem-solving situation that gave rise to the Enrichment Triad Model. The only difference between the natural learning that takes place in real-life situations and the use of the triad model within the more structured world of the school is that the researchers at the Neag Center view products as vehicles through which a wide variety of more enduring and transferable processes can be developed. Learning that focuses on the interaction between product and process results in the kinds of learning experiences that enhance both the present and the future.

More Than a Sum of the Parts

A second general consideration about the Enrichment Triad Model is that the *interaction* between and among the three types of enrichment is as important as any one type of enrichment or the collective sum of all three types. In other words, the arrows in Figure 4.5 are as important as the individual cells because they give the model dynamic properties that cannot be achieved if the three types of enrichment are pursued independently. A Type I experience, for example, may have value in and of itself, but it achieves maximum payoff if it leads to Type II or III experiences. In this regard, it is a good idea to view Types I and II enrichment as "identification situations" that may lead to Type III experiences, which are the most advanced type of enrichment in the model. As Figure 4.5 indicates, the regular curriculum and the environment in general (i.e., non-school experiences) can also serve as pathways of entry into Type III activities. An identification situation is simply an experience that allows students and teachers an opportunity to (1) participate in an activity, (2) analyze their interest in and reaction to the topic covered in the activity—and the processes through which the activity was pursued, and (3) make a purposeful decision about their interest in the topic and the diverse ways further involvement may be carried out. Types I and II are general forms of enrichment that are usually pursued with larger groups of students. Type III enrichment, on the other hand, is pursued only on a voluntary and self-selected basis.

The interactiveness of the three types of enrichment also includes what might be called the "backward arrows" in Figure 4.5 (e.g., the arrows leading back from Type III to Type I, etc.). In many cases, the advanced work of students (i.e., Type III) can be used as Types I and II experiences for other students. Thus, for example, a group of students who carried out a comprehensive study on lunchroom waste can present its work to other groups for both awareness and instructional purposes, and for the purpose of stimulating potential new interests on the parts of other students. In this regard, the model is designed to renew itself and to bring students "inside" the pedagogy of the school enterprise rather than viewing learning from a spectator's perspective.

Personal Knowledge

A third consideration about the Enrichment Triad Model in general is that it is designed to help students gain personal knowledge about their own abilities, interests, and learning styles. If, as Socrates said, "The unexamined life is not worth living," then we should also consider a corollary to this axiom about life in school: "The unexamined lesson is not worth learning." While it would be desirable to apply this corollary to all school experiences, the types of enrichment advocated in the triad model are excellent vehicles for examining personal preferences, tastes, and inclinations that will help students gain a greater understanding of themselves.

This corollary is operationalized in the model by recommending debriefings and postlearning analyses (sometimes called metalearning) about both *what* has been learned and *how* a particular segment of learning has been pursued. Following exposure to a particular instructional style, a careful postlearning analysis should be conducted that focuses on the unique properties of the purposefully selected instructional technique. Students should be encouraged to discuss and record in personal journals their reactions to the instructional technique in terms of both efficiency in learning and the amount of pleasure they derive from the technique. The goal of the postlearning analysis is to help students understand more about themselves by understanding more about their preferences in a particular learning situation. Thus, collective experiences in learning styles should provide (1) exposure to many styles, (2) an understanding of which styles are the most personally applicable to particular subjects, and (3) experience in how to blend styles in order to maximize both the effectiveness and the satisfaction of learning.

> "The unexamined lesson is not worth learning."

In the sections that follow, a brief description of each component of the triad model is presented. It is helpful to keep in mind that the triad model is part of the service delivery component that is targeted at three school structures: the regular curriculum, enrichment clusters, and the continuum of special services. In many ways, enrichment learning and teaching can be thought of as an overlay that can be applied to these three school structures.

Type I Enrichment: General Exploratory Experiences

Type I enrichment consists of general exploratory experiences that are designed to expose students to new and exciting topics, ideas, and fields of knowledge not ordinarily covered in the regular curriculum. This type of enrichment is carried out through a variety of procedures such as visiting speakers, demonstrations, mini visits, video presentations, interest centers, and the use of other audiovisual and technological materials. Type I enrichment and the debriefing that accompanies this type of enrichment represent an invitation to more advanced levels of involvement with the topic or area of interest.

Type II Enrichment: Group Training Activities

Type II enrichment consists of methods, materials, and instructional techniques designed to develop higher-level thinking processes, research and reference skills, and processes related to personal and social development. Type II enrichment is provided for all students within the regular curriculum, as well as students who are involved in enrichment clusters and self-selected, independent investigations. For example, science class students involved in determining water quality of a local river above and below the location of a major industrial park may need training in hypothesizing, data analysis, and research report writing. This training serves as motivation for participation in a self-selected independent investigation. A small group of students engaged in a real-world investigation related to oral history may need training in interview protocol, the use of tape recorder devices, and data analysis.

Type III Enrichment: Individual and Small-Group Investigations of Real Problems

Type III enrichment is the highest level of enrichment in which students can engage because they exchange their role from traditional lesson learner to firsthand inquirer. Type III enrichment is distinguished from other types of enrichment by five essential elements: (1) a personal frame of reference, (2) a focus on advanced-level knowledge, (3) a focus on methodology, (4) a sense of audience, and (5) authentic evaluation.

First, a Type III enrichment experience must be based on the interest of the individual or small group of students; students must "own" the real problem they will investigate. Second, this type of enrichment requires that students draw upon the roles and skills of practicing professionals. These skills include, for example, judging problem difficulty, apportioning time, and predicting outcomes. Third, Type III enrichment requires that students utilize authentic methodology. Students involved in a scientific investigation will employ the scientific method, while students involved in video production will use the methodology of media experts in the field. A sense of audience is the fourth essential element in Type III enrichment. It is the presence of a real audience that encourages students to improve the quality of their product and develop new and effective ways of communicating their findings. Finally, Type III enrichment is characterized by authentic evaluation. Type III projects are products produced using the methodology of a field; by necessity, the products must be evaluated according to criteria provided by experts in the field and whether or not they have the desired impact on the intended audience.

SCHOOLWIDE ENRICHMENT AND EDUCATIONAL REFORM

Most efforts to make major changes in schooling have failed. Although there is endless speculation about why schools are so resistant to change, most theorists and policy makers have concluded that tinkering with single components of a complex system will give only the appearance of school improvement rather than the real and lasting change so desperately sought by educational leaders. Examples of single-component tinkering are familiar to most educators. More rigorous curriculum standards, for example, without improved curricular materials and teachers able to use the materials effectively negate any potential value that new standards may have for improving academic performance. Similarly, single-component tinkering designed to force change in classrooms (e.g., high-stakes testing) may create the illusion of improved achievement, but the reality becomes an increased pressure on schools to expand the use of compensatory learning models that, so far, have contributed only to the "dumbing down" of curriculum and the overall lowering of

> Tinkering with single components of a complex educational system will give only the appearance of school improvement rather than the real and lasting change so desperately sought by educational leaders.

academic standards. Teacher empowerment, school-based management, an extended school day and year, and revised teacher certification requirements are merely apparitions of change when state or central office regulations prescribe the curriculum by using tests that determine whether schools get high marks for better performance.

How, then, do we establish an effective change process—one that overcomes the long record of failed attempts? The leverage for meaningful change depends upon breaking two mind-sets: (1) that one person or single group knows the right answer and (2) that change is linear. The only reasonable solution is to develop a process whereby the adoption of policy and the adoption of practice proceed simultaneously. Policy makers and practitioners in schools need to collaborate during all phases of the change process by examining local capacity and motivation in conjunction with the desired changes. Thus, neither policy makers nor practitioners, by themselves, can reform schools; instead, both must come together to shape a vision and develop the procedures needed to realize and sustain that vision. Senge (1994) compares "visioneering" to the hologram, a three-dimensional image created by interacting light sources:

> When a group of people come to share a vision, . . . each sees his or her own picture. Each vision represents the whole image from a different point of view. When you add up the pieces of the hologram, the image does not change fundamentally, but rather becomes more intense, more lifelike, more real in the sense that people can truly imagine achieving it. The vision no longer rests on the shoulders of one person [or one group], but is shared and embodies the passion and commitment of all participants. (Senge, 1994, p. 312).

This article is based on my book *Schools for Talent Development,* which has been developed around a shared vision that my colleagues in the Neag Center for Gifted Education and Talent Development and I have had for a number of years. This vision is also embraced by thousands of teachers and administrators with whom we have worked in academic programs and summer institutes that date back to the 1970s. *Simply stated, this vision is that schools are places for talent development.* Academic achievement is an important part of the vision and the model for school improvement described in *Schools for Talent Development;* however, we also believe a focus on talent development places the need for improved academic achievement into a larger perspective about the goals of education. The things that have made our nation great and our society one of the most productive in the world are manifestations of talent development at all levels of human productivity. From the creators and inventors of new ideas, products, and art forms, to the vast array of people who manufacture, advertise, and market the creations that improve and enrich our lives, there are levels of excellence and quality that contribute to our standard of living and way of life.

> *Everyone* has an important role to play in societal improvement, and those roles can be enhanced if we provide all students with the opportunities, resources, and encouragement to aspire to the highest levels possible.

This vision of schools for talent development is based on the beliefs that *everyone* has an important role to play in societal improvement and that everyone's role can be enhanced if we provide all students with opportunities, resources, and encouragement to aspire to the highest level of talent development humanly possible. Rewarding lives are a function of the ways we use our individual potentials in productive ways. Accordingly, the SEM is a practical plan for making our vision of schools for talent development a reality. We are not naive about the politics, personalities, and financial issues that often supersede the pedagogical goals that are the focus of *Schools for Talent Development*. At the same time, we have seen this vision manifested in schools ranging from urban areas and isolated and frequently poor rural areas to affluent suburbs and combinations thereof. We believe that the strategies described in this book provide the guidance for making any school a place for talent development.

There are no quick fixes or easy formulas for transforming schools into places where talent development is valued and vigorously pursued. Our experience has shown, however, that once the concept of talent development catches on, students, parents, teachers, and administrators begin to view their school in a different way. Students become more excited and engaged in what they are learning; parents find more opportunities to become involved in all aspects related to their children's learning, rather than peripheral activities; teachers begin to find and use a variety of resources that, until now, seldom found their way into classrooms; and administrators start to make decisions that affect learning rather than "tight ship" efficiency.

Everyone has a stake in schools that provide all of our young people with a high-quality education. Parents benefit when their children lead happy and successful lives. Employers and colleges benefit when they have access to people who are competent, creative, and effective in the work they do and in higher educational pursuits. Political leaders benefit when good citizens and a productive population contribute to a healthy economy, a high quality of life, and respect for the values and institutions in a democracy. And professional educators at all levels benefit when the quality of schools for which they are responsible is effective enough to create respect for their work and generous financial support for the educational enterprise.

Everyone has a stake in good schools because schools create and recreate a successful modern society. Renewed and sustained economic growth and the well-being of all citizens means investing in high-quality learning the same way that previous generations invested in machines and raw materials. Our schools are already dumping millions of functionally illiterate young people into the workforce, more and more colleges are teaching remedial courses based on material formerly taught in high school, and college graduates in almost all fields are experiencing difficulty entering career areas of choice.

Although everyone has a stake in good schools, America has been faced with a "school problem" that has resulted in declining confidence in schools and the people who work in them, drastic limitations in the amount of financial support for education, and general public apathy or dissatisfaction with the quality of education our young people are receiving. The parents of poor children have given up hope that education will enable their sons and daughters to break the bonds of poverty. And the middle class, perhaps for the first time in our nation's history, is exploring government-supported alternatives such as vouchers and tax credits for private schools, home schooling, charter schools, and summer and afterschool programs that enhance admission to competitive colleges. A great deal has been written about America's "school problem," and studies, commissions, reports, and even a Governor's Summit Conference have been initiated to generate solutions to the problems facing our schools.

> Renewed and sustained economic growth and the well-being of all citizens means investing in high-quality learning the same way that previous generations invested in machines and raw materials.

But the hundreds, if not thousands, of conferences, commissions, and meetings and the tons of reports, proclamations, and lists of goals have yielded minimal results, mainly because they generally focused on tinkering with traditional methods of schooling.

THREE KEY INGREDIENTS OF SCHOOL IMPROVEMENT

If the traditional methods of schooling have failed to bring about substantial changes, we must look to different models that show promise of achieving the types of school improvement we so desperately need. New models must focus their attention on three major dimensions of schooling—the act of learning, the use of time, and the change process itself.

The Act of Learning

School improvement must begin by placing the *act of learning* at the center of the change process. Organizational and administrative structures such as vouchers, site-based management, school choice, multiaged classes, parent involvement, and extended school days are important considerations, but they do not address *directly* the crucial question of how we can improve what happens in classrooms where teachers, students, and curriculum interact with one another. One of the things we have done in developing the SEM is to base all recommendations for school improvement on the learning process. It is beyond the scope of this summary to explain all components of the act of learning, but a figural representation of the learning process is depicted in Figure 4.6. The "Learner Circle" highlights important components students bring to the act of learning. Thus, when examining the learner we must take into consideration (1) the present achievement levels in each area of study, (2) the learner's interest in particular topics and the ways in which we can enhance present interests or develop new interests, and (3) the preferred styles of learning that will improve the learner's motivation to pursue the material being studied. Likewise, the teacher and learner dimensions have subcomponents that must be considered when we place the act of learning at the center of the school improvement process (Renzulli, 1992).

Figure 4.6   Figural Representation of the Act of Learning

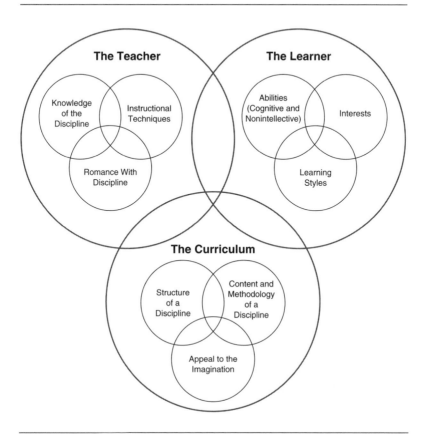

The Use of Time

Although it would be interesting to speculate about why schools have changed so little over the centuries, at least part of the reason has been our unwillingness to examine critically the issue of school time. If the ways we currently use school time were producing remarkably positive or even adequate results, there might be an argument for maintaining the traditional schedule and calendar. But such is not the case.

A universal pattern of school organization that has emerged over the years has contributed to our inability to make even the smallest changes in the overall process of learning. This universal pattern is well known to educators and laypersons alike. The "major" subject matter areas (reading, mathematics, science, language arts, and social studies) are taught on a regular basis, five days per week. Other subjects, sometimes called "the specials," such as music, art, and physical education, are taught once or twice a week. So accustomed have we become to the rigidity of this schedule that even the slightest hint of possible variation is met with a storm of protest from administrators and teachers: "We don't have time *now* to cover the regular curriculum." "How will we fit in the specials?" "They keep adding new things [drug education, sex education, etc.] for us to cover." Our uncontested acceptance of the elementary and secondary school schedule causes us to lose sight of the fact that at the college level, where material is ordinarily more advanced and demanding, we routinely drop from a five-meetings-per-week schedule to a three-day- (and sometimes even two-day-) per-week schedule of class meetings. And our adherence to the "more time is better argument" fails to take into account research that shows quite the opposite. For example, international comparison studies report that eight of the eleven nations that surpass U.S. achievement levels in mathematics spend less time on math instruction than do American schools (Jaeger, 1992). In the Schoolwide Enrichment Model, a number of alternative scheduling patterns are based on selectively "borrowing" one or two class meetings per month from the major subject areas. This approach guarantees that a designated time will be available each week for advanced-level enrichment clusters.

The Change Process

The approach to school improvement being recommended in the SEM is realistic because it focuses on those aspects of learning and development over which schools have the most influence, and, therefore, the highest probability of achieving success. Schools are being bombarded with proposals for change. These proposals range from total "systemic reform" to tinkering with bits and pieces of specific subjects and teaching methods. Oftentimes, the proposals are little more than lists of intended goals or outcomes, and limited direction is provided about how these outcomes can best be achieved. Even less information is provided about the effectiveness of recommended practices in a broad range of field test sites. Worse yet are the mixed messages that policy makers and regulators are beaming at schools at an unprecedented rate, messages often incompatible with one another. One state, for example, mandated a core curriculum for students but then evaluated teachers on the basis of generic teaching skills that had nothing to do with the curriculum. Schools are encouraged to raise their standards, and advocates of site-based management encourage teachers to become more active in curriculum development. But these same schools are rated on the basis of test scores tied to lists of state-specified, outcome-based competencies. A recent study (Madaus, 1992) showed that the most widely used tests measure low-level skills and knowledge and that teachers are under pressure to emphasize this kind of material because it shows up on the tests. The study also reported that teachers and administrators believed the tests forced them to compromise their ideals about good teaching. In another study, researchers asked a group of teachers how they would evaluate school reform initiatives in their schools. The group of teachers replied, "There's nothing but chaos. Our best strategy is to ignore them and close our doors and go about our business" (Olson, 1992, p. 1).

The researchers at the Neag Center for Gifted Education and Talent Development believe that school improvement can be initiated and built upon through gentle and evolutionary strategies for change. These strategies must first and foremost concentrate on the act of learning as represented by the interactions that take place between and among learners, teachers, and the curriculum. In the early stages of the change process, these strategies should make minimal but specific suggestions for change in existing schedules, textbook usage, and curricular conventions. And these strategies should be based on practices that have already demonstrated favorable results in places where they have been used for reasonable periods of time and with groups from varying ethnic and economic backgrounds. We also believe that the individual school building is the unit of change for addressing school improvement and that effective and lasting change can only occur when it is initiated, nurtured, and monitored from within the school itself. Outside-of-school regulations and remedies have seldom changed the daily behaviors of students and teachers or dealt effectively with solutions to inside-of-school problems (Barth, 1991). A simple but sincere waiver of top-down regulations, a plan that involves consensus and shared decision making on the parts of administrators, parents, and teachers and incentives for specific contributions to the change process are the starting points and the only "big decisions" policy makers need to make in order to initiate a gentle and evolutionary school improvement process.

Our goal in the Schoolwide Enrichment Model is not to replace existing school structures but rather to apply the strategies and services that define the model to improve the structures to which schools have already made a commitment. Thus, for example, if a school has adopted national standards or outcomes, whole language learning models, or site-based management, the purpose of SEM is to influence these structures in order to maximize their effectiveness. We view this process as an infusion rather than an add-on or replacement approach to school improvement. The main targets of the process are those factors that have a direct bearing on the act of learning. Evaluations of SEM programs (Olenchak & Renzulli, 1989) have indicated that the model is systematic, inexpensive to implement, and practical in a common-sense sort of way that makes it appealing to both professionals and laypersons.

> The goal of the Schoolwide Enrichment Model is to apply the strategies and services that define the model toward improving the structures to which schools have already made a commitment.

A COMPUTERIZED STRENGTH ASSESSMENT AND INTERNET-BASED ENRICHMENT PROGRAM

Every teacher has had the satisfaction of seeing a child "turn on" to a topic or school experience that demonstrates the true joy and excitement of both learning and teaching. Teachers are also painfully aware of the boredom and lack of interest that so many of our young people express about so much of the work they do in school. Highly prescriptive curriculum guides, endless lists of standards to be covered, and relentless pressure to increase achievement test scores often prevent us from doing the kind of teaching that results in those joyous but rare times when we have seen truly remarkable engagement in learning.

One teacher we interviewed as part of a research project dealing with high engagement in learning said, "I could easily improve student enthusiasm, enjoyment, and engagement if I had about a dozen teaching assistants in my classroom!" It was comments like this plus the almost infinite resources that are now available through the Internet that inspired the development of the Renzulli Learning System (RLS) at the University of Connecticut's Neag School of Education. The University of Connecticut Research and Development Corporation sponsors the program, with income from subscriptions used to support further research.

The use of instructional technology, and especially the Internet, has evolved rapidly over the past decade. Technology has evolved from "first generation" use, consisting mainly of what might be called worksheets-online, to current technology that allows students to navigate Web pages, using hypermedia to pursue additional, more advanced information.

The Renzulli Learning System might best be viewed as the next generation of applying instructional technology to the learning process. It is a totally unique use of the Internet that combines computer-based strength assessment with search engine technology, allowing true differentiation in the matching of thousands of carefully selected resources to individual strengths. The RLS also has what might best be called theoretical integrity. It is based on a high-end learning theory called the Enrichment Triad Model (Renzulli, 1977) and numerous research studies dealing with model implementation (Renzulli & Reis, 1994). With minimal skills in the use of the Internet, and only a small amount of the teacher's time, all schools can easily make use of a system that will give teachers the equivalent of "a dozen assistants" in their classrooms. The Renzulli Learning System is a four-step procedure that is based on more than 30 years of research and development dealing with the diagnosis and promotion of advanced level thinking skills, motivation, creativity, and engagement in learning. An overview of the system is presented in Figure 4.7.

Step 1. Strength Assessment:
Using the Electronic Learning Profile

The first step consists of a computer-based diagnostic assessment that creates a profile of each student's academic strengths, interests, learning styles, and preferred modes of expression. The online assessment, which takes about thirty minutes, results in a personalized profile that highlights individual student strengths and sets the stage for Step 2 of the RLS. The profile acts like a compass for the second step, which is a differentiation search engine that examines thousands of

Figure 4.7   Renzulli Learning System Overview At-a-Glance

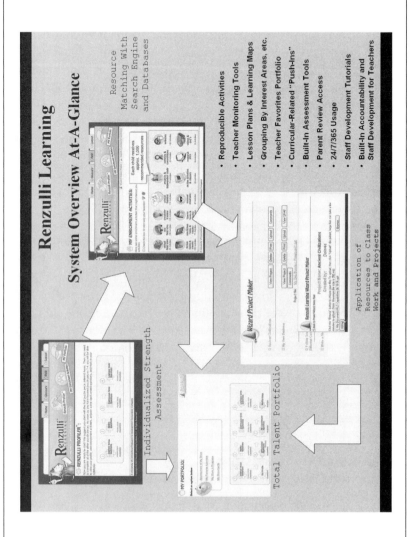

resources that relate specifically to each student's profile. Student profiles can also be used to form groups of students who share common interests. A project management tool guides students and teachers to use specifically selected resources for assigned curricular activities, independent or small group investigative projects, and a wide variety of challenging enrichment experiences. Another management tool enables teachers to form instructional groups and enrichment clusters based on interests and learning style preferences. Teachers have instant access to student profiles, all sites students have visited on the Web, and the amount of time spent in each activity. Parents may also access their child's profile and Web activities. In order to promote parent involvement, we suggest that students actually work on some of their favorite activities with their parents.

Step 2. Enrichment Differentiation Databases

In Step 2, the differentiation search engine matches student strengths and interests to an enrichment database of 15,000 enrichment activities, materials, resources, and opportunities for further study. These are grouped into the following categories:

Virtual Field Trips

Real Field Trips

Creativity Training

Critical Thinking

Projects and Independent Study

Contests and Competitions

Web sites

Fiction Books

Nonfiction Books

How-To Books

Summer Programs

Online Classes and Activities

Research Skills

Videos and DVDs

These resources are not merely intended to inform students about new information or to occupy their time surfing around the Web. Rather, they are used as vehicles for helping students find and focus on a problem or creative exploration of personal interest that they might like to pursue in greater depth. Many of the resources provide the methods of inquiry, opportunities for advanced level thinking and creative problem-solving skills, and the investigative approaches that form the modus operandi of the practicing professional. Students are guided toward the application of knowledge through the development of original research studies, creative projects, and action-oriented undertakings that put knowledge to work in personally meaningful areas of interest. The resources also provide students with suggestions for outlets and audiences for their creative products.

Step 3. The Wizard Project Maker

A special feature of Renzulli Learning is a project organization and management plan for students and teachers called The Wizard Project Maker. This software allows teachers to help students use their Web-based explorations for original research, investigative projects, and the development of a wide variety of creative undertakings. The sophisticated software used in this tool automatically locates potentially relevant Web-based resources that can be used in connection with the student's investigative activity. This management device is designed to fulfill the requirements of a Type III Enrichment experience, which is the highest level of enrichment previously described in the discussion of the Enrichment Triad Model. Specifically, the Project Maker provides students with the metacognitive skills to:

Define a project and set a goal;

Identify and evaluate both the resources to which they have access and the resources they need (e.g., time, Internet sites, teacher or mentor assistance);

Prioritize and refine goals;

Balance the resources needed to meet multiple goals;

Learn from past actions and project future outcomes; and

Monitor progress, making necessary adjustments as a project unfolds.

As one teacher recently said, "The Wizard Project Maker helps my students understand 'the why' of using the Internet."

Step 4. The Total Talent Portfolio

The final step in the Renzulli Learning System is an automatic compilation and storage of all student activity from Steps 1, 2, and 3 into an ongoing Total Talent Portfolio. This management tool allows students to evaluate each site visited and resource used, and then complete a self-assessment of what they derived from the resource. If they choose, students can store favorite activities and resources in their portfolio. This feature allows easy access to on-going work.

The Total Talent Portfolio "travels" with students throughout their educational career. It serves as a reminder of previous activities and creative accomplishments that students might want to include in college applications, and as an ongoing record, the Portfolio can help students, teachers, guidance counselors, and parents make decisions about future educational and vocational plans.

The Theory and Research Underlying the Renzulli Learning System

The RLS is based the Enrichment Triad Model and has been implemented in thousands of schools in the United States and several overseas nations since being developed in 1977. Classroom teachers using the model worked very hard to access resources to provide enrichment for students, but their many responsibilities and the amount of time required to track down individual resources made this a daunting task. In the Renzulli Learning System, thousands of resources and enrichment materials are provided for teachers and students with the click of a mouse. And what makes this system unique is that these resources are individually tailored to students' abilities, interests, and learning styles. The resources can be accessed in school, during after-school programs, or even at home when students want to pursue enriched learning opportunities on their own.

The Value-Added Benefits of Learning With Technology

The conditions of learning have changed dramatically for young people going to school today. Don Leu and his team of New Literacies researchers at The University of Connecticut (2004) have pointed out that the Internet is this generation's defining technology for literacy and learning. Profound changes have already taken place in higher education, adult learning, and the workplace—all situations for which we are preparing the young students who are in our classrooms today. There was a time when teachers and textbooks were the gatekeepers of knowledge, but today virtually all of the world's knowledge is accessible to any student who can turn on a computer and log into the Internet. One of the dangers of a content-abundant resource such as the Internet, however, is that we might use it simply to cram more information into students' heads! But by applying a learner-centered pedagogy rather than a traditional drill-and-practice approach, we can harness the power of the Internet in a way that respects principles of high-level learning developed by the Task Force on Psychology of the American Psychological Association (APA, 1997).

> By applying a learner-centered pedagogy rather than a traditional drill-and-practice approach, teachers can harness the power of the Internet in a way that respects the principles of high-level learning.

A number of crucial questions follow. Will we use this information wisely? Or will we simply turn the powerful resources available through the Internet into electronic work sheets, test-prep tutorials, and online courses that adhere to the same prescriptive model for learning that almost all reform initiatives have followed thus far—a model that has left many young people bored, disengaged, and lagging behind? Or will the new technologies be the workhorse that finally allows teachers to truly differentiate learning experiences for all students? These technologies now make it possible to apply the pedagogy typically used with high-achieving students to all students. A "gifted education approach" can improve engagement and achievement for all students (Renzulli, 1988).

The Renzulli Learning System—Summing It All Up

The Renzulli Learning System is designed to be an aid to busy teachers who seek the tools for effective differentiation as they go about the process of dealing with a broad range of individual differences, diverse student needs, and increased pressures to improve student achievement. Through the use of technology and an approach to learning that is the opposite of highly prescriptive instruction, the RLS provides teachers with the assistance that every teacher would like to have in his or her classroom. The main goal of the RLS is to simultaneously increase the achievement and enjoyment of learning by making available an inexpensive, easy-to-use, research-based system that promotes student engagement. Although student engagement has been defined in many ways, we view it as the infectious enthusiasm that students display when working on projects of personal interest that challenge them to "stretch" in the use of materials and resources that are above their current comfort level of learning. Research on the role of student engagement is clear and unequivocal. High engagement results in higher achievement, improved self-concept and self-efficacy, and more favorable attitudes toward school and learning. Numerous students involved in our field tests of the RLS summed it up with one word: "Awesome!" Interested readers can examine the RLS by going to www.ren zullilearning.com and clicking on "Test Drive Renzulli Learning."

WHY SHOULD SCHOOLS FOCUS ON TALENT DEVELOPMENT?

Many people view America's public education system as a failed public monopoly. Policy makers, parents, educational leaders, and the corporate and business communities are expressing the lowest level of confidence in public education in our nation's history. Parents of economically disadvantaged youth have all but given up on expectations that schools can improve their children's future, and they have grown weary and suspicious of endless rhetoric and flavor-of-the-month reform initiatives that devour more and more of our limited dollars without producing any noticeable results. It is clear to all stakeholders that the billions of federal and state dollars spent on remedial and compensatory education models have not produced achievement gains of any significance.

Lack of confidence in public education is also being expressed by middle-class parents who have watched the slow but steady decline of SAT scores at the top end of the achievement continuum. In an article entitled "The Other Crisis in Our Schools," Daniel Singal documented the effects of what happens when our brightest students receive a "dumbed-down" education. "For the first time in the history of our country, the educational skills of one generation will not surpass, will not equal, will not even approach those of their parents. This failure will bring a lower sense of professional fulfillment for our youngsters as they pursue their careers, and will hamper their ability to stay competitive with European and Asian countries" (Singal, 1991, p. 59). The middle class has become so disenchanted with the quality of public education that for the first time in history they are asking for *public* funds to pursue private educational alternatives.

Dr. Leon Lederman, the Nobel Prize–winning physicist, recently said, "Once upon a time, America sheltered an Einstein, went to the moon, and gave the world the laser, electronic computer, nylons, television, and the cure for polio. Today we are in the process, albeit unwittingly, of abandoning this leadership role" (Hilts, 1991, p. A16). Every school and classroom in this country has in it young people capable of continuing this remarkable tradition. But our tradition of leadership will not survive without a national resolve to invest in developing the talent potentials of *all* of our young people. Every school also has within it students who possess the highest potential for advanced level learning, creative problem solving, and the motivation to pursue rigorous and rewarding work. As the United Negro College Fund aptly puts it, a mind is a terrible thing to waste. It's time to recognize that we have been wasting far too many minds.

Notes

The work reported herein was supported under the Javits Act Program (Grant No. R206R00001) as administered by the Office of Educational Research and Improvement, U.S. Department of Education. The opinions expressed in this article do not reflect the position or policies of the Office of Educational Research and Improvement or the U.S. Department of Education.

1. Although it is beyond the scope of this article to review the work of these eminent thinkers, the group includes William James, Alfred North Whitehead, John Dewey, Maria Montessori, Jean Piaget, Paul Torrance, Jerome Bruner, Philip Phenix, Howard Gardner, Robert Sternberg, and Albert Bandura.

REFERENCES

Adler, M. J. (Ed.). (1990). *The syntopicon: An index to the great ideas.* Chicago: Encyclopedia Britannica.

Ainley, M. D. (1993). Styles of engagement with learning: Multidimensional assessment of their relationship with strategy use and school achievement. *Journal of Educational Psychology, 85*(3), 395–405.

Amabile, T. M., & Gryskiewicz, N. (1989). The creative environment scales: Work environment inventory. *Creative Research Journal, 2,* 231–254.

APA Work Group of the Board of Educational Affairs. (1997). *Learner-centered psychological principles: A framework for school reform and redesign.* Washington, DC: American Psychological Association.

Bandura, A. (1986). *Social foundation of thought and action: A social cognitive theory.* Englewood Cliffs, NJ: Prentice Hall.

Barth, R. S. (1991). *Improving schools from within* (reprint edition). San Francisco: Jossey-Bass.

Bloom, B. S. (Ed.). (1985). *Developing talent in young people.* New York: Ballantine Books.

Brown, A. L. (1987). Metacognition, executive control, self-regulation and other mysterious mechanism. In F. E. Weinert & R. H. Kluwe (Eds.), *Metacognition, motivation, and understanding.* Hillsdale, NJ: Lawrence Erlbaum Associates, Inc.

Butler, D., & Winne, P. H. (1995). Feedback as self-regulated learning: A theoretical synthesis. *Review of Educational Research, 65,* 245–281.

Corno, L., & Mandinach, E. (1983). The role of cognitive engagement in classroom learning and motivation. *Educational Psychologist, 18,* 88–109.

Dunn, R., Dunn, K., & Price, G. E. (1984). *Learning style inventory.* Lawrence, KS: Price Learning Systems.

Flavell, J. H., Miller, P. H., & Miller, S. A. (2001). *Cognitive development* (4th ed.). Upper Saddle River, NJ: Prentice Hall.

Gardner, H. (1993). *Frames of mind: The theory of multiple intelligences* (10th annual ed.). New York: Basic Books.

Greenwood, C. R. (1991). Longitudinal analysis of time, engagement, and achievement in at-risk versus non-risk students. *Exceptional Children, 57*(6), 521–536.

Hacker, D. J., Dunlosy, J., & Grassner, A. E. (Eds.). (1998). *Metacognition in educational theory and practice.* Mahwah, NJ: Lawrence Erlbaum Associates, Inc.

Hilts, P. (1991, January 6). Nobel physicist raises alarm on U.S. science. *New York Times,* p. A16.

Jaeger, R. M. (1992). "World class" standards, choice, and privatization: Weak measurement serving presumptive policy. *Phi Delta Kappan, 72,* 118–128.

Kettle K., Renzulli, J. S., & Rizza, M. (1998). Products of mind: Exploring student preferences for product development using my way—An expression style instrument. *Gifted Child Quarterly, 42*, 48–61.

Leu, D. J., Jr., Castek, J., Henry, L., Coiro, J., McMullan, M. (2004). The lessons that children teach us: Integrating children's literature and the new literacies of the Internet. *The Reading Teacher, 57*, 496–503.

Madaus, G. F. (1992). *The influence of testing on teaching math and science in grades 4–12.* Boston College: Center for the Study of Testing, Evaluation, and Educational Policy.

McLaughlin, M. W., & Talbert, J. E. (1994). *Contexts that matter for teaching and learning: Strategic opportunities for meeting the nation's education goals.* Stanford, CA: Center for Research on the Context of Secondary School Teaching.

Olenchak, F. R., & Renzulli, J. S. (1989). The effectiveness of the Schoolwide Enrichment Model on selected aspects of elementary school change. *Gifted Child Quarterly, 33*, 36–46.

Olson, L. (1992). Fed up with tinkering, reformers now touting "systemic" approach. *Education Week, 12*(1), 30.

Paris, S. G., Byrnes, J. P., & Paris, A. H. (2001). Constructing theories, identities, and actions of self-regulated learners. In B. Zimmerman & D. Schunk (Eds.), *Self-regulated learning and academinc achievement: Theoretical perspectives* (pp. 253–288). Mahwah, NJ: Lawrence Erlbaum Associates, Inc.

Phenix, P. (1986). *Realms of meaning: A philosophy of curriculum for general education.* New York: McGraw-Hill.

Pintrich, P. R. (2001). The role of goal orientation is self-regulated learning. In M. Boekaerts, P. Pintrich, & M. Zeidner (Eds.), *Handbook of self-regulation* (pp. 452–502). New York: Academic.

Reeves, T. C., Herrington, J., & Oliver, R. (2002). Authentic activities and on-line learning. In A. Goody, J. Harrington, & M. Northcote (Eds.), *Quality conversations: Research and Development in Higher Education* (Vol. 25, pp. 562–567). Jamison, ACT: HERDSA.

Reis, S. M., & Renzulli, J. S. (1992). Using curriculum compacting to challenge the above-average. *Educational Leadership, 50*(2), 51–57.

Reis, S. M., & Renzulli, J. S. (1994). Research related to the Schoolwide Enrichment Triad Model. *Gifted Child Quarterly, 38*(1), 7–20.

Renzulli, J. S. (1977). *The enrichment triad model.* Mansfield Center, CT: Creative Learning Press.

Renzulli, J. S. (1998). A rising tide lifts all ships: Developing the gifts and talents of all students. *Phi Delta Kappan, 80*(2), 105–111.

Renzulli, J. S. (1998). The three-ring conception of giftedness: A developmental model for creative productivity. In Baum, S. M., Reis, S. M., & L. R. Maxfield (Eds.), *Nurturing the gifts and talents of primary grade students.* Mansfield Center, CT: Creative Learning Press.

Renzulli, J. S. (1992). A general theory for the development of creative productivity through the pursuit of ideal acts of learning. *Gifted Child Quarterly, 36,* 170–182.

Renzulli, J. S. (1994). Schools for talent development: A practical plan for total school improvement. Mansfield, CT: Creative Learning Press.

Renzulli, J. S., & Reis, S. M. (1985). *The school wide enrichment model: A comprehensive plan for educational excellence.* Mansfield Center, CT: Creative Learning Press.

Renzulli, J. S., & Reis, S. M. (1994). Research related to the Schoolwide Enrichment Model. *Gifted Child Quarterly, 38,* 2–14.

Renzulli, J. S., & Smith, L. H. (1978). *The learning style inventory: A measure of student preference for instructional techniques.* Mansfield Center, CT: Creative Learning Press.

Schunk, D. (2001). Social cognitive theory of self-regulated learning. In B. Zimmerman & D. Schunk (Eds.), *Self-regulated learning and academic achievement: Theoretical perspectives.* (pp. 125–152). Mahwah, NJ: Lawrence Erlbaum Associates, Inc.

Senge, P. M. (1994). *The fifth discipline.* New York: Currency.

Singal, D. J. (1991). The other crisis in our schools. *The Atlantic, 268,* 59–62.

Sternberg, R. J. (1984). Toward a triarchic theory of human intelligence. *Behavioral and Brain Sciences, 7*(2), 269–316.

Sternberg, R. J. (1988). Mental self-government: A theory of intellectual styles and their development. *Human Development, 3,* 197–224.

Sternberg, R. J., and Lubart, T. I. (1992). An investment theory of creativity and its development. *Human Development, 34,* 1–31.

Weiner, P. P. (Ed.). (1973). *Dictionary of the history of ideas.* New York: Scribner's Sons.

Zimmerman, B., & Schunk, D. (Eds.). (2001). *Self-regulated learning and academic achievement* (2nd ed.). Mahwah, NJ: Lawrence Erlbaum Associates, Inc.

Creating the Climate and Conditions for Children to Learn

James P. Comer

James P. Comer *has worked to bring inner city, low-income elementary schools from chaos to stability and academic and social achievement by creating the Comer School Development Program. Dr. Comer, the Maurice Falk Professor of Child Psychiatry at the Yale University School of Medicine's Child Study Center, has been a Yale medical faculty member since 1968. Dr. Comer is a noted author and columnist and serves as a consulting editor for* Parents *magazine. He is the recipient of some 40 honorary degrees, numerous awards and honors, and has served as a consultant to the Children's Television Workshop, which produces programs such as* Sesame Street.

My interest in factors that contribute to life success and the role of intelligence in all of this began in 1960 with an observation and with a question. I went back to my hometown to become a general practitioner in medicine and I observed that my childhood friends were going on a downhill course in life. The question of what happened to them turned me away from my plan to become a general practitioner, and I began to pursue the question:

Why were my friends going on a downhill course and how could we prevent it? The ability of my low-achieving friends and other observations made me suspicious of intelligence tests and of our concerns about the question of intelligence in the first place. So over the years I have been watchful, continually asking why we are paying so much attention to intelligence and intelligence tests instead of how to create conditions that make the most of whatever a child has to offer. That is why I am pleased about this conference, where the emphasis is not on test scores, but on how we create the climate and the conditions that make it possible for children to learn and to achieve at the highest level possible.

> Intelligence is reflected in the utilization of information to solve problems, general or specific, and to do that consistently. Creativity may be much more important than what we traditionally call and attempt to measure as intelligence.

As a young psychiatrist, a couple of times I had brothers and sisters, once twins, in the same treatment. The twin who possessed the higher IQ test score performed less well than the twin with the 20-points lower score. That raised a question for me about the efficacy of IQ tests to measure what really contributes to achievement. I grew up in a tough, low-income, steel mill town. As a teenager I would go out to the bars, to church and the barbershop, and I would listen to uneducated, low-achieving people (by somebody's standards) who were very creative, very smart, reflective and analytical, and had great memory skills, and I realized these were bright people. Why didn't they do well in school and why didn't they do well on achievement tests?

I also remember early in my training a colleague, a white psychologist, told me of her experience in a Harlem hospital while testing a black youngster. He was testing as developmentally delayed. She took a break and as she went out of the room, she met a black colleague who had given a party for her. They embraced in the hallway, and clearly they were friends. The black youngster was watching. When the psychologist resumed testing after the break, this youngster scored in the above-average range. I began to think about the work of Ogbu[1] and many others who point out that there is about a 15-point IQ difference between groups who have been stigmatized and those who have not been stigmatized within the same society (e.g., the Baraku of Japan, the West Indians in Great Britain, the Maoris of New Zealand) in favor of the nonstigmatized group.

Claude Steele,[2] a psychologist at the University of Michigan, observed that black students with the same ability level as white students were not achieving as well. The longer they stayed in college, the worse they did, increasing the disparity between people of the same ability level. He created a program in which students were randomly selected at the same ratio that they were represented at the college, except with an overrepresentation of blacks and of nonblack minorities. The only intervention given was a challenging calculus workshop and once-a-week meeting, a group discussion in which they talked about everything—all aspects of their lives. The students also all lived in the same wing of a large dormitory. They held this program for about ten weeks. Over a two-year period, they absolutely wiped out the previously observed difference in achievement levels— the black youngsters did as well as the white youngsters.

So what is this business of intelligence all about? Why are we so committed to the IQ test, which is no more than a score based on something that we claim to be a measure of intelligence? There is serious question as to whether it really is. It seems to me that we really use the information to protect and promote privilege. Intelligence is reflected in the utilization of information to solve problems, general or specific, and to do that consistently. Creativity may be as important, maybe much more important, than whatever it is that we call and attempt to measure as intelligence.

I have always loved my daughter, but I particularly loved what she did and what she observed once when she was a senior in high school. She was on an honors track where students drove hard and fought to be at the top of the class. She decided to take a course they were offering called Outward Bound. One day she said to me, "Dad, how do you explain the fact that many of the kids who don't do well in school have the best answers about how you get out of a ditch without a shovel?" I was delighted by that observation and that concern, because there are too many PhDs who haven't considered that question.

The only thing we can say for certain about intelligence is that social and behavioral scientists, biological scientists, and all of us really have a lot to learn. In the meantime, we should be careful not to use intelligence as an absolute, a gatekeeping force in the way that we are beginning to use it. I believe there is a threshold[3] level of general intelligence that is needed in order to perform most tasks, and that most people have a high enough level to perform well in school. Swedish psychiatrists have shown that children can learn to read with IQs of 70 to 75. It doesn't take great intelligence.

But to perform adequately in school and in life, we really need to be motivated, flexible, to have social and emotional intelligence,[4] to have a culture that promotes learning, to have the opportunity structure that makes it possible for us to learn, and then most of all, to be lucky in one way or another. The expression of intelligence is an outgrowth of all these things, rather than the innate potential that we are born with. But I return to the question of what our preoccupation with the intelligence test and the achievement test scores is really all about.

Almost from the beginning, we have used intelligence in this country to justify the unfair distribution of opportunities and privileges. Because the system of slavery was so central to our economy and so contrary to our stated founding purposes and beliefs, we had to justify the system. Intelligence was used as a primary justification. As a result, deeply ingrained in much of our thinking in this society is this preoccupation with intelligence. We ignore that outcomes in life are determined only partially by your intelligence. Once you are above a general threshold of intelligence, it is your access to the political, economic, and social structure of the society that really determines your outcome.

Although we know that this is true, we still cling to the notion that it is intelligence alone that determines outcomes. Whether it is the media or scholars, every five or ten years someone comes out with a report that shows that blacks or some other group are not capable, and we use those reports to justify the distribution of opportunities in our society. We do this in spite of the vast social and behavioral science literature that tells us that intelligence and achievement are greatly influenced by the quality of the child-rearing experience that we receive. I want to point out that I am talking here not only about the child rearing that comes from mother and father, although they are most important. There is a child rearing that takes place in the social network of mother and father, or mothers and family, which is important—a network of friends and kin and the institutions they are a part of. There is also child rearing that takes place in schools and community organizations. We have a great opportunity in schools to promote child rearing, and yet we ignore child rearing in schools. We think of the schools as a place where we pass on information to children. That is only one part of what we do in schools. We should really be in the business of helping children grow.

What I would like to do briefly at this point is to cite some of the literature that talks about the importance of child rearing. Then I want to tell you about my own experience as a son of a "child of extreme poverty and abuse" and the way that education broke the cycle and permitted the development and expression of the potential that my brothers, sisters and I had. I'd like to show how that experience has led to my work in schools, and how it suggested what must be done to make it possible for all children to achieve and to meet their highest potential—the greatest expression of their intelligence.

The key point that we pull from the literature on child rearing is that the interaction between the parents and the child is critical.[5] Positive parent-child interaction allows bonding to occur, and it is bonding with the caretaker that prepares and enables the caretaker to lead the child along important developmental pathways. This makes learning at an increasingly high level possible. The use of reasoning is important; the IQ of children whose parents use reasoning more than punishment is greater.[6] Parents who are attentive and responsive to the behaviors of their children produce children with higher IQs.[7] Warmth and setting appropriate limits is important. Positive interaction between parents is also important in improving IQs.[8] Where fathers are supportive of mothers and vice versa, family stress decreases and children have higher IQs.

> Almost from the beginning, we have used intelligence in this country to justify the unfair distribution of opportunities and privileges.

Parental depression lowers children's IQs.[9] In situations with little verbal interaction and where the quality of this verbal content is poor, children's IQs tend to be depressed.[10] By high-quality verbal interaction, I mean that parents talk to their children about everything that is going on around them. In low-quality verbal interaction, parents use language mostly for control. Parents, who organize the environment so that their children can take advantage of educational opportunities in it, including materials to play with, produce children with higher IQs.[11] Parents who emphasize the importance of hard work and persistence at a task until they get good outcomes produce children with both good academic achievement and higher IQs.[12] Parents who model what they want their children to do, rather than just talk at the children, also produces better outcomes.

Now I want to turn and talk about my own family because my family was low income, working class. The point I want to make is that it is not the education of the parent alone that is critically important, it is how the parent carries out all of the other functions related to learning that I have mentioned that researchers have found important.

My mother was born in rural Mississippi into extreme poverty. Her father was a sharecropper and a good man, but lightning killed him when she was six years of age. Because there were no support programs during that period, a cruel stepfather came into her life. He was abusive in every way, and he would not allow the children to go to school. My mother decided when she was about eight years of age that the way to a better life was through education. When she was sixteen, she ran away to live with a sister in East Chicago, Indiana, and tried to go to school. But she didn't receive the support she needed, and had to drop out and become a domestic worker.

> Children also need protection—not only physical protection, but protection of their dreams and ideas, and their hopes and wishes.

She declared at that point that if she ever had children, she was going to make certain that all of them got a good education. Then she set out very, very carefully to find my father. She wanted to make certain that she didn't make the same mistake that her mother had made. My father had been married once before so she wasn't certain that he was the right choice. She insisted that he get a letter of recommendation from his ex–mother-in-law. It worked out okay in the end—my mother, with no education at all, working as a domestic, and my father, with about a sixth-grade rural Alabama education, working as a steel mill laborer, eventually sent the five of us to college for a total of thirteen college degrees.

All of this took place in a social network of friend and kin and church that was supportive and protective, promoting our development. The three friends who I went to elementary school with, and who were starting on a downhill course when I went back home to become a general practice physician, were in the same neighborhood, the same school. Their fathers worked in the same steel mills as my father, and yet they had a very different developmental experience. I realized that it was development that made the difference for me, and it is development that makes the difference for all of our children. One of my friends became an alcoholic and died early, one spent a good part of his life in jail, and the other had been in and out of mental institutions all of his life until he died recently.

I want to emphasize the point of development and go into some detail about my developmental experience. It is critically important in thinking about all children from all income groups, but especially important in thinking about low-income children. Their parents, even when they want to do the right thing, even when they want to give their children the best experiences to succeed in school, very often have not had those experiences themselves and are not able to provide them to their children.

Let us think about my own experience. The first point is that we were very much wanted. My mother had a plan. She wanted to send her children to school and make certain that every one of them got a good education. My father shared the vision and fully supported the plan. We received enormous care, sometimes to the point of overprotection, but this was not harmful. I recall every Sunday evening, we four younger children would gather around my mother, two at her legs, one on her lap, one at her shoulder, and she would read us the funny papers. Now my mother could just barely read, but that didn't matter. That wasn't the point. We were there to be close to her. When she finished reading the paper, one would ask her to read another cartoon, and then another cartoon, and then another, until she had read the paper all over again. The whole point was time together and closeness. There was also popcorn and malted milk on the front porch. We would sit and talk with our parents on the swing almost every summer evening.

We lived in a very predictable household. Every evening at the same time, my father came around the corner on his way home from work. The four of us would jump up and run down and all leap into his arms and grab his legs. On one occasion, I remember we were talking about a baseball glove that we were going to play with and how we were going to share it when my mother said, "But your father didn't say he was going to buy that glove." We replied that he said he would think about it, and we knew from experience that when he says he'll think about it, that means he is going to do it. Reliability and predictability were terribly important.

Children also need protection—not only physical protection, but protection of their dreams and their ideas, and their hopes and their wishes. When I was a little boy of two years of age, I said I wanted to become a doctor. My parents bought me a doctor's kit for Christmas. I would fix an arm, a leg, or whatever the problem was of anybody around. A neighbor came by and said, "Why are you encouraging him to be a doctor? We're poor people. You know he's not going to be a doctor." My mother retorted, "If you say that one more time you're going to have to leave this house!"

In fifth grade, a youngster moved into my school and said, "I know your mother." I was wondering how she knew my mother so I went home and asked her. My mother pointed out that she had worked for the girl's mother as a domestic years before. My mother saw that that bothered me a little bit because you're very status conscious in fifth grade. My mother looked at me and said, "You're just as clean as she is, just as smart as she is, and you can do just as well as she can," and then gave me her no-nonsense look and said, "and you had better!" Again, protection.

Dinnertime was a very special time. We were always expected to be home at dinnertime and to be on time. Dinner was five o'clock. During dinner there was always discussion. In the process we were taught how to listen, and no one could take over the conversation. Sometimes we were helped to make a point. Thus, all of the rules and the skills of discussion were learned around the dinner table. Many of those discussions would spill over into the evening as informal debates. We had vigorous debates; the four younger children and sometimes my older sister would get into it. We would debate about everything. Those debates were very important to us. Sometimes it was not good to lose in our house because you'd get teased, and there was a rule that you couldn't fight—no matter how badly you lost a debate, you couldn't fight. And so, you might practice your argument, what you had to say, on the way home from school, because you didn't want to lose. The habit of thinking was well established in our household.

On one occasion, my brother, who was usually on the conservative side of the argument, caught me arguing against public welfare. He was giving it to me about how I was cruel, and so on. My mother, who usually stayed out of those discussions and just listened, said, "Jim, but what about the poor people?" I suggested that the government become an employer of last resort. She said, "Okay," and that was the end of her involvement. And so, my parents did not intrude but instead promoted thinking and the appreciation of fair and rational thinking.

The worst sin you could commit as a child in my family was of disrespect for my father. My father was a very religious man, but we had some questions about religion and we would ask them. My mother would try to stop us, but he wanted to hear those questions. There was no area where thinking, challenging, and raising questions was unacceptable when age appropriate. Values were caught more than taught. You can't just sit children down and tell them what they ought to value. They have to experience in an actual living and working environment values that are important.

We were Baptists. At the Baptist Young People's Training Union, my father was the moderator. When my brother correctly answered a question at the same time as another child, my father acknowledged the other child so as not to appear to favor his own. With my father, fairness was fairness, and that's what we learned. My mother would come to the steps where we were playing in the streets below. In those days, there were no grooves in the candy bars where they could break apart easily. She used a ruler to break the candy bar into four even parts so each of us got the same amount. So fairness was an important value that we learned in everyday situations.

> Values are caught more than taught. You can't just sit children down and tell them what they ought to value.

Social skills were also important. My mother said when you see trouble coming from one way, you go the other way. In other words, learn to read the environment and negotiate it wisely. We had many developmental experiences as a family. When we were young children, my mother and father together took us to the lakefront and bundled us all up to go to see Franklin D. Roosevelt's caravan come through town. They exposed us to anything and everything they thought was educational. On one occasion, this involvement got pretty close to being illegal. My mother worked at the polls, and as I was passing she invited me to come in. She took me into the voting area, which was probably illegal. I actually pulled a lever, which *was* illegal. But to this day, voting is important to me because of that involvement and that particular experience.

Issues related to race are very important because all children in our society are exposed to them in one way or another. They must understand and learn how to manage race-related issues at a young age so that they are not thrown by them when they are seven and eight years old and begin to ask the question, "Who am I?" The answer must be "You are someone worthwhile, you need not be embarrassed about your roots, you are okay, you are very good." My mother and father never denied that there was a problem, but they taught us how to manage it. For example, my mother would always say, "If you think that your teacher is unfair, don't you bother with the teacher, tell me, and I will talk with the teacher." She did this on occasion and we would listen and learn.

In ninth grade I had a teacher who gave me a B and gave students who were one and two points ahead of me A's. She gave the next highest student, who was thirty points behind me, a B. I thought that was unfair. After talking with her for about half an hour, she said, "Well, you know, I just don't think you're capable of making A's." I understood what that meant, and that was the end of that discussion. I went back and worked very hard the next ten weeks. At the end of that time, I had the top score in the class. But instead of taking her my grade book, I waited until the end of the day. I had worked very hard the entire semester and I had all A's. I took the card to her and got my A. I learned how to manage that environment from living in a home where people managed their environment in a way that made bad matters better.

> The school is a developmental venue—a place where we can and must support the development of children.

My mother wasn't operating off the top of her head. She had a child-rearing theory that said that the good times we have together make it possible for me and your father to chastise you when there are bad times, and for you to understand that chastising is in your best interest. The support and discipline that we received from our parents is what allowed us to go to school prepared to manage ourselves in the school environment and balance and understand the expectations of the school. All that I have described about my family meets the conditions that researchers in child rearing say produce improved IQ test scores and achievement.

I tell you my story because I know and you know that most of the low-income children that you deal with—black, white, Asian, Latino, or others—are not receiving the kind of experiences that I'm talking about. And yet, some do. The underachievement that we observe among so many children is because they are not receiving the kinds of experiences that I was privileged to have. But we can't give up on those children. We can't say they are underdeveloped and therefore they can't learn, and that's too bad. The school is a developmental venue. It is a place along the developmental pathway where we can and must support the development of children. We can compensate for underdevelopment. And when we fully support the development of children, they will do well in school.

So let me turn now and tell you about our work in schools. The two initial schools in New Haven, and our continued work, have made a difference. I directed a team from the Yale Child Study Center that went into two elementary schools in New Haven, Connecticut, in 1968. What we literally did was simply to recreate the community. We recreated a community that supported the rearing and development of children so that they could perform at a high level. The schools were 99 percent black, almost all poor, and had the worst achievement, worst attendance, and worst behavior in the city. They were thirty-second and thirty-third out of 33 schools in achievement on nationally standardized tests. By the time we left those schools, they were tied for the third and fourth highest levels of achievement in the city, a year above grade level in one school, and seven months above grade level in the other. They had the best attendance in the city, and there were no serious behavior problems.

What we initially found in those schools was chaos and apathy. When we go into such settings as educators, we have a tendency to blame. We blame the teacher, the union, the parents. We blame everyone involved. What we discovered was that teachers, the union, the parents, the custodian, and all of those people wanted to succeed, but they were in an environment in which they couldn't succeed. They couldn't succeed because the "community" of the past no longer existed to support the development of the children. The family support of the children was not there. I would say, as one way of stating it, that the kitchen table was gone. Families didn't sit around and organize their lives—think, reflect, and transmit values—like in the past.

The school remained a cognition factory where information was passed on. Some got it and others did not. The former were thought to be smart and the others not. That worked all right until the 1960s and 1970s because we could sweep everybody who was undereducated into an economy that did not require an education and they could take care of all their adult tasks and responsibilities and be okay. But that is no longer so. We were dealing with children who were underdeveloped, who needed to have an experience in which there was support for their continued development. Yet the staff, through no fault of their own, was not prepared to support the development of the children. What we did was create a community in school that supported development.

We put the kitchen table of the home into the school program. We begged those parents who came to throw us out to give us a chance. We created a governance and management team that was made up of parents, teachers, and administrators. They became the organizing, value-setting, skill-teaching mechanism within the program. That governance and management team developed a comprehensive school plan: staff development, assessment, and modification were done on an ongoing basis so that the school could keep changing and improving. There was a parents program that supported the governance and management team. There was a school support team (we called it the mental health team at the time) that dealt with overall conditions in the school and made it a child-supporting place.

Most importantly, I think, was a change in the attitude and the climate and the way we understood and went about doing things. We developed three guiding principles. First, we called "no fault." We stopped pointing the finger of blame, and we asked instead, "How do we solve this problem?" In some ways, that's what I hear us doing now. We don't want to know IQ scores; we want to know what kind of conditions to create to make the most of what we have. That is the way the no-fault principle works; the emphasis is not on who is to blame, but on how to solve the problem.

The second principle is consensus. Consensus means that decisions are made by common agreement rather than by voting. Decisions are based on what's good for the children, not what's good for the parents, teachers, or administrators, but what's good and necessary for the children to function well. The third principle is collaboration; working together rather than paralyzing the principal on the one hand or ignoring the governance group on the other. Again, the three principles are no-fault, consensus, and collaboration.

Let me give you two examples of how these principles have worked. We had a child who on a Friday was in rural North Carolina, a small, tight-knit, warm community, supported by his friends, his neighbors, and his family. An aunt from New Haven brought him to live with her. He was brought to King School on the following Monday. The principal took him directly to the classroom. The teacher had had three transfers the week before, and she was frustrated by all of this turnover and confusion. She nodded her head in frustration, and the youngster, eight years of age, looked at her and perceived rejection. Frightened, he panicked, kicked the teacher in the leg, and ran out.

We thought that was a fairly healthy response for an eight-year-old. But that's the kind of response that gets a child sent to the principal, punished, and sent back. Somebody laughs, he punches him in the mouth, he goes back to the principal, and it goes around and around and around, until he is labeled "disturbed," and then he is sent off to somebody like me to have his head "fixed."

Our mental health team had a discussion with the staff. We asked them what it might be like to be eight years of age and have your entire support system removed and to find yourself in a strange place. Everybody began to think about that and about what could be done in the classroom to help with his transition. Suggestions included things like put up "Welcome, Johnnie" signs and assign him to some youngster who is very competent, capable, and well liked in the classroom to help him be accepted in that group. We called on the creativity of the teachers. We did not tell them what they had to do. We presented the problem and had them think about what they could do. Teachers come up with ideas very, very well.

> Wherever there was a problem, we worked together as a school and as a team to address the needs of the children. We modified the school to support the development and functioning of each child so that all children could succeed in the school.

How do you change your school and make it a child-centered, friendly place for children? First, you don't take children and dump them into strange classrooms. You give them an orientation. You show them what they can do if they have a problem. You do whatever is reasonable and possible to help them make it in school. That is what happened with this transfer student and many more children. They made it because we began to think differently about children: how to support their functioning in that system and how that promotes their social development, behavior, and academic performance.

A second example: We had a child who for seven months did not look at or smile at the teacher. She had been traumatized by adults and didn't trust them. At the end of seven months, with a predictable, caring, responsible teacher, she finally looked up and smiled. The teacher was devastated, because in two more months she would have to pass that child on. She wouldn't be able to build on the positive relationship that was emerging. She went back to the teachers' lounge and expressed her concern. We held a mental health meeting, and we talked about the discontinuity in the lives of so many low-income children (many children across the socioeconomic spectrum now have discontinuity in their lives). We talked about what we could do to promote continuity in the school. We worked out a program of keeping children with the same teacher for two years. Some children who made no academic gain the first year caught up to grade level or better. Some even made two years or more of academic gain in the second year. In short, wherever there was a problem, we worked together as a school, as a team, to address the needs of the children. We modified the school to support the development and functioning of each child so that all children could make it in the school. In this way, we reduced many of the behavioral problems in that school. We went from forty-three major referrals of behavior problems in one school in the first year to three in the second.

At that point, we began to think about children and how they learn and grow. We thought about how they grow along different developmental pathways—six that are critically important: physical, social-interactive, psycho-emotional, moral-ethical, linguistic, and intellectual-cognitive. We began to think about how all of our work supports development along those pathways, or doesn't.

The teachers no longer believed that they were teaching people who were destined to become the dregs of the earth. They began to see bright, able young people.

We delayed deep involvement in this work until very recently, but we are picking it up again. We delayed because at that point people were still adamant in saying that low-income children can't learn, that what happened in school didn't matter. We felt it was very important to first go out and create enough good schools where low-income children did learn, rather than to initially go deeply into understanding the process. The fact that low-income children can learn has, and is, being established, and oddly enough, through an approach that I think is wrong. High stakes accountability—loss of job if test scores don't go up—does not get at the real problem. It forces us to teach to the test. But what is implicit in this approach is the expectation that children will be able to learn. At any rate, providing evidence that low-income children can learn was our past concern and we didn't go deeply into integrating the developmental pathways into teaching and learning. We are now working on that.

Another approach we took in the past is very important. We developed a program that would provide low-income children with the same kinds of experiences that middle-income children receive simply by growing up with their parents. We are renewing in a modified way this program that we called the Social Skills Curriculum for Inner City Children. We think of the school as a venue, along with the home and the parents, for the support and development of children. By systematically playing the role of a developmental venue, schools can overcome the underdevelopment of children.

Many low-income families have either never been connected to the mainstream or have been marginally involved. A good part of what we need to be doing in schools is to connect or reconnect low-income children to mainstream activities. Because of everything that we want adults to be able to do, we need to start having little children practice from the very early years.

When we started work on the curriculum, we did not tell the parents "We want you to develop a social skills curriculum." What we asked was "What do you want for your children?" They wanted the same thing that every one of us in this room wants for our children. We then asked, "What kind of experiences would your children need to be able to carry out these activities?" Together, we thought about it and decided they would need activities in politics and government, business and economics, health and nutrition, spiritual and leisure time activities. Then we developed a program in each of these areas that allowed the integration of basic academic skills, social skills, and an appreciation of the arts.

When we started this social skills curriculum, there was a mayoral contest going on in the city. The children wrote letters inviting the candidates to come and speak to them, and sent thank-you notes after their visit. The parents took money from their activities and rented a bus, and with the teachers took the children through the town. They had discussions about the relationship of government to the conditions that they observed in the city. The children came back and wrote about it in their language arts and social science classes.

The children put on a dance and drama program and hosted the event. They learned all the skills associated with being the hosts. These were all of the things that I learned at home with my parents and that most middle-income children learn at home with their parents. All of these activities created great excitement in the school. The teachers no longer believed that they were teaching people who were destined to become the dregs of the earth. They began to see bright, able young people. For example, a young man who stood up and spoke to an audience in an articulate way with great presence had not been a good student. Staff began to see the children in very different ways because the curriculum allowed students more than a single way to perform.

An activity called "The Life and Times of Jackie Robinson" was developed as part of this project. The staff prepared to take the children to an exhibit in New York about Jackie Robinson. The academic program was centered around his life and times: what was going on in America at the time of Jackie Robinson and what his experience represented. Many such experiences turned those schools into very exciting places. We experienced the first significant jump in academic achievement after these experiences.

We were not doing anything magical. We helped underdeveloped children from marginalized families catch up and began the process of connecting them to mainstream society. We helped them and their teachers develop a future orientation. Their parents were involved in a way that avoided the conflict between their own family and social network, and mainstream institutions and culture. There is a natural conflict for children who grow up in low-income environments. We ask them to succeed in school and in the workplace in ways that their own parents had often not succeeded. But involving parents in planning all of these activities and working through them gives students and staff the go-ahead signal.

I wish I could tell you that all of the schools we have worked with—almost 700 in 26 different states—just jumped up and performed in the same way as those two initial schools. Some have, but far too many have not performed in that way. I estimate that about a third have made significant improvement, a third have made some improvement, and a third have made no improvement. You cannot get the kind of improvement the country needs in environments where there is huge turnover, where people play political, economic, and social games of one kind or another, where there is a simple lack of sensitivity, where there is a deep-seated belief that these children cannot learn, or where there is inadequate investment in teacher and administrative preparation.

One school in Virginia using our model went from twenty-fourth in achievement to first, ahead of the middle-income school. The central office was suspicious and they sent people out to retest the children. They did slightly better the second time than they did the first. Another school, thirty-fourth in New Jersey, went from thirty-fourth to first. They created a climate of trust and collaboration to the point where the teachers were willing to take the math test that the children took. The teachers didn't do very well so the principal, previously a math supervisor, tutored the teachers. These low-income eighth-grade students soared to within 0.3 of a point of their affluent counterparts. This means that the children can. The teachers, through no fault of their own, weren't adequately prepared. It wasn't their fault. It was the fault of our national education system. If we want a world-class tennis team, wouldn't we make certain that the coaches know how to play and to teach tennis?

> I am not convinced that everybody wants low-income children to achieve. In addition to creating ways to change schools, we have to create the will to make certain that all our children achieve at a high level.

These conditions must change. We know that the children can learn. We know that school staffs start out eager and willing to learn and perform at a high level. We must arrive at a consensus and develop the political pressure to make the system change so that our children, all of our children, will have an opportunity to learn at the needed level. We must insist on the training, the selection, support, and the time to make these changes in our schools.

The new directions that we are going in—vouchers, charters, privatization, and all of those things—are really not the answer. Those models are basically economic and political. They are not developmental. But unless we pay attention to the development of children—train people and create programs that can support it—we're not going to improve our system of education.

Let me stop on that point. I am not convinced that everybody wants low-income children to achieve. We have a good idea what to do and how to do it, but we seem to lack the will. Therefore, in addition to creating ways to change schools, we've got to create the will to make certain that all our children achieve at a high level. The two schools that changed dramatically in 1996 and 1997 received limited news reports. There was a flurry of reports when they thought there might be cheating in one of the schools. When it was found out that the schools weren't cheating, the news interest ended. Unusually high achievement among low-income students would seem to deserve much inquiry.

Not only were the newspapers not interested, there have not been researchers asking questions about what went on in those schools. This suggests to me that the will is not there. We have to work to create the will. All of us—not me, not the parents, but everybody in this room and everybody concerned about the future of this country—must do so because we cannot have a society where we have large numbers of people who are educated and doing well, and large numbers of people who are denied an education and who are not doing well. If we do that, all of us will pay, and there is no need for it. We can create a country that will survive and thrive in the twenty-first century if we do the right thing.

NOTES

1. Ogbu, J. (1986). The consequences of the American caste system. In U. Neisser (Ed.), *The school achievement of minority children: New perspectives* (pp. 19–56). Hillsdale, NJ: Erlbaum.

2. Steele, C. M. (1997). A threat in the air. *American Psychologist, 52*(6), 613–629.

3. Renzulli, J. (1998). The three ring conception of giftedness: A developmental model for creative productivity. In S. M. Baum, S. M. Reis, & L. R. Maxfield, (Eds.), *Nurturing the gifts and talents of primary grade students.* Mansfield Center, CT: Creative Learning Press.

4. Goldman, D. P. (1997). *Emotional intelligence: Why it can matter more than IQ.* New York: Bantam Books.

5. Hart, B., & T. D. Risley. (1992). American parenting of language-learning children: Persisting differences in family-child interactions observed in natural home environments. *Developmental Psychology, 28*(6), 1096–1105.

6. Mills, B. C., Stevens, A., & Weidner, V. R. (1989). Effects of maternal child-rearing practices on school readiness and achievement of young children. ERIC Document ED 329337.

7. Beckwith, L., & Parmelee, A. (1986). EEG patterns of preterm infants, home environment, and later IQ. *Child Development, 57,* 777–789.

8. Pianta, R. C., & Egeland, B. (1994). Predictors of instability in children's mental test performance at 24, 48, and 96 months. *Intelligence, 18*(2), 145–163.

9. Lyons-Ruth, K., Zoll, D., Connell, D., & Grunebaum, H. (1986). The depressed mother and her one-year-old infant: Environment, interaction, attachment and infant development. *New Directions for Child Development, 34,* 61–82.

10. Hart, B., & Risley, T. R. (1992). American parenting of language-learning children: Persisting differences in family-child interactions observed in natural home environments. *Developmental Psychology, 28*(6), 1096–1105.

11. Gottfried, A. W. (1984). Home environment and early cognitive development integration, meta-analyses, and conclusions. In A. W. Gottfried (Ed.), *Home environment and early cognitive development: Longitudinal research* (pp. 329–342). San Diego, CA: Academic Press.

12. Olszewski, P., Kulieke, M. J., & Buescher, T. (1987). The influence of the environment on the development of talent: A literature review. *Journal for the Education of the Gifted, 11*(1), 6–28.

Credits

Grateful acknowledgment is made to the following authors and agents for their permission to reprint copyrighted materials.

SECTION 1

SECTION 2

Student Learning," by Linda Darling-Hammond. From February, 1998 *Educational Leadership*, *55*(5), pp. 6–11. Used with permission. The Association for Supervision and Curriculum Development is a worldwide community of educators advocating sound policies and sharing best practices to achieve the success of each learner. To learn more, visit ASCD at www.ascd.org.

"Did You Ask a Good Question Today?" is from a paper based on a presentation at the Fourth International Teaching for Intelligence Conference, April 24, 1998, New York, NY. © 2007 by John Barell. Reprinted with permission. John Barell is Professor Emeritus, Montclair State University and can be reached at jbarell@nye.rr.com or www.morecuriousminds.com.

Elliot W. Eisner and Phi Delta Kappa for "The Misunderstood Role of the Arts in Human Development." From *Phi Delta Kappan*, April 1992, pp. 591–595. © 1992 by Elliot W. Eisner. Published with permission of the author.

International Reading Association and Richard L. Allington for "What Really Matters in Teaching Children to Read." From a portion of the introduction to Help for Struggling Readers. © 1998 by International Reading Association. Newark, DE. Dr. Allington is now a professor at the University of Tennessee. Reprinted with the permission of the International Reading Association.

SECTION 3

Robert R. Spillane, Ph.D., Director of the Center for Education, CNA Corporation, for "Teaching for Intelligence: The Intellectual Life of Schools." © 1998 by Robert R. Spillane. Reprinted with permisssion.

Robin Fogarty for "The Intelligence-Friendly Classroom: It Just Makes Sense." Used with permission. Robin Fogarty, Ph.D.

James Bellanca for "Teaching for Intelligence: In Search of Best Practices." © 1998 SkyLight Training and Publishing Inc. A similar version of this article was first published in *Phi Delta Kappan,* May 1998, pp. 658–660.

"Mediative Environments: Creating Conditions for Intellectual Growth" is from a paper based on a presentation at the Fourth International Teaching for Intelligence Conference, April 25, 1998, New York, NY. © 2007 by Arthur L. Costa. Reprinted with permission.

"Differentiating Instruction in the Classroom: Tapping into the Intelligence of *Every* Learner" is from a paper based on a presentation at the Fourth International Teaching for Intelligence Conference, April 24, 1998, New York, NY. © 2007 by Dorothy S. Strickland. Used with permission of Dorothy S. Strickland, Rutgers, The State University of New Jersey.

Section 4

Index

CORWIN
PRESS

The Corwin Press logo—a raven striding across an open book—represents the union of courage and learning. Corwin Press is committed to improving education for all learners by publishing books and other professional development resources for those serving the field of PreK–12 education. By providing practical, hands-on materials, Corwin Press continues to carry out the promise of its motto: **"Helping Educators Do Their Work Better."**